WRONG SIDE of the LAW

WRONG SIDE of the LAW

True Stories of Crime

EDWARD BUTTS

DUNDURN
TORONTO

Editor: Shannon Whibbs
Design: Jesse Hooper
Printer: Webcom

Library and Archives Canada Cataloguing in Publication

Butts, Edward, 1951-, author
        Wrong side of the law : true stories of crime / by Edward Butts.

Includes bibliographical references.
Issued in print and electronic formats.
ISBN 978-1-4597-0952-2 (pbk.).--ISBN 978-1-4597-0953-9 (pdf).--ISBN 978-1-4597-0954-6 (epub)

        1. Crime--Canada--History. 2. Criminals--Canada--Biography. I. Title.

HV6803.B88 2013   364.971   C2013-900836-5
                                          C2013-900837-3

1 2 3 4 5   17 16 15 14 13

We acknowledge the support of the **Canada Council for the Arts** and the **Ontario Arts Council** for our publishing program. We also acknowledge the financial support of the **Government of Canada** through the **Canada Book Fund** and **Livres Canada Books**, and the **Government of Ontario** through the **Ontario Book Publishing Tax Credit** and the **Ontario Media Development Corporation**.

Care has been taken to trace the ownership of copyright material used in this book. The author and the publisher welcome any information enabling them to rectify any references or credits in subsequent editions.

J. Kirk Howard, President

Printed and bound in Canada.

VISIT US AT
Dundurn.com | *Pinterest.com/dundurnpress* | *@dundurnpress* | *Facebook.com/dundurnpress*

Dundurn
3 Church Street, Suite 500
Toronto, Ontario, Canada
M5E 1M2

Gazelle Book Services Limited
White Cross Mills
High Town, Lancaster, England
L41 4XS

Dundurn
2250 Military Road
Tonawanda, NY
U.S.A. 14150

To the memory of Mac Jamieson,
Integrated Studies, University of Waterloo.
Friend and mentor.

CONTENTS

ACKNOWLEDGEMENTS

I would like to express my appreciation to the many people and institutions who assisted me in researching and writing this book: Michael Carroll and Shannon Whibbs of Dundurn; Edward (Ted) and Jane Cobean and the Brocton Heritage Committee; Monica Graham; A.E. Dalton; Peter Edwards; the Colorado Historical Society; the Metropolitan Toronto Reference Library; the Rooms of St. John's, Newfoundland and Labrador; the Ontario Provincial Archives; the Alberta Provincial Archives; Pinkerton's Inc.; the Walkerton Public Library; Library and Archives Canada; Mary Moriarty, Damien Rodden, Kingston Penitentiary Museum; and as always the staff of the Guelph Public Library.

INTRODUCTION

Living on the wrong side of the law has never been an enviable existence. Those who have experienced it have often been among the first to warn juvenile offenders against falling into the trap of lawlessness — advice that they themselves failed to heed in their youth. Life on the run can certainly have moments of adrenaline-pumping excitement, but one can get the same thing from any number of legitimate challenges, from bungee-jumping to working as a professional in search-and-rescue operations.

There is nothing glamorous about being a fugitive from the law, no matter how much Hollywood romanticizes it. The highly successful organized-crime boss with a fine house and an offshore account full of tainted money is in many ways no different from the two-bit burglar who resides in cheap rooms and lives from one robbery to the next. Both live in fear of making a mistake, of being betrayed, or of any unforeseen clue that will bring the police to their door.

Of course, there is always the threat of punishment. In colonial Canada that could mean flogging, imprisonment, or being hanged and then having your body gibbeted as a warning to others. Over the years the more barbaric punishments were discarded as unfit for a civilized and enlightened nation. It was also obvious that they were ineffective as deterrents to crime.

Some people who live on the wrong side of the law are drawn by the prospect of "easy money." Like career criminal Micky McArthur, they might think that working is for fools. Or, like the outlaw Newton brothers, they might have seen how years of honest toil got their families and neighbours nowhere, and decided that armed robbery would be an acceptable method not only of survival, but also of financial success. As the Newtons put it, robbery was their "business." Such criminals don't fear punishment because they don't expect to get caught. They believe they are smart enough to always stay one jump ahead of the police.

Other people, like Sydney Lass, wander over to the wrong side of the law while they are still very young and never find their way back. Lass spent more time in prison than he did out of it and never learned to be anything but a thief. For Lass and many others like him, jail becomes an occupational hazard — part of the game. Harsh sentences meted out only to only punish do nothing to help them change their ways. If anything, they turn out criminals who are only more bitter and all the more seasoned in the cynicism of underworld life. Short-sighted "get tough" policies of populist "law and order" governments fill jails, but history has shown that they don't do a thing to address the social problems that are at the root of crime.

This doesn't mean that the criminal is absolved of all responsibility. No matter how dire an individual's circumstances, it still comes down to a matter of choices. Verne Sankey could have pursued an honest career as an engineer for the CPR. He chose the wrong side of the law and became a bootlegger, bank robber, and kidnapper. The Newton boys in the 1920s, and Micky McArthur in the 1970s said that they only wanted money and didn't intend to hurt anybody. "We wasn't thugs," said Willis Newton. But the Newtons didn't hesitate to shoot bank messengers during a holdup in downtown Toronto. McArthur was responsible for the shooting of four police officers. When a person uses a weapon to commit robbery, that person is a thug, whether or not physical harm is done to other people. The potential for extreme violence is always at hand, and tragedy can be but a heartbeat away, for those who live on the wrong side of the law.

CHAPTER 1
NEWFOUNDLAND DESPERADOES:
A Rogues' Gallery

The recorded history of the province of Newfoundland and Labrador is the oldest of any part of Canada, predating even the earliest documented use of the word *Canada*. Lawlessness on the island of Newfoundland began early in the seventeenth century, when it was a base for pirates like Peter Easton and Henry Mainwaring. Later, the interior became a haven for the outlawed Masterless Men, escaped indentured servants and Royal Navy deserters who sought freedom in the wild.

Throughout their long colonial period, Newfoundlanders were subject to the same harsh laws as the common people of Britain. In the earliest years, the usual punishment for theft was hanging. It didn't matter if the culprit had stolen a few shillings or a cow. In time, the number of crimes punishable by death was reduced, but penalties were still severe. They included whipping, branding with a hot iron, banishment, and the confiscation of property.

In 1777, for example, Lawrence Hallohan was hanged for forging a bill for eight pounds. That same year, Lawrence Dalton followed him to the gallows for forging bills for twenty shillings and seventeen shillings. However, when Patrick Knowlan was convicted of stealing an item valued at ten pence, he wasn't sentenced to hang. Instead, he had a halter put around his neck and was dragged to whipping posts set up at various locations in St. John's where he was given a total of sixty lashes on his back by the "common whipper." He forfeited all of his goods and property, was obliged to pay the court costs, and then was banished from the colony forever. If he returned to Newfoundland, he would be imprisoned and subjected to sixty lashes every Monday until passage on a ship could be found for him.

Offences such as public drunkenness, disorderly conduct, or sticking your tongue out at your employer could result in lashes or a day locked in the stocks, where you were an object of ridicule and the target for all the manure and other filth passersby wanted to throw at you. Most of the individuals subjected to these harsh punishments could hardly be considered hardened criminals. The existence of such measures is far more telling of the legal system that applied them than of the unfortunates who received them. Nonetheless, old time Newfoundland did have its share of ne'er-do-wells who were willing to risk everything for personal gain, and so slipped over to the wrong side of the law.

DOWNING AND MALONE

In 1832, Patrick Downing and Patrick Malone were working on the farm of Robert Crocker Bray at Harbour Grace. As they bent their backs to raising stumps with crowbars, Malone allegedly told Downing that following the recent fire that had destroyed much of Harbour Grace, he had carried a bag into Bray's house. That bag, he said, had been buried to protect it from the fire because it contained money. Forty or fifty pounds! That was more money than either of them had ever seen. Malone said he slept in a room next to the one in which Bray kept the money bag, and that stealing it would be easy. Downing had no qualms about robbing Bray, but he thought the job would require four men. He wanted to bring his two brothers in on it. Malone said he didn't trust them, and the matter was dropped for the time being.

The following spring, Malone went out on the ice for the annual seal hunt. That was a hazardous way to earn a few shillings and it had Malone thinking once again about the money in Bray's house. He plotted with Downing, and they came up with a scheme that involved not just robbery, but murder. Malone said he had enlisted the Bray's housemaid, Ellen Coombs, as an accomplice by promising to marry her.

One night in July 1833, Downing and Malone went into the Bray house. They killed Robert in the kitchen with two blows of a tomahawk. Mrs. Bray was out of town, but little Samuel Bray and Ellen Coombs were in an upstairs bedroom. Whether the housemaid was really involved in the plot would never be known, because she and the child were both hacked to death.

The murderers ransacked the house, but found no bag of money. They took whatever cash and valuables they could find; a total value between thirty and forty shillings. Then they started a fire in an upstairs bedroom and another one at the foot of the stairs before leaving the house.

Downing and Malone slipped off to Bear's Cove, a little over a mile away, to hide their loot. They were certain that all evidence of the crime would be consumed by the flames. On their way back they met some men who told them the Bray house was on fire. They joined in spreading the alarm.

To the killers' dismay, neighbours had gone into the house and put out the fires before the building could be engulfed. The butchered bodies had been found. Suspicion immediately fell on Malone, since he had been living in the house.

The Harbour Grace Magistrate, a doctor named Stirling, told Malone that if he confessed, he wouldn't hang. In a signed statement, Malone placed the blame on Downing. He said that he had been sitting in the Bray house, rocking little Samuel, when Downing burst in and committed the murders. He admitted that he had helped hide the loot and disclosed the location. Downing was arrested, and both men were bound over for the next assize. Of course, Downing gave a different version of the crime, saying that Malone had done the killing.

The trial was held in St. John's on January 3, 1834, and lasted nine hours. The presiding judge, Henry John Boulton, wouldn't allow Malone's statement to be read to the jury because it had been made after Malone had been told it would save his life. The accused men blamed each other. Boulton told the jury, "I believe the confessions of the two culprits were fully much of the same tenor and character, only that each charged the other with being the actual murderer. They differed only as to which one did the bloody deed."

Amazingly, the judge also told the jury to disregard anything Downing had said against Malone, as he believed the evidence against Malone was very slight. It took the jury less than an hour to reach a verdict of "guilty" for both men. Downing was condemned to death, but to the astonishment of all, Malone was sentenced to life in prison. "His life may be spared," Boulton said. "He will never again be allowed to infest society with his presence."

At that time there was no process of appeal. Two days after the trial, Patrick Downing was publicly hanged on a scaffold set up on Market House Hill. According to the local press, he showed "the most astonishing composure and fortitude." The reporter also noted that, "The execution was witnessed by an immense concourse of people, who behaved in the most decorous and orderly manner."

By the standards of the time, the Bray murders had been judiciously avenged. But there were some who felt that justice hadn't been served. They believed that Malone had done the killing, and then made a spurious "confession" to save his own life. By court order, Downing's body was cut down and taken to Harbour Grace, the scene of the crime. There it was gibbeted — hung in chains — as a warning to would-be lawbreakers.

Some of Downing's friends held Dr. Stirling responsible for a miscarriage of justice because he had illegally obtained Malone's confession with a promise of clemency. One night, Downing's decomposing corpse was cut down from the gibbet by persons unknown and the chains were removed. Dr. Stirling found the grisly remains on his doorstep the next morning. There was an accompanying note: "Dr. S. This is your man you were the cause of bringing him here take and bury him or Lookout should you be the cause of allowing him to be put up again we will mark you for it so Do your duty and put him out of sight. truly A friend from Carbonear. [sic]"

Dr. Stirling heeded the warning. He had the body placed in a coffin and buried in the yard of the Harbour Grace courthouse. It was never determined who really struck the blows that killed the three victims.

JOHN FLOOD

Colonial Newfoundland was better known for pirates than highwaymen, but at least one Newfoundlander who lived on the wrong side of the law met his demise because of highway robbery. Today we associate the term *highwayman* with images of flamboyant mounted robbers like England's Dick Turpin, romantically portrayed in verse and fiction as dashing "knights of the road." In fact most of them — including Turpin — were thugs, and they were as likely to be on foot as on horseback. Any petty holdup of a traveller on a public road was classified as highway robbery.

Because of missing documents, little is known of Newfoundland highwayman John Flood. Sometime in 1834, he robbed the stagecoach that ran between St. John's and Portugal Cove, an important port for passenger vessels that served communities in Conception Bay. Flood stopped the coach on the Portugal Cove Road, in the vicinity of Kent's Pond. It isn't known if he called out the famous highwayman command, "Stand and deliver!"

Flood was soon arrested. On December 9, 1834, he was tried for robbery and assault, convicted, and sentenced to death. No documentation survives to confirm that the sentence was carried out. However, evidence indicates that a man who was hanged on January 12, 1835, was John Flood. The highwayman (if it was indeed he) was the last person to be publicly executed in Newfoundland.

BRADY AND NAUGHTON

In January 1842, a pair of British criminals named Thomas Brady and William Naughton looted the Manchester branch of the Bank of England of nineteen thousand pounds — well over a hundred thousand dollars in today's currency. While Scotland Yard detectives searched for them the length and breadth of Great Britain, the bandits were enjoying a luxurious Atlantic crossing on the steamer *Britannia*, the most famous passenger ship of the day. One of their fellow passengers was Charles Dickens. Brady and Naughton would later claim that they shared Dickens's company at meals and took strolls around the deck with him. The truth of that is questionable, since Dickens was seasick for almost the entire voyage.

When the ship reached New York, Brady and Naughton were confident that they were beyond the long arm of British law. However, they soon learned from the newspapers that back home the police had discovered their identities and their means of escape. If they were found in New York, they'd be arrested and put on the first ship back to England.

Brady and Naughton went to the New York docks in search of a ship that would take them to any place they thought the police wouldn't be likely to look for them. They found a vessel that was bound for Fogo, Newfoundland. Rather than pay for passage and leave a money trail, they signed aboard as deck hands.

At Fogo, Brady and Naughton helped unload the cargo. After being paid off, they took a schooner to St. John's. Now they felt they had given Scotland Yard the slip. The colonial capital wasn't New York, but it was still a place where a pair of crooks with a lot of money could enjoy themselves.

The bank robbers passed themselves off as debonair, well-educated gentlemen of means named Thomas Bradshaw and William O'Kelly. They were soon the toast of the small, elite social circle of St. John's, and were invited to dine in the best homes. When they astounded listeners with the news that they had crossed the ocean with Charles Dickens, people pumped them with questions about the great man and about the fate of Little Nell, the heroine of the serialized novel, *The Old Curiosity Shop*.

Things were going well enough for the pair until they ran out of small currency and had to dip into the swag from the bank. They went into the Dublin Bookstore and asked the proprietor, Bernard Duffy, if he could change a one-hundred-pound note. Duffy was astonished to see a bill of such large denomination — and suspicious. He told them he didn't have that much money on the premises. They agreed to leave the note with him, and come back after supper when he'd had time to gather up some cash.

As soon as they were gone, Duffy took the note to Bishop Michael Fleming, who sent him to the manager of the British Bank of North America. The manager had recently received some newspapers from England, and he recalled reading about the Manchester bank robbery. He sorted through the papers and found the article. It included a list of serial numbers of the stolen notes. The bill "Bradshaw and O'Kelly" had given Duffy had one of those numbers. The manager immediately alerted the chief of police. The robbers were arrested in their room at Johnson's Hotel, where the constables also found the loot.

News of the arrest swept through St. John's. When the high society people heard it, they were shocked; not because their new friends had been exposed as criminals and imposters, but because they thought the police had made an incredible blunder. Several of them went to the jail on Signal Hill to vouch for the two and protest such undignified treatment of gentlemen.

A few days after the arrest, Brady and Naughton appeared in court for a preliminary hearing. They had hired a lawyer, John Little, who argued that a newspaper article was hardly strong enough evidence to keep them in jail. W.B. Rowe, Q.C., representing the Crown, countered that possession of a large amount of money that had been identified as stolen was indeed good enough reason for them to be held in custody, especially since they could not satisfactorily explain how they came to be travelling with such an incredible sum of money. The court ruled that the pair remain in jail until arrangements could be made to send them back to England. The editor of the St. John's *Times* commented:

> We are not, technically speaking, learned in the law; but we may be allowed to observe, that with the strong circumstantial evidence there is of their guilt, in addition to what is determined as newspaper information, their immediate release would not only defeat the ends of justice, but go for the encouragement of delinquency in others.

According to one story, a friend smuggled files to the prisoners in a cake. Whether or not that's true, Brady and Naughton did manage to get out of their cell one foggy night and make a run for it. Naughton tripped and fell and a guard shot him in the leg. Brady kept running down the hill until he reached Maggoty Cove. He dove into the water and swam across the Narrows. He then made his way to a squatter community in the Southside Hills and vanished from documented history.

Naughton was recaptured and taken back to jail, where an army surgeon tended to his bullet wound. He finally admitted that he and his partner were the Manchester bank robbers, and said he intended to plead guilty when he got back to England. Soon after, Naughton was put aboard the *Vesuvius* for the voyage to England. His police escort, High Constable Finlay, also had charge of the stolen money.

In spite of an intense search, Brady was never found. It's possible that he managed to slip off the island undetected. However, legend has it that the squatters hid him and he married a fisherman's daughter and became a fisherman himself.

PHILIP BRADY

For centuries, outlaws have been the inspiration for songs and legends. Real-life desperadoes like Billy the Kid, Jesse James, and Pretty Boy Floyd have been made into Robin Hood–like folk heroes, whether they deserved it or not. In Newfoundland, where it has been said that an event doesn't officially become history until someone writes a song about it, one such inspiration was Philip Brady (not to be confused with the Manchester bank robber).

In September of 1906, eighteen-year-old Philip Brady, an immigrant from England, was sentenced to eighteen months in His Majesty's Penitentiary in St. John's for stealing money from a home in Holyrood. He stood just five foot four, and didn't appear to be a person who would give the guards much trouble. But what Brady lacked in size, he made up for in nerve and resourcefulness. Brady had served about six weeks of his sentence when he decided he'd had enough of prison, with its harsh conditions and bad food. He and his cellmate, John Farrell, plotted an escape.

Brady managed to steal a coil of rope from the prison's industrial room and hid it in a barrel of kitchen waste. Later, he was one of the prisoners who took the barrels to be emptied in a part of the yard that was used as a dump. Brady made sure the rope was covered with slops so the guards wouldn't see it.

His Majesty's Prison in St. John's, Newfoundland and Labrador. Philip Brady became a local folk hero after his escape in 1906.
THE ROOMS ARCHIVES, ST. JOHN'S, NEWFOUNDLAND.

At 5:45 p.m. on October 6, when all of the prisoners were in their cells and many of the guards had gone home for the night, Brady and Farrell asked to be taken to the toilet. A single guard escorted them to the privy. While he waited outside for them to answer nature's call, they slipped out of the latrine area, made their way along a roof to the dump, and jumped down. They pulled the coil of rope out of the slops and scurried to the lower end of the prison yard where there was a turnip patch. Darkness was falling and the two lay low there until they thought it was safe for them to make their break.

Brady was the first to go over the wall. But by this time the guard at the privies had become suspicious and had raised an alarm. The prison dogs were turned loose and guards seized Farrell before he could clamber up the wall. Brady ran to Mount Carmel Cemetery where he hid until midnight. Then he disappeared into the darkness. Meanwhile, the warden ordered a thorough search of the prison and the surrounding area and alerted the police.

In the weeks that followed, little Phil Brady rose from being a lowly felon to a Newfoundland folk hero. Hard-working, law-abiding people who would never have condoned Brady's crime of theft, nonetheless cheered him on as he made fools of the police who were trying to catch him.

There were repeated sightings of Brady everywhere, especially after the offer of a reward for information leading to his capture was posted. A farmer named Patrick Coughlan told police that Brady had broken into his house in the night and stolen food and clothing. As proof, he had Brady's discarded prison uniform, which he'd found on the floor. Then Coughlan claimed that Brady had also stolen a can containing one hundred dollars. That part of Coughlan's story was soon proven untrue. But it inspired one of the first songs in the saga of Phil Brady. "Who Stole Paddy Coughlan's Can?" became a popular humorous ditty.

Days passed, with police searching high and low. Reports came to St. John's of Brady being seen in the countryside and other communities and each time constables had to go and investigate. One day John Roche McCowan, inspector general of the Newfoundland Constabulary, received a report that Brady was in Pleasantville, on the eastern edge of St. John's. A resident there said he was holding the fugitive in his home. All of McCowan's men were out chasing down (false) leads, so the inspector had to recruit a pair of firemen as special constables. When they arrived at Pleasantville, two policemen joined the little posse.

The resident met McCowan in front of his house and proudly explained how he had lured Brady inside with the promise of a meal. McCowan and his men burst into the kitchen and surprised a young man who was sitting at the table having lunch. It wasn't Brady, but a simple-minded fellow named Paul Gorman. He somewhat resembled Brady and both young men had blond hair. The case of mistaken identity was frustrating for McCowan. It was downright embarrassing when, one day later, the police responded to another tip, and once again found Paul Gorman.

Sightings of young, blond-haired men had constables running everywhere on wild goose chases. One led to a man eating lunch on a schooner in St. John's Harbour. He was a well-known local vagrant. Other searched turned up a Danish sailor and two German sailors.

The citizens of St. John's were having a great laugh at the expense of the police. They told jokes about the constables arresting bums, the simple-minded, and innocent foreigners while the elusive Brady thumbed his nose at them. Inspector General McCowan's patience was wearing thin.

Then McCowan received a telegram that Brady had been arrested at Brigus, a community on Conception Bay. Constables were bringing him to St. John's on the train — the *Newfie Bullet* — that very day. Stung by the ridicule to which the police had been subjected, McCowan helped spread the word that Brady was in police custody and would be handed over to him on the arrival of the afternoon train.

A crowd of people turned up at the station to get a look at the notorious Brady. A horse-drawn police wagon was on hand to take the escapee back to His Majesty's Penitentiary. When the *Bullet* squealed to a stop, two constables stepped out of a coach with a blond-haired man in handcuffs. The crowd roared with laughter. The police had once again picked up Paul Gorman. Humiliated and exasperated, Inspector General McCowan went to Gorman's father and told him to keep his son at home until Brady was captured.

McCowan's woes continued. Patrick Coughlan accused the police of stealing the money he'd originally said Brady had taken. People wrote letters to the local newspapers, making fun of the constabulary's failure to catch Brady. One sarcastic letter asked, "Where is our wandering boy tonight?"

The merry chase on which Phil Brady led the police ended suddenly in mid-November. The police somehow learned (possibly from an informer) that Brady was working on a farm near Petty Harbour and had a hiding place in the potato cellar. When the police cornered him, Brady tried to fight with a pitchfork, but two constables subdued him and got handcuffs on him.

Brady was taken to St. John's in a police wagon. Crowds of people lined the streets to watch him pass by. When he was taken before Inspector General McCowan, Brady said he had read the newspaper reports on the trouble he'd caused the police and had been very amused by them. No doubt Brady wasn't laughing when told he would serve an extra year in prison for escaping.

Brady's story has a tragic ending. He was released on March 5, 1908, suffering from tuberculosis. Three months later, he died in the old hospital on Signal Hill, still not twenty-one years old. He was buried in Mount Carmel Cemetery. However, he did get to bask a little in his notoriety. Shortly after Brady's capture, Johnny Burke, the "Bard of Prescott Street," wrote a short play about him that delighted St. John's audiences. There was also a popular song that went in part:

> The jailers are all nearly wild
> Their grief is awful sad
> Because they've lost their darling boy
> Their little English lad.
> Oh Brady wise, you fooled us boys
> And left us in a trance
> Filled up with holy horrors 'cause
> You stole Pad Coughlan's pants.

CHAPTER 2
BAD-MEN ON THE BORDER:
Six-Guns and Running Irons

To American outlaws on the run from sheriffs and marshals in their own country, Canada often seemed to beckon as a safe haven. American lawmen had no authority in Canada and the desperadoes believed that as long as they broke no laws in Canada, they would be safe from arrest. There are many yarns about notorious American bandits slipping across the border to enjoy a little peace and quiet in a country where nobody with a badge was looking for them. There is even a legend that Jesse James once hid out in the vicinity of Hanover, Ontario.

Of course, because of the Webster–Ashburton Treaty that existed between the United States and Great Britain, suspected criminals could be extradited from Canada to the United States, and vice versa. In 1868, the train-robbing Reno gang of Indiana, wanted for a long list of crimes that included murder, fled to Windsor, Ontario, a favourite hang-out for American bad-men on the lam. They were trailed there by Pinkerton agents and arrested by Dominion Police. The Canadian government turned the Renos over to the Americans on the condition that the outlaws be given a fair trial. Unfortunately, American vigilantes had no regard for the legalities of international treaties. A mob stormed the jail in which the Renos were being held and lynched them from the rafters. This lawless act placed a severe strain on Canadian–American relations and almost resulted in the cancellation of the extradition treaty. Ottawa's position on the matter was, "We don't care if you hang the villains; just have the decency to do it legally."

The problem was even greater in the West. The sparsely populated Canadian West drew American bad-men like a magnet. Fugitives from

American justice drifted north of the forty-ninth parallel not only to escape their own lawmen, but also because some of them believed they could carry on their marauding ways with impunity. Who was there in the Great Lone Land to stop them?

The Canadian West, during its very brief "wild" period, didn't have gunslinging lawmen like Wyatt Earp, Wild Bill Hickok, or Bat Masterson to enforce law and order. After 1874, Canada did have the North-West Mounted Police. Those men weren't always the knights in scarlet most Canadians like to believe they were. But they were, in general, much more effective as policemen than the pistol-packin' sheriffs of American cow-towns and mining camps. A Mounted Police constable was trained in police work, whereas the average sheriff was not. Moreover, a Mountie had the authority of the federal government behind him throughout Canada. An American sheriff or marshal worked in a limited jurisdiction. An American desperado who had committed a crime at one location in Canada would be surprised to learn that a Mountie could come after him in a place hundreds of miles away. Not surprisingly, in towns like Fort Benton, Montana, a place so wild and woolly it was dubbed "The Sagebrush Sodom," criminals who heard of the exploits of the Mounted Police referred to the redcoat constables as agents of British tyranny.

DUTCH HENRY

Dutch Henry was one of those Old West desperadoes whose story is such a mixture of fact and legend that it's difficult to separate one from the other. Part of the reason for this confusion lies in the fact that more than one American outlaw went by the moniker "Dutch Henry." At least three bandits used the name. There was a Dutch Henry Yauch, a Dutch Henry Baker, and a Dutch Henry Born (or Borne). Even though these men were real historical figures, not the creations of the dime-novel writers, their criminal careers were nonetheless embellished by those chroniclers of Wild West fantasies. "Dutch Henry" was a name that helped sell pulp magazines, just like Billy the Kid, Wild Bill Hickok, and the fictional Deadeye Dick.

The Dutch Henry who made a nuisance of himself to the North-West Mounted Police was one Henry Yauch (or Yeuch). He was probably born in Holland and immigrated to the United States with his family as a child. He became a cowboy in Texas and moved north during the time of the great cattle drives. He allegedly participated in the Second Battle of Adobe Walls on June 27, 1874. In that clash, a group of about twenty buffalo hunters, including young Bat Masterson, armed with high-powered rifles, stood off about two hundred southern Plains warriors led by the legendary Comanche Chief Quanah Parker.

When the ranching industry spread to the northern plains with the coming of the railroads, Dutch moved to Montana. However, in the mid-1880s, a decline in beef prices caused many ranchers to go broke. Unemployed cowboys who knew no other trade turned to rustling. Dutch Henry found that a man could make more money driving stolen cattle and horses over the Canadian border than he could ever hope to earn as an honest cowpoke. He soon learned how to use a running iron, an illegal tool used to alter the brands on livestock.

Apparently Dutch passed himself off as a legitimate stockman, while at the same time operating as a rustler with an assortment of shady characters. Among them was a former NWMP constable named Frank Carlyle. Carlyle had given up his scarlet tunic for an outlaw's duster. He would wind up dead at the bottom of a coulee, gunned down by a criminal colleague.

Thanks to the vast stretches of wide-open country and a sparse population, the outlaws could carry on their trade almost with impunity. It helped, too, that the rustlers' victims were often reluctant to go to the police (or sheriff) out of fear of reprisal. Like the gangsters of a later day, the rustlers knew that a threat could go a long way in keeping memories blank and lips sealed. When a rancher named Frank King complained to the police about the outlaws, the gang kidnapped him and kept him in their camp for two weeks. He was blindfolded most of the time and subjected to rough treatment. When the outlaws finally let King go, they warned him to stay away from the police posts. King left for parts unknown.

James Marshall, a former Mountie, was another rancher whose life was made miserable by the rustlers. His stock had been shot and run off and on at least one occasion the desperadoes had lain in ambush for him. Marshall wouldn't be frightened off as King had been, but he never left his house without his rifle and even slept with it close at hand.

It would be impossible to say how many horses and cattle Dutch Henry stole or how much money he made during his criminal career. The profits must have been substantial, because stealing, driving, and disposing of rustled livestock involved a certain amount of hard work — something most outlaws hated with a vengeance. Had the returns not been worth the effort, they'd have drifted into other enterprises — like robbing banks and trains.

Dutch Henry and his gang got away with their depredations until the summer of 1904, when Dutch ran into a Canadian rancher who was not too timid to report a robbery to the Mounted Police. In 1903 Paschal Bonneau of Willow Bunch, in what is now Saskatchewan, entered into negotiations with R.E. Hamilton of Lewiston, Montana, for the purchase of 230 horses. Bonneau hired Dutch Henry to drive the herd from Montana to his ranch at Willow Bunch. Bonneau had heard rumours that Dutch was involved with rustlers, but Dutch also had a reputation as a top-notch cowboy who could be relied upon. He decided to trust Dutch with the horses. Bonneau went to Montreal for the winter, expecting that when he returned in the spring, the horses would be at his ranch.

Instead of taking the horses to Canada, Dutch and a partner named Frank Jones, leader of one of the worst of the rustler gangs, tried to sell off the horses in Montana. But Hamilton's brand was well known, and nobody would buy the animals. Early in 1904, Dutch and Jones had a hundred of the horses taken across the border, paying the duty on them at the police post at Wood Mountain. The horses were taken to Moose Jaw and advertised as being for sale. The outlaws' agents for this business were Edward Shufelt, John Sally, and Sally's wife. They had a bill of sale "proving" they had bought the horses from Dutch Henry.

Paschal Bonneau was still in Montreal when he got word of a crooked deal involving *his* horses. He was soon on a train to Moose Jaw, where he took legal action against Shufelt and the Sallys. However, he couldn't find anyone willing to testify against Dutch Henry, so great was people's fear of the outlaw. Meanwhile it was discovered that Shufelt had a long criminal record, was known to have killed at least one man in Montana, and was wanted on a variety of charges. He was sentenced to five years and died in prison.

The honest ranchers in the area came to Bonneau's support. His stand against the rustlers was a dangerous one, but everyone knew that sooner or later the day of the outlaw had to come to an end. On the Canadian side of the line, the Mounties increased the manpower at their posts and began to crack down on the rustlers. On the American side of the line, the notorious Frank Jones tried to shoot it out with a couple of lawmen, and lost. As had happened in so many other parts of the West, the border country was becoming very uncomfortable for those men who chose to ride the Outlaw Trail.

Just what eventually became of Dutch Henry is uncertain and that may be due to people confusing the three historical Dutch Henry stories. Dutch Henry Baker's fate is lost in the mists of time. He is believed to have been shot dead, but no one knows when, where, or by whom. Dutch Henry Born spent a long time in prison and died of natural causes around 1930. As for Dutch Henry Yauch, he seems to have been killed several times over.

In 1905, it was reported that one of Dutch's own friends had murdered him in Minnesota. Then in January 1910, a Montana newspaper claimed that Dutch had been killed in a blazing gunfight with a Mountie near Moose Jaw. Dutch allegedly shot the constable's horse out from under him before the officer drilled him with a bullet in the chest. But there doesn't seem to be any documentation supporting this story. Another tale has it that, with the Mounties making life difficult for rustlers in Canada, Dutch drifted south to continue his criminal ways in Mexico, where he was finally hanged. Yet another story says Dutch gave up his evil ways, got married, and settled down in Minnesota, only to be shot dead in 1928 or 1929. There is also a claim that he travelled to South America before vanishing from history. Whatever the truth may be, Dutch Henry remains as elusive in death as he was in the years when he was the most feared rustler on both sides of the forty-ninth parallel.

FRANK SPENCER

Frank Spencer left his home in Tennessee at the age of sixteen and drifted west. He worked as a cowboy and knew Dodge City in its wild and woolly heyday when Bat Masterson and Wyatt Earp were lawmen there. He followed the stream of fortune hunters drawn by the silver strike at Tombstone in Arizona Territory. By that time, Spencer had discovered that a rustler who was handy with a rope, a running iron, and a six-gun could make a lot more money than an honest cowboy. He allegedly ran with the Clanton-McLaury gang, whose specialty was rustling cattle on both sides of the Mexican border, and selling the beef to the U.S. Army and restaurants and hotels in Tombstone. After the climactic gunfight at the OK Corral between the Clanton-Mclaury bunch and the Earp brothers and Doc Holliday, Spencer made tracks for Colorado and then Montana. He resumed his old practice of working as a cowboy by day and a rustler by night.

In 1886, Spencer fled across the international line into the Canadian territory that would one day be called Alberta. He was allegedly just a jump ahead of vigilantes who preferred lynch law over putting rustlers on trial in a legitimate court. Once he was safe in Canada, Spencer headed west. That summer, he rode into Kamloops, British Columbia.

Spencer got a job as a cowhand on Lewis Campbell's big ranch about ten miles out of town. He seemed to like it there, perhaps because his past wasn't known. For the first time in years, nobody with a badge was after him. Spencer did his job and kept out of trouble — for a while.

Frank Spencer liked his whiskey. On his days off he would ride into Kamloops for a binge in a saloon. Sometimes he'd pass a bottle around with the other cowboys in the bunkhouse. Sharing a jug of "popskull" was part of the camaraderie of ranch hands everywhere. But a misunderstanding over the etiquette of sharing liquor would lead to bloody violence at the Campbell ranch.

On Friday, May 20, 1887, Spencer was saddled up and about to ride into Kamloops. A twenty-two-year-old cowhand named Pete Foster gave him five dollars and asked him to bring back four bottles of whiskey. Spencer agreed. He bought the four bottles, but got thirsty on the ride back from town. He decided that Foster owed him something for his trouble. Any cowboy would understand that! Spencer pulled a cork from one of the bottles and took a drink.

By the time Spencer got back to the ranch, the bottle was almost empty and he was drunk. Foster met him in the corral and became angry when Spencer gave him only three bottles. It didn't ease the situation when Spencer said he'd guzzled the fourth bottle as his "share."

His temper flaring, Foster demanded that Spencer pay him for the whiskey. Spencer merely shrugged and began to unsaddle his horse.

Foster grabbed Spencer by the shoulder, spun him around, and punched him in the face, knocking him to the ground.

Foster was a tough, strapping young man and Spencer had never been one to slug it out in a fistfight. He'd always resorted to an "equalizer." He wasn't wearing a gun, but he had a knife in his belt. Drunk as he was, Spencer was on his feet quickly, with the menacing blade in his hand.

Foster wasn't about to go unarmed against a knife, so he turned and ran. Spencer chased him, but the younger man easily got away. Winded and staggering, Spencer gave up the pursuit.

Foster evidently thought that was the end of the affair, and indeed it should have been. But now Spencer was consumed with a drunken rage. He lurched into the ranch house and grabbed a Winchester rifle that Lew Campbell kept hanging on a wall. He went outside and spotted Foster walking toward the bunkhouse.

When Foster saw the rifle in Spencer's hands he started to run for cover. He didn't get far. Before any of the cowboys who had witnessed the quarrel could make a move, Spencer levered a cartridge into the firing chamber, aimed the rifle, and squeezed the trigger. The .44-calibre bullet struck Foster in the right arm and deflected into his body, tearing through his stomach. Foster spun around from the impact and dropped to the ground.

While the startled cowboys dashed to Foster's aid, Spencer ran into the barn and saddled Campbell's fastest horse. When he came out, he waved the rifle at the other cowboys and warned them to stay away from him. Then he galloped off.

At the moment, the cowhands were less concerned about apprehending Spencer than they were about getting Foster to the hospital in Kamloops. They put him in a buckboard and raced to town. A doctor removed the bullet, but the internal damage was too great. Foster died early the next morning. That same day a coroner's inquest held in the Kamloops court house came to the conclusion that: "Pete Foster came to his death by means of a rifle ball, shot from a rifle in the hands of Frank Spencer and that he [Spencer] is guilty of willful murder."

Posses of British Columbia Provincial Police and volunteer cowboys scoured the countryside in search of the killer. But Spencer stayed off the main trails and camped without fires. A week after the shooting, he crossed the border into the state of Washington. A few weeks later,

Lew Campbell posted a reward for the return of his horse, saddle, and Winchester. Nobody came forward with information. Frank Spencer had left a cold trail. As far as Canadian authorities knew, he had fled all the way to Mexico.

In fact, Spencer had gone no farther than Oregon, where he again hired out as a cowboy and kept out of trouble. Two years passed after the Foster murder and nobody came looking for him. Spencer thought that the trouble in Canada had blown over.

In the spring of 1889, Spencer was working for an Oregon rancher who asked him to accompany a group of cowboys who were taking some horses by steamer to New Westminster. Spencer cheerfully agreed. It didn't even seem to occur to him that it would be unwise for him to set foot in British Columbia.

After the steamer had docked and the horses were unloaded, the cowboys were paid. Spencer headed straight for the nearest saloon. He spent the next few days making the rounds of the grog shops on Columbia Street. Spencer was standing at a bar, quietly enjoying a drink, when a policeman put a hand on his shoulder, and, to his astonishment, told him he was under arrest. Someone from Kamloops had recognized him. Spencer was unarmed and had no choice but to accompany the officer to the New Westminster jail, protesting all the way that it was a case of mistaken identity.

Spencer was taken to Kamloops. At a preliminary hearing held in the fall, eight witnesses identified him as Frank Spencer, the man wanted for killing Pete Foster. He was bound over to the spring assizes to be tried for murder. A reporter for the *Inland Sentinel* wrote, "He does not present the appearance of a man who would commit so serious a crime as that with which he is charged." Evidently, the reporter was unfamiliar with Spencer's outlaw history.

Spencer was tried on June 2, 1890. He was convicted and sentenced to hang on July 21. When that morning dawned, Spencer had been awake all night, pacing his cell in his leg irons. He refused a last breakfast, but drank a cup of tea. He was thirty-six years old and had outlived many of his rustler comrades, most of whom had died with their boots on in gunfights or vigilante lynchings. Before he was taken from his cell, Spencer made a last request: a pair of slippers that he could wear to the gallows instead of his boots. The request was granted.

JACK DUBOIS

Jack Dubois, a.k.a. Jim Palmerston, settled on Big Knife Creek near Galahad, Alberta, in 1902. A robber and rustler, he was a wanted man throughout the American West. Dubois had shot and killed a man in Arizona, but managed to have himself acquitted of a murder charge.

In Canada, Dubois started up a ranch with about fifty head of cattle. From all appearances, he was a legitimate American stockman who had come north to take advantage of cheap grazing land. But the ranch was just a cover. Dubois was an expert with a running iron and the cowboys who worked for him were veteran rustlers.

Dubois's neighbouring ranchers began losing a lot of cattle. They couldn't help but notice that his herd was not only untouched by cattle thieves, it was also growing larger. Several times angry ranchers charged Dubois with stealing their livestock, but they couldn't prove it in court. In Montana or the Dakotas, a vigilante gang might have paid the Dubois ranch a midnight visit, but lynch law was a rarity in Canada.

Dubois was making big money off stolen cattle while he thumbed his nose at the Royal North-West Mounted Police, who just couldn't produce solid evidence against him. Flush with success, he expanded his rustling operation in 1908. Dubois moved into the Hand Hills, from which it would be easier to drive rustled cattle across the American border.

Determined to break up the rustler gang, the Mounties assigned a single officer to nail Dubois. Sergeant Robert Weld Ensor was a tough, tenacious, and dedicated policeman. His assignment was to shadow Dubois and his riders. He was to document every move they made and investigate every reported incident of cattle theft.

Connecting the wily American rancher to the rustling epidemic was a daunting task. Ensor had a thousand square miles of territory to cover and the men he was after were experts who knew how to make cattle disappear. Ensor's biggest advantage lay in the support of the beleaguered ranchers.

To avoid drawing attention to himself, Ensor put aside his uniform and dressed in the plain clothes of an ordinary cowboy. Instead of a police mount, he had a string of four cow ponies. If he needed fresh horses, ranchers gladly provided them. They also gave the Mountie every scrap of information they heard about Dubois and his men.

Ensor drifted around the territory like a cowboy riding the grub line. He discreetly asked questions and wrote down descriptions of missing cattle. At night he would slip in amongst Dubois's herd, looking for other ranchers' brands and brands that appeared to have been altered. Whenever he found a suspect animal, he quietly cut it out of the herd and took it to a neighbouring ranch where it would be kept hidden while he continued to gather evidence. Rustling from the rustlers was dangerous, because the Dubois riders wouldn't hesitate to reach for their guns if they caught him.

Meanwhile, a young homesteader from England named Henry Brace lost his entire small herd to rustlers. Brace had worked hard to get established on a parcel of land about a hundred miles northeast of Red Deer. He wasn't going to take the theft lying down. He convinced his fellow ranchers to form a delegation to take their complaints against Dubois right to Charles Cross, the attorney general of Alberta. They did that, but Cross passed them on to Superintendent A.E.R. Cuthbert of the Royal North-West Mounted Police.

As he had done many times before, Cuthbert explained to the ranchers the difficulty of building a legal case against the Dubois gang. Then he suggested that if one of the ranchers could infiltrate the gang, he might be able to provide valuable inside information for Sergeant Ensor. Brace, who was the youngest and unmarried, accepted the risky job.

Brace rode to the Dubois ranch, posing as a novice cowboy looking for work. His British accent helped him pass himself off as a greenhorn. He must have made a good impression on Dubois because he was hired. Brace had already mastered such cowboy skills as horsemanship and roping, but he put on a convincing act of learning on the job.

As a spy for the Mounties, Brace proved to be invaluable to Sergeant Ensor. He rode with the gang when they ran stolen cattle across the border. He learned the identities not only of the rustlers, but also of their shady business contacts on both sides of the line. He found that Dubois lorded it over a rustling empire that included much of southern Alberta, northern Montana, and part of Idaho. Brace was also able to report that years of committing his crimes with impunity had made Dubois cocky. He was getting careless about covering his trail. Ensor built up a considerable file of evidence. By late March 1909, he felt he was ready to move in on the Dubois gang.

On March 25, wearing his scarlet tunic and accompanied by two constables, Sergeant Ensor rode out to a ranch at Battle River. The owners, brothers named Jim and Irven Holt, were known confederates of Jack Dubois. Irven had served five years in the Idaho territorial prison for horse theft. Ensor was certain that these hard cases would try to shoot it out. But he took them completely by surprise and they gave up without a fight.

The next day the Mounties continued their round-up with the arrests of Abe and Louis Solway and Joe Cardinal. All three were principal Dubois henchmen. The police took the prisoners to the town of Stettler where they could be locked up while Ensor went after the main quarry, Jack Dubois.

However, at Stettler, Ensor learned that Dubois had somehow got word of the Mountie sweep and had fled. He sent the two constables to watch the ranch at Hand Hills in case Dubois showed up. Then Ensor resumed the painstaking task of gathering evidence.

Dubois didn't return to the ranch. Instead, he boarded a train for Calgary. The local Mountie detachment heard he was in town and arrested him in the office of lawyer Paddy Nolan, a hard-drinking Calgary legend who was known for his success in defending bootleggers, horse thieves, disorderly persons, and prostitutes. Dubois was packed off to join his men in the Stettler jail.

Sergeant Ensor had seized almost four hundred head of cattle from the Dubois and Holt ranches. Stockmen examined them and identified several as their property. Nonetheless, the legal fight with the rustler boss was just beginning.

Irven Holt was sentenced to nine years in the provincial penitentiary at Edmonton. His brother Jim got two years. Joe Cardinal and Louis Solway received relatively light sentences of a few months and Louis's brother Abe got off scot-free. Sergeant Ensor was certain that the evidence he and Henry Brace had compiled would put Jack Dubois behind bars for a long time. He was in for a great disappointment.

As a career criminal, Dubois knew how to work all the angles. He had a lot of money, and therefore a lot of influence. He allegedly spent more than $20,000 on his defence; a princely sum at that time and still just a fraction of the fortune he had accumulated over years of selling other people's cattle.

Dubois hired the very best legal talent. He was able to delay proceedings so that it took months for the prosecution to drag the case through the courts. This was an enormous drain on the slender provincial budget. Ensor looked on with disgust as finally the charges against Dubois were dismissed. The judge ruled that actual ownership of the allegedly stolen cattle had not been clearly established.

For the first time in Alberta history, the Crown appealed a court ruling. The Supreme Court of Alberta overturned the decision of the lower court and ordered a new trial. This time Jack Dubois was sentenced to five years in prison.

But the outlaw wasn't finished. While Dubois sweated at hard labour in the penitentiary at Fort Saskatchewan, his lawyers went to work. They appealed his conviction and finally convinced a court that the allegedly stolen cattle had been branded by mistake without his knowledge. Dubois was released after serving only nine months in prison. With his rustling operation broken, he got out of Alberta. Members of his gang who hadn't been arrested had long since fled to parts unknown. Alberta was at last rid of what one rancher called "a pest worse than mange."

SAM KELLY

Butch Cassidy's Wild Bunch was the last of the big outlaw gangs of the American Old West. The gang's principal hideout and headquarters was an isolated place called Hole-in-the-Wall, in Wyoming. But Cassidy (real name Robert Leroy Parker) was smarter than most bandit gang leaders. Rather than rely on one place of refuge where he and his riders could be safe from the law between robberies and large-scale rustling operations, he had a string of hideouts that stretched from Mexico to Canada. The northernmost Wild Bunch sanctuary was a cave in the Big Muddy region of Southern Saskatchewan, just across the international border.

Originally a wolf's den in the side of a butte, the cave had been enlarged so that several men could live there in relative comfort. It had an emergency escape tunnel and a water supply. A nearby high point called Peake's Butte made a good lookout post. Like other Wild Bunch hideouts, the Big Muddy cave was kept well-stocked with food. Horses could be stabled in another cave nearby.

Butch Cassidy's gang included a number of desperadoes whose names are among the most infamous of Old West bandits: the Sundance Kid (Harry Longbaugh), Kid Curry (Harvey Logan), Ben "The Tall Texan" Kilpatrick, and Bill Carver. There is no evidence that Butch Cassidy himself ever visited the Big Muddy cave, but legend has it that the Sundance Kid was often there. Sundance was in fact well acquainted with Canada, having worked on ranches in the Calgary area between bank and train robberies in the United States. He even briefly went into partnership in a Calgary saloon with a man named Frank Hamilton. Foolishly, Hamilton tried to cheat the Kid out of his share of the profits. Sundance collected his money — at gunpoint — and dissolved the partnership.

The Wild Bunch rider whose name is most often associated with the cave was Sam Kelly, one of the most successful outlaws never to have a movie made about him. "Sam Kelly" was the alias of Charles Nelson,

Canadian outlaw Sam Kelly rode with the Wild Bunch, also known as the Hole-in-the-Wall Gang, led by Butch Cassidy, seated at right. Kelly wasn't present for this photo. Seated at left is the Sundance Kid, who sometimes visited Alberta between bank and train robberies.
PINKERTON'S INC.

who was born in Nova Scotia around 1859. He was six feet tall, with a muscular 180-pound frame. His hair earned him the nickname "Red." According to those who knew him, Kelly had eyes "as cold as a fish."

Sometime in the 1880s Nelson headed west. Like so many other young easterners, he might have been drawn by the idea of living the adventurous life of a cowboy. Popular magazines were full of stories that romanticized life on the prairies. At that time, however, the cattle industry had been hard hit by dry summers, extremely cold winters, and a steep drop in the price of beef. Cowboys found themselves out of work all across the West. Some rode the "grub line," wandering from one ranch to another in search of honest work, but having to settle for a meal and a night in the bunkhouse before moving on. Others, with nothing but a horse and a Colt .45 to their name, became outlaws. Red Nelson was one of those. Because it was not safe for a bandit to operate under his own name, he became Sam Kelly.

As a Wild Bunch rider, Sam Kelly mingled with some of the border country's worst criminals. Among them were Dutch Henry, Frank Jones, and an outlaw called the Pigeon-Toed Kid, whose Colt bore five notches for men he had killed. Those bandits and others periodically shared the cave at Big Muddy with Kelly. Apparently Kelly was not the killer some of his outlaw cronies were. But he could certainly handle a gun, as he demonstrated on one occasion when he shot the rifle out of the hands of a Montana sheriff who had the drop on him.

Kelly would not turn down an armed robbery if the job looked promising, but as a professional he specialized in rustling. Kelly would steal cattle and horses on either side of the international line — sometimes as many as two hundred at a time — then run them over the border to be sold in the other country. He was even known to re-steal rustled stock he had just sold, and take the animals back over the border to be sold again. Kelly became very adept in the use of a running iron. Mere possession of that rustler's tool could send a man to jail in Canada. In the United States it could very well get him lynched.

In May 1895, Kelly was instrumental in breaking two outlaws out of the jail in Glasgow, Montana. He learned that a friend named Trotter had been locked up by the Glasgow sheriff, Sid Willis. Kelly somehow managed to have a duplicate made of the key to Trotter's cell. On May 25 a rumour spread through Glasgow — possibly started by Kelly himself

— that Sam Kelly was holed up somewhere outside of town. Sheriff Willis sent a deputy with an armed posse to apprehend the outlaw, but Kelly had stayed in town.

With most of the men in Glasgow off on a wild goose chase, Sam Kelly and a man known as Smitty rode in to liberate Trotter. Sheriff Willis had gone for lunch when the two outlaws dismounted in front of his office. When they entered the jailhouse they found the sheriff's wife sitting at her husband's desk. The woman could do nothing as the intruders unlocked the cell and released not only Trotter, but also a suspected killer — a man named Seffick who was a sometime partner of Dutch Henry. Kelly thought Seffick might be a worthy recruit for the Wild Bunch. As the outlaws left the jail, one of them gallantly tipped his hat to Mrs. Willis. Then they jumped on their horses and galloped out of town.

The sheriff's lunch was rudely interrupted when he was told of the escape. He had no one to call on to form a posse, but he bravely went after the fugitives alone. He had them in sight when one of the outlaws looked back and took a shot at him. The bullet missed, but the sound of the gunshot frightened the sheriff's horse. The animal reared up and threw the lawman to the ground. The outlaws made good their escape and were soon over the border in the safety of Big Muddy.

Sheriff Willis would have further cause to develop an intense dislike for Sam Kelly. About a year after the bust-out, he learned that Kelly and Seffick were in a Dakota town. He sent a deputy to investigate, but told the man that under no circumstances was he to try to arrest the outlaws on his own. For whatever reason — perhaps he wanted the rewards on the bandits' heads — the deputy ignored the sheriff's orders. When he encountered Kelly and Seffick, the deputy pulled a gun, fired — and missed!

The outlaws reached for their guns and the deputy dove for cover. He was a lucky man that day. Kelly and Seffick were more interested in getting away than they were in shooting a lawman. They leaped onto their horses and dashed away, leaving the deputy with the problem of explaining his rashness to Sheriff Willis.

Most of the men associated with The Wild Bunch died bloody, gunned down by lawmen or vigilantes. Butch Cassidy and the Sundance Kid fled to Bolivia where they continued their bandit ways until they died in a gunfight with Bolivian soldiers in 1908. However, one story has it that another man was killed with Sundance and Cassidy quietly returned to the United States and lived to a ripe old age under an alias.

Butch Cassidy's actual fate might be a mystery, but historians do know how Charles Nelson, alias Sam Kelly, ended his days. Kelly and his pals had things pretty much their own way until 1902, when the North-West Mounted Police set up a post at Big Muddy. The Mounties didn't like the idea of ne'er-do-wells from the United States using Canadian territory as a sanctuary from their own police. Kelly could do nothing about the police post right on his doorstep. This was nothing like the United States, where the outlaws simply had to shoot the man with the badge to blow a town wide open again. If you shot a Mountie, not only did others immediately take his place, but the redcoats also hunted you to the ends of the earth and delivered you up for trial and hanging.

By 1904, Kelly was sick and tired of outlaw life. Most of the men who had ridden with the Wild Bunch were either dead or in prison. It was remarkable that Kelly had not already shared their fate. He knew that sooner or later the Mounties would trap him, or some deputy or bounty hunter would shoot him down for the reward on his head.

Kelly rode into the town of Plentywood, Montana, and gave himself up to the sheriff there. To his astonishment (or maybe not) he was soon released. No one could produce enough evidence to convict him. Many potential witnesses could not be found. Others refused to testify. All charges were dropped. Sam Kelly rode out of town a free man, and a waste of a bullet as far as bounty hunters were concerned.

Kelly returned to the only home he had known for years, the cave in Big Muddy. He had nowhere else to go and his home in Nova Scotia was probably just a distant memory. Kelly might have made his living by hiring out as a cowboy, and he might even have done a little small-scale rustling when the Mounties weren't looking. He still knew how to use a running iron. Or maybe he had a nest egg he'd built up during his bandit days.

Kelly bought a ranch in the Big Muddy in 1909. Then in 1913 he bought another spread near Debden, Saskatchewan. The property was around a body of water that became known as Kelly's Lake. Sam's partners in the purchase were all former outlaws. Neighbours said that Kelly and his friends were frequently visited by strangers from south of the border.

Moreover, Kelly used a specially painted rain barrel as a signal to let visitors know if the Mounties were poking around.

Sam Kelly, formerly Charles Nelson of Nova Scotia, outlived all of his outlaw friends. In 1937 he fell ill and was taken to a hospital in Battleford, Saskatchewan. He died there in October of that year, at the age of seventy-eight. He was the last of the Wild Bunch.

CHAPTER 3
THE SMUGGLERS OF NOVA SCOTIA:
The Tale of the Four Sisters

For much of the eighteenth century, Nova Scotia was a popular lair for pirates. Its wild coastline provided hundreds of hidden coves that were excellent hiding places where freebooters like Captain Edward Low could put in to replenish stores of food and water, or careen a ship, unseen by naval patrols. Such isolated natural harbours were also perfect bases from which to ambush merchant vessels. There is hardly a bay or inlet along the Nova Scotia coast that doesn't have its tale of buried treasure, usually associated with the legendary Captain William Kidd. The dock at Halifax was frequently decorated with the gibbeted bodies of pirates, hung in chains and left to rot.

The Royal Navy had pretty well put an end to piracy in Nova Scotian waters by the early nineteenth century, although the last significant trial in Halifax for piracy didn't take place until 1844. However, during the War of 1812, Nova Scotia was the base for some of the most successful privateers in history. In times of war, a privateer sailed with a document called a Letter of Marque, issued by his government, which allowed him to plunder the commercial shipping of an enemy nation. It was basically a licence to commit piracy. Nova Scotian privateers wreaked such havoc with American shipping that the maritime commerce of the United States was almost brought to a halt. The Nova Scotian economy boomed as a steady stream of captured prizes sailed into Halifax. Privateer vessels like the notorious *Black Joke* became the subjects of songs and stories.

Nova Scotia's pirates and privateers contributed to the lore and mystique of sea-faring adventurers who risked their lives in the pursuit of fortunes. It was largely due to Nova Scotia's long history of sea-going marauders that the smuggler became a fact of life in colonial Nova Scotia and continued to be a thorn in the side of the law well after Confederation.

The smuggler of the nineteenth century wasn't like the modern-day smuggler who tries to sneak illegal narcotics into a country. There were no illegal narcotics then. Drugs like morphine were widely used as painkillers and were readily available. The nineteenth-century smuggler's challenge was to bypass the customs collector, the government official whose responsibility it was to ensure that duties were paid on imported goods.

The smuggler dealt in just about any commodity that could be sold on the black market: manufactured goods, liquor, tobacco, tea and coffee, sugar, clothing, and silk. Once he got his merchandise into the country, he sold it to storekeepers and travelling peddlers. They in turn sold it to their customers at lower prices than legal imports on which duties had been paid. For that reason, the smuggler was often seen as a Robin Hood type of outlaw, while the customs collector was cast in the role of the villainous agent of the Crown.

Often the smuggler had to unload his cargo at an isolated cove or at some quiet little port where the locals could be trusted to keep their mouths shut. Would-be snitches were bought off or threatened. With a well-placed bribe or two, the smuggler might also sail into a major port like Halifax and unload his goods while the customs collector looked the other way.

Because of its geography, Nova Scotia was a smuggler's paradise. It was a major point of entry for merchandise coming to Canada from Britain and continental Europe, and from ports along the eastern seaboard of the United States, particularly Boston. Also, lying just a few miles off the coast of Newfoundland were the islands of Saint Pierre and Miquelon, the last specks of the French empire in North America. The two mainstays of the islanders' economy were fishing and smuggling. The French brandy sipped in the finer homes of Halifax, Montreal, and Toronto was as likely to have been smuggled into the country via Nova Scotia as to have legally passed under the eye of an official in a customs house.

As unpopular as the customs collector was, he didn't stand alone against the smugglers. In all coastal Nova Scotian communities, every person of authority responsible for enforcing the law and keeping the peace, from magistrates down to village constables, was duty-bound to watch out for these robbers of the government purse. One of the most diligent was police detective Peter Owen "Peachie" Carroll.

Born in Pictou, Nova Scotia, in 1860, Carroll was an adventurer. He was big, bull-strong, tough, and took guff from no man. A veteran sailor, Carroll had been "round the horn," and had once thwarted mutineers. He had served as chief of police in Pictou and Yarmouth. As a police detective, Carroll had apprehended enough lawbreakers to earn a reputation equal to that of John Wilson Murray, the nineteenth-century Ontario sleuth who became known as Canada's Great Detective. One of Carroll's most notable accomplishments was his 1892 capture of one of the murderers of Constable Joseph Steadman of Moncton, New Brunswick. If Peachie Carroll had been American, his life story might well have been the inspiration for a movie, because at times he was as much a bounty hunter as he was an officer of the law. The Canadian government offered rewards for the capture of smugglers.

Peter Owen "Peachie" Carroll, right, Nova Scotia's legendary detective.
A.E. DALTON.

In the summer of 1892, Carroll was self-employed as a private detective, one of just a few in the Maritimes. He'd been officially sworn in as a constable by the Pictou Police Department so he had the legal authority to make arrests. That July he was hired by Captain LeMaistre of the coastal steamer *St. Olaf*, and ship's purser William Tait to investigate a theft.

A year earlier, the Quebec firm of Richards & Company had shipped two crates of fishermen's long boots to Grand Entry in the Magdalen Islands, an archipelago belonging to Quebec, though geographically closer to Prince Edward Island and Nova Scotia. The crates had been taken by train to Pictou, and then loaded aboard the *St. Olaf*, which made a regular run to Souris, Prince Edward Island, and the Magdalens. Grand Entry had no wharf at the time, so ships anchored a half-mile offshore, and passengers and freight were ferried ashore in boats. Somewhere between Pictou and Grand Entry, one crate containing forty-eight pairs of boots disappeared. Richards & Company held the *St. Olaf*'s owners responsible for the lost merchandise.

The theft of a crate of fishing boots might seem a trivial reason for engaging the services of a private detective. However, the ship's owners would have been concerned that someone within their firm or connected to it was pilfering. If so, the problem had to be nipped in the bud. For Carroll, the case quickly became something larger than one of petty larceny.

While Carroll was still in Pictou, preparing for the trip to Grand Entry on the *St. Olaf*, he received a tip that smugglers carrying liquor from Saint Pierre and Miquelon often put in at the Magdalens before heading for the St. Lawrence River and Quebec City. Carroll smelled opportunity. He obtained a warrant from the Pictou customs collector that gave him the power of arrest and seizure within Canada's three-mile offshore limit. When Carroll boarded the *St. Olaf*, he carried a rifle and a fishing rod so he'd appear to be a sportsman on holiday. He also packed two revolvers, a .38 and a .44.

En route to the islands, Carroll met Captain Alexander O'Brien, an evangelical missionary on his way to Grosse-Île. Considering the preacher trustworthy, Carroll told him what his own real mission was. He asked O'Brien to contact him by telegraph if he heard any information about smugglers in the area. O'Brien agreed.

Carroll also made the acquaintance of a man named Fly, who was the manager of the Portland Packing Company in the Magdalens. The detective knew that the crate of boots that had *not* been stolen was safely delivered to Fly's company. Mr. Fly didn't make a very good impression on Carroll, who found his demeanor suspicious. Carroll would later say that the man was "Fly by name and fly by nature."

On Grand Entry, Carroll stayed at the home of the port master while he poked around for information about the stolen boots. He'd been there only two days when he received a wire from O'Brien telling him to come to Grosse-Île at once. A smuggler's ship was lying at anchor just off the island.

Carroll didn't lose a minute. Armed with his warrant and his two pistols, he hired a man with an open boat to take him to Grosse-Île. There he met O'Brien and a local man named Alexander MacLean. They pointed to a schooner anchored about a mile and a half from shore. "There is a smuggler," one of them said. They suspected the ship was outward bound from the French islands with a cargo of liquor.

With his veteran sailor's eye, Carroll could tell from the set of the sails that the schooner was about to get underway. He had to act quickly or she'd be gone. Spotting four fishermen sitting by a boat on the beach, Carroll hired them to row him out to the schooner. He left O'Brien and MacLean on the beach.

As his boat drew alongside the schooner, Carroll saw her name: *Four Sisters*. He climbed aboard while the fishermen waited in the boat. At first Carroll could see no one on deck, but within moments he was confronted by the captain, a man named Cormier who spoke to him in French. Realizing that the stranger didn't understand him, Cormier demanded in English, "Who are you? What do you want?"

Carroll showed Cormier the warrant and told him he was going to search the ship for contraband liquor. While the angry captain stood by, Carroll opened the main hatch. The hold was half full of cases of liquor. Then Carroll looked in the cabin and found more cases. The detective had caught a smuggler red-handed! Carroll went to the main mast and marked it with an official symbol of the Crown that branded the *Four Sisters* as legally seized and now the property of Her Majesty Queen Victoria's Canadian government.

But Captain Cormier wasn't about to just hand his ship and cargo over to this meddling intruder. He shouted in French to the fishermen who were waiting for Carroll. The men immediately pushed off from the schooner and then put their backs to it as they rowed for shore. When Carroll saw that they were abandoning him, he shouted that he'd pay them twenty dollars each if they'd come back and get him. Twenty dollars was a lot of money in 1892, but for whatever reason — doubt in Carroll's word or fear of the smugglers — the men didn't respond. They kept rowing as though they hadn't heard him.

It was now twilight, with darkness quickly rolling in across the water, and Carroll was alone on a smuggler's ship that he had officially seized. Although the schooner had been made ready to sail when he first saw her from the beach, the crew had gone below to have their supper by the time he climbed aboard. Now the crewmen were all out on deck, seven of them plus the captain!

Cormier spoke to his men in French, and from the laughter that followed, Carroll guessed that the captain must have explained the situation to them. A detective had come aboard to catch them, but instead *they* had caught *him*! The question now was what to do about him. Carroll had no doubt that he was in a dangerous predicament. The captain *might* decide to put him ashore somewhere, but then Carroll could still make his way to some place where he could report to the authorities and Cormier's days as a smuggler would be over. The captain just might consider other, darker, alternatives.

Keeping his distance from the crewmen, Carroll warily backed to the schooner's bow. The confines were narrower there, so he'd have a better chance of defending himself if they tried to rush him. The smugglers didn't know about the two pistols in his pockets.

Cormier tried putting on a friendly face. He invited Carroll to join him for supper and a glass of wine or brandy. Carroll refused the offer and then used a ploy of his own. He told Cormier that he was a government agent from the Canadian revenue cutter *Acadia*, which was based in Halifax. The *Acadia* was armed with a cannon and was famous for chasing down smugglers. The prospect that she might be nearby evidently worried Cormier, but he wasn't sure if he should believe Carroll.

Cormier asked why, if Carroll had just come from the *Acadia*, he couldn't see the cutter. Knowing that his life might depend on how convincingly he could spin a yarn, Carroll said that the *Acadia*'s captain had sent him ahead to intercept the *Four Sisters*. The cutter, he lied, was on her way from Grand Entry, sailing around Grosse-Île to cut off the smuggler's escape.

Captain Cormier fell for Carroll's story. He ordered the crewmen into their quarters in the main cabin and he went into his own, leaving Carroll on deck alone. The crewmen climbed into their bunks, fully dressed in case they should be suddenly called on deck. Cormier sat up, trying to think of a way to get rid of Carroll and give the *Acadia* the slip.

At around 10:00 p.m., with the night around the *Four Sisters* as dark as the water below, Carroll began to creep around the deck to do a little sabotage. He removed the brakes from both windlasses, throwing one overboard and hiding the other in case he should need it. With the wind-lasses disabled, the crew couldn't hoist the ship's two anchors. There was a possibility that the schooner could run aground in rising winds, but Carroll was a strong swimmer and believed he could make it to shore if that happened.

There was still lamplight in the main cabin window. Carroll crept aft and peered inside. The seven crewmen were all dozing in their bunks. Carroll sat by the window and watched them. The one thing he couldn't afford to do now was fall asleep himself.

At about midnight, Captain Cormier came out on deck. He asked Carroll if he'd seen any sign of the *Acadia*. Carroll said he'd just seen her lights flickering in the distance. Cormier looked across the dark, heaving sea and saw nothing. A light wind had come up and he decided to take advantage of it. Convinced now that Carroll had been bluffing, Cormier shouted orders in French to his men. Jolted awake, the men leaped out of their bunks.

"What's the idea?" Carroll demanded.

Cormier said they were weighing anchor and going back to Saint Pierre. That's when Carroll drew his revolvers and aimed them at Cormier. "Get back in your cabin, or I'll shoot," he ordered.

Taken by surprise, Cormier hesitated. Then, looking down the muzzles of two pistols, he realized Carroll meant business. He withdrew to his cabin and closed the door.

Carroll turned to the crewmen at the door of the main cabin. None of them spoke English, but they understood Carroll's meaning when he used his guns to wave them back inside and into their bunks. Spotting a rifle hanging on the cabin wall, Carroll took it. The gun was fully loaded with six cartridges. If one of the sailors had thought to grab it earlier, Carroll's adventure aboard the *Four Sisters* might have ended in an unsolved mystery of the sea.

Carroll tied the captain's and the crew's cabin doors shut with cords. He also shoved a piece of deck machinery against the main cabin door. Then, with the rifle cradled in his arms, Carroll paced the deck, fighting off sleep and waiting for dawn. He still didn't know how he was going the get the *Four Sisters* to a port where Cormier and his crew of smugglers could be taken into custody.

At sunrise, Carroll saw a small boat approaching from Grosse-Îsle. He shouted and waved his arms to get attention. The boatman was a lobsterman heading out to retrieve his traps. Carroll gave him five dollars to go back and send a telegram. The message was for Mr. Joncas, the customs collector at House Harbour Island. It said, "Aboard seized schooner Four Sisters bay Grosse-Îsle."

About noon the lobsterman returned with Joncas's response. He was on his way and he wanted Carroll to hold the *Four Sisters*. The lobsterman also brought the hungry detective some sandwiches and a bottle of milk, courtesy of his friend O'Brien.

Later that afternoon Joncas arrived with seven men, much to Carroll's relief. He undid the cords securing the captain's door, and Joncas went in to talk to Cormier. The captain must have been furious when he finally knew for certain that the *Acadia* wasn't in the vicinity at all. The *Four Sisters'* crew were kept locked in their cabin. The sailors who'd accompanied Joncas got the schooner underway. Since one windlass brake was missing, they had to use a crowbar as a substitute.

The *Four Sisters* arrived at House Harbour at eight o'clock the next morning. Carroll helped Joncas's men unload the contraband liquor and carry it into the Customs House. Records showed a previous smuggling charge against Cormier and the *Four Sisters*. That time, Cormier had gotten off with a fine. Now he'd used up his last chance. His schooner was officially confiscated by the Canadian government. She'd be sold at auction the following spring. Captain Cormier and his men were fined for smuggling. No doubt they cursed the name of Detective Carroll all the way back to Saint Pierre.

The seizure of the *Four Sisters* meant a handsome reward for Carroll, not to mention a boost to his prestige as a private detective. But he hadn't forgotten the case that had taken him to the Magdalens in the first place. Carroll went back to Grand Entry to resume his investigation concerning the missing boots.

Carroll had sensed something dishonest about Mr. Fly, so he went to the office of the Portland Packing Company to talk to him. He was told that the manager was away. Using his authority as a police constable, Carroll demanded to look at Fly's account books. The ledger showed that Fly had sold forty-eight more pairs of fishermen's boots than he had ordered from Richards & Company.

When Fly returned, Carroll confronted him with the evidence. Fly admitted to stealing the boots. To avoid prosecution, he gave Carroll the money the owners of the *St. Olaf* had lost, to be passed on to them. He also paid Carroll's expenses.

Of course, the age-old game of cat-and-mouse that smugglers played with the law continued along Canada's east coast. The lure of a cash payoff was too great for many fishermen and other sailors to resist. Five years after his single-handed capture of the *Four Sisters*, Carroll was involved in the seizure of another liquor smuggler right in Pictou harbour; the schooner *Union*, commanded by Captain Lawrence Lavache of Cape Breton. However, it was the story of the night he stood alone on the deck of a smuggling ship in the Magdalen Islands that helped make Peachie Carroll a Nova Scotia legend.

CHAPTER 4
THE NEWTON GANG:
Texas Bandits in Canada

Willis Newton stood on a corner in downtown Toronto one July morning in 1923, and could hardly believe what he saw. Five pairs of men were coming down the sidewalk from a building at the corner of Yonge and Wellington Streets, each pair carrying a large leather bag. The bags appeared to be heavy. Behind each pair walked a guard with a holstered pistol. As Willis watched, the little groups split up, heading off down different streets. Willis followed one of them because he had a strong hunch those bags contained money. Sure enough, the men went into a bank.

It seemed almost unbelievable to Willis that bags fat with money were conveyed through city streets by men on foot, protected only by guards armed with weapons he considered mere pop-guns. In the United States, money shipments went by armoured car. Willis's bewilderment gave way to the excitement of a man who has just struck gold. Willis Newton was the leader of one of the most prolific bandit gangs in American history. He had just lost a lot of money in oil speculation in the United States, and had gone to Toronto to scout possibilities for recouping his finances the way he knew best — robbery!

Over the next few mornings, Willis followed the men with the bags, studying their daily routine. He learned that in addition to Canada's official currency, Canadian financial institutions like the Bank of Commerce, the Bank of Nova Scotia, and the Standard Bank each issued their own paper money. The banks all honoured one another's bills when customers brought them in. Every morning at nine o'clock, the banks in Toronto's downtown core sent messengers with hundreds of thousands of dollars in cash to the clearing house at the corner of Yonge and Wellington for sorting. Less than an hour later, the messengers carried bags full of bills back to the banks to which they belonged. Some of the banks had started using cars to transport the money, but others still employed foot messengers. Sometimes one man carried a bag, but if it was especially heavy, two men would carry it between them. Willis thought it was the silliest system he had ever seen. But it looked like a bank robber's dream come true. Willis sent for his brothers: Joe, Wylie (Doc), and Jess.

Born to a large, hard-working, but dirt-poor Texas family, the Newton boys had known tough times all their lives. The family roamed around south Texas earning a meagre living picking cotton and other crops. Sometimes they had a shack for a home; other times they lived in a covered wagon. James, the boys' father, taught them to hunt rabbits and deer to put meat on the table. Once a year their mother, Janetta, bought material from which she made their clothes by hand. Education was a luxury the Newtons couldn't afford. Willis didn't see the inside of a school until he was twelve. He learned to read and write, but within a year he stopped going to school because he was embarrassed by his ragged pants. Joe and Doc didn't have much more schooling than Willis, and Jess was illiterate.

Janetta told the boys stories about Frank and Jesse James and the Dalton gang. To the young Newtons, these legendary outlaws were Robin Hood–like folk heroes. In the summer of 1902, the notorious desperado Harry Tracy broke out of the Oregon State Penitentiary and became the object of a highly publicized manhunt. Thirteen-year-old Willis followed the unfolding drama day-by-day, thrilled by newspaper accounts of the outlaw's defiance and narrow escapes. Then, after being on the run for almost two months, Tracy was wounded in a gunfight and cornered. To avoid capture, he committed suicide. Willis Newton wept at the news.

In spite of their fascination with Wild West outlaws, the Newton brothers weren't troublemakers growing up. Then in 1909, eighteen-year-old Doc stole a bale of cotton worth about fifty dollars. When the local sheriff couldn't find Doc, he decided that Willis, age twenty, was an accomplice and arrested him instead. A "tough on crime" judge felt it was in the best interests of society to make an example of Willis and sentenced him to two years' hard labour in the Texas State Penitentiary. Soon after, Doc was arrested for pilfering stamps from a post office. Again, the punishment was excessive for a minor offence. Sentenced to two years, Doc joined Willis in prison.

The Texas State Penitentiary was a brutal place where prisoners were starved and beaten. Medical facilities were non-existent. Willis and Doc didn't want to end up like the many inmates who were buried in the prison's large cemetery, so they escaped. They were recaptured, and had time added to their sentences. In four years of incarceration, the young men mixed with criminals of every sort. If they weren't hard cases when they entered the prison, they were by the time they got out. Moreover, once they'd been released they found it difficult to get honest employment because they were "jailbirds."

Bitter over spending four brutal years in prison for a petty theft he hadn't committed, Willis was determined to get even. He and a partner robbed a train and got away with $4,700. Now Willis Newton really was an outlaw like Jesse James and Harry Tracy. Doc also walked out of prison and into a life of crime.

Over the next few years, both brothers were sent to jail several times and then escaped. Willis once obtained a pardon by means of a series of forged letters. They also found that some sheriffs and judges could be bribed. Willis usually operated as a burglar, stealing clothing from stores at night and then selling it at bargain prices to people who asked no questions. In 1916 he joined a gang for a bank robbery in Oklahoma and made his getaway on horseback. He then joined a gang of bank burglars and learned the art of blowing safes and vaults open with nitroglycerine.

While Willis and Doc were running afoul of the law, Joe and Jess were earning honest livings as cowboys and bronc busters. It was gruelling work that didn't pay much. In 1920, Willis convinced them to join him in forming an outlaw gang. He'd been unimpressed with most of the criminals he'd worked with, considering them reckless and stupid. He thought his brothers would be more reliable and trustworthy. That year Doc broke out of prison where he was doing time on a robbery conviction and joined the gang. From time to time Willis would bring one of his ne'er-do-well cronies in on a job if he thought the boys could use an extra hand.

The Newton Gang plundered banks in Texas, Oklahoma, Kansas, Arkansas, Nebraska, Colorado, Iowa, Missouri, North Dakota, Wisconsin, and Illinois. They also stole company payrolls and robbed trains. In later years, Willis and Doc would boast that the Newton Gang robbed six trains and at least eighty banks. They stole more money than the James-Younger Gang, the Dalton Gang, and Butch Cassidy's Wild Bunch combined. In their heyday, the Newton boys lived in a manner their parents had never dreamed of. They wore expensive suits and diamond tie pins. They bought new cars every year. They stayed in the best hotels. As Willis put it, "We wasn't thugs. All we wanted was the money. Just like doctors and lawyers and other businessmen. Robbing banks and trains was our way of getting it. That was our business."

The Newton Gang usually preyed on small-town banks. In the dead of night they would cut the telephone and telegraph wires, shutting off outside communication. Night guards and interfering sheriffs or deputies were waylaid and then tied up. Breaking into the banks was easy. Then, while the robbers on the inside worked on the safe, the others waited outside in case the noise of the exploding nitro attracted attention. If it did, the men standing guard warned the people to keep away. A shotgun blast fired into the air was usually enough to send them scurrying back indoors. Then the gang made its getaway in a fast car. However, on one occasion, some of the townsmen grabbed guns and began shooting. The four brothers escaped without a scratch, but a man who was with them was killed. Because they preferred to avoid shootouts, the Newton Gang only occasionally pulled daytime stick-ups. Looting a bank at night was less troublesome and there was less chance of being identified.

For a long time police didn't know who was behind the rash of bank burglaries. After all, the Newtons weren't the only bandits who were blowing safes at night. The Texas Bankers Association, enraged at the frequency of the robberies and frustrated with the failure of the law to apprehend the culprits, eventually had a notice posted in every bank in the state:

REWARD

FIVE THOUSAND DOLLARS FOR DEAD BANK ROBBERS

NOT ONE CENT FOR LIVE ONES

The trip Willis Newton took to Toronto in the summer of 1923 wasn't his first visit to Canada, nor even to Toronto. The previous September, the Newton boys, posing as tourists on a fishing vacation, had rented a cabin at Pelican Lake, Manitoba. It was their base while they raided banks in local communities. A colleague had told Willis that Canadian banks used old-fashioned safes that were easier to blow than the tough new models that American banks had started to install.

"We never worried about the Mounties," Willis said years later. "Canadian Mounties don't amount to a hill of beans ... Mounties can do no more than anybody else, and anyway, they couldn't put guards on the banks because they didn't know what bank was going to be robbed." It's worth noting that Willis was just as contemptuous of the Texas Rangers.

From their lair at Pelican Lake, the Newton boys pillaged the banks in Melita, Manitoba, and Moosomin, Saskatchewan. They might also have been responsible for the robbery of the Bank of Montreal in Ceylon, Saskatchewan, on September 27. The *modus operandi* would have been familiar to American police: communication wires cut, safe blown with nitro, quick getaway by automobile. In the Melita job, the brothers learned of the Canadian bankers' practice of having someone sleep in an upstairs room. This was supposed to discourage robbers. When the nitro blast brought cries of alarm from upstairs, Willis shouted, "You go back to bed and stay put, and you ain't going to get hurt."

According to Willis, because of the robberies he and his brothers pulled, "They quit having people sleep up over them places. They took everybody out. At least in that country they did."

The few people who had encountered the bandits reported that they had American accents. Police picked up several suspects and then let them go. After three weeks at Pelican Lake, the Newton boys drove to Winnipeg. They had their automobile loaded into a boxcar and then travelled separately by train to Toronto.

To avoid drawing attention, the Newtons got rooms in different Toronto hotels. That would also make it more difficult for police to trace them later. Then they scouted the small towns near the city, looking for a promising target. Willis later recalled, "First day we was out, we found a good one. Good location and everything, wasn't but twenty-five miles outside of Toronto there. We drove the getaway, working out a route so that we wouldn't run into nobody and could stay off the main roads."

On the night of October 24, the Newton Gang hit the Standard Bank in Stouffville. They cleaned out the safe and then drove back to Toronto. The robbers were dropped off at different locations to take streetcars to their respective hotels, with the exception of the driver, who left that very night for Detroit. Over the next couple of days, the bandits boarded trains for different American destinations. The brothers soon got together in Chicago to divide the loot.

The Stouffville bank robbery was a big news story in Toronto. More than $100,000 had been taken. However, $90,000 of it was in registered Dominion of Canada bonds, which were utterly valueless to the bandits. They had no way of fencing them the way they did stolen, unregistered American bonds. Nonetheless, the boys were pleased with the cash they'd taken; between ten and thirteen thousand dollars. Willis's fond memory of Stouffville was, "It was a pretty good little town."

Ontario Provincial Police investigated the crime, assisted by the Toronto Police. They had no idea who had pulled the robbery. They believed it was the work of American professionals who had learned about Canadian banks through bootlegging connections. The police were certain, however, that there was no connection between the Stouffville robbery and the bank robberies in Manitoba and Saskatchewan. Those western robberies, the police said, had probably been committed by American border bandits who had also robbed a bank in Alberta before running back to the United States.

Willis had no worries about returning to Toronto less than a year later. He went there with the intention of scouting another small-town bank that he and his brothers could knock over without any trouble. Instead, he saw the golden opportunity of bags of money in the bank messengers' hands, ripe for the taking.

Joe, Doc, and Jess answered Willis's call and put up in Toronto hotels. They watched the bank messengers and agreed that the pickings should be easy. But they didn't want to rush things. The brothers took a side trip to Montreal just because they'd never been there before. While he was there, Willis bought a Browning automatic twelve-gauge shotgun. Back in Toronto, Willis sawed "six or eight inches off of it so it would be short and I could handle it easy."

Besides firepower, the gang also needed a getaway car. They had always favoured the Studebaker, with its big six-cylinder engine. By sheer luck, Willis happened to be on the street when he saw a man park a maroon Studebaker Big Six at the curb and dash into a store. Willis looked inside and saw the key in the ignition. He hopped in and drove the car to a garage the gang had already rented. There he removed the licence plates and put on a stolen set.

On the morning of July 24, the Newtons were ready to strike. For their ambush they had chosen the intersection of Jordan and Melinda Streets, a block east of Yonge Street and a block south of King. The brothers were all armed with pistols and two of them had shotguns. Willis had planned for them to grab five big money bags.

The foot messengers left the clearing house and headed north on Yonge Street, soon to be followed by two cars carrying money for the Molson's Bank and the Standard Bank. They turned left on Melinda and proceeded toward Jordan Street. At 9:45, the usually staid Toronto streets suddenly resembled the OK Corral. The account given by Joe and Willis years later differed in some details from those that appeared in Toronto newspapers within hours of the holdup. The one point they had in common was that the robbery wasn't the easy job the gang thought it would be.

Left to right, Willis and Joe Newton, Texas bandits who shot it out with bank messengers in downtown Toronto.
CLAUDE STANUSH AND DAVID MIDDLETON.

As the messengers made their way along Melinda Street, the mauve Studebaker drove past them and pulled over to the curb on the other side of Jordan. It was facing south, toward Wellington Street. Willis, Jess, and Doc got out, leaving Joe at the wheel with the motor running.

Wielding his sawed-off shotgun, Willis confronted James Brown and William Duck of the Union Bank. "Give me that bag!" he ordered. The startled messengers refused. Willis fired a blast into a telephone pole to show them he meant business. Brown let go of his bag and backed off. But Duck, a veteran of the Great War, held on to his and struck at Willis with his fist.

Willis tried to shoot at Duck's feet, but the shotgun jammed, so he used it to club Duck to the ground. Then Willis went for the pistol in his coat pocket. It got caught in the lining, and he had to drop the shotgun so he could use both hands to free it. Brown grabbed the money bag he had dropped and raced for a doorway. Duck got up and followed, leaving his bag, but attempting to draw his revolver as he ran. Before Duck reached the shelter of the doorway, he turned and faced the bandit. Willis shot him. The bullet struck him in the left side above the heart and tore right through his body. Duck staggered and fell to the pavement.

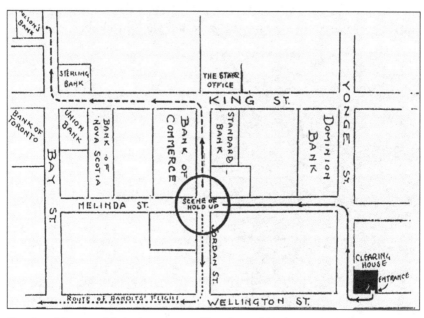

Overview of the scene of the bank-messenger robbery. Some of this area is now the site of Commerce Court Plaza

THE *GLOBE AND MAIL.*

At the same time, David Campbell of the Sterling Bank refused to hand his bag over to Doc. Like William Duck, he tried to put up a fight. According to Willis, "He was coming out with his gun and Doc had to shoot him, but he didn't shoot to kill him. Just shot to hurt him." Actually, Campbell was unarmed. Doc shot him at almost point-blank range, and Campbell went down with a bullet in his left lung.

Jess had seen Doc struggling with Campbell and thought his brother was in trouble. He started to run to his assistance. That left the way clear for a couple of messengers to dash for safety. Meanwhile, the men in the two bank cars had seen the attacks on the foot messengers. The driver of the Molson's Bank car pulled into a lane beside the Toronto *Globe* building. The Standard Bank car stopped partway into the intersection, and guards Peter Robb and James Harris jumped out. Robb crouched beside the car and fired at the bandits with his revolver. Harris, another Great War veteran, ran to Campbell's aid with his gun drawn. Doc shot him in the shoulder. Harris fell to his knees and returned fire. Jess fired a shotgun blast at him and some of the buckshot struck Harris in the stomach. He sank to the pavement, but fired the last rounds in his gun at the bandits' car.

A street corner that had been quiet just a minute earlier was now chaotic. The echo of gunfire rang off buildings. Passersby ducked for cover as people poured out of buildings to see what all the commotion was about. Bandits shouted at people to get out of the way if they didn't want to get blown to hell. Bullets smacked into telephone poles, walls, and the windshield and door of the Standard Bank car. A Bank of Nova Scotia messenger named A. Smith handed over his bag when ordered to do so because he was looking down the muzzle of a shotgun. Even after he'd handed over the money, a bandit shot the hat off his head.

A Sterling Bank guard named R. Davis was at the rear of the messenger group when he saw the bandits leap out of their car and attack. Seeing another bandit at the wheel of the car, Davis advanced on it with his gun blazing. Joe got out and fired back. He later claimed that he wasn't trying to hit the guard; just scare him off. Davis had to back off when he ran out of ammunition. Guards like Robb and Davis were at a disadvantage; they had to take care not to accidentally shoot innocent bystanders.

An unlikely participant in the melee was Alan Lord, an elevator operator in the McKinnon Building on Melinda Street. He'd been drawn outside by the racket. Lord saw Duck struck down, and rushed to his aid. It's possible that because of his work uniform, the bandits mistook Lord for a guard or a policeman. He later told a Toronto *Star* reporter:

> I grabbed at the bandit and another man struck me over the back and shoulders with the stock of a large new shotgun. He was swearing terribly and telling me he'd knock my brains out if I didn't let go. I did let go, but they fired four shots at me. One of them got me in the leg. I thought it was all over as I fell like a ton of lead, but that is probably what saved me. I crawled underneath an auto standing close by. The buckshot simply riddled the body and windows of the car.

The Newtons managed to grab three money bags. They threw them into the Studebaker and then piled in. Guards fired at the back of the car as it roared down Jordan Street. Eighteen-year-old William Young, driving a Salvation Army truck, had turned onto Jordan in time to witness almost the whole event. He tried to chase the bandit car, but his truck couldn't keep up with the fast Studebaker.

Joe drove down Jordan and turned right on Wellington. Willis later recalled:

> How we ever got away, I don't know. Then we hit a main street going to the right. I said, 'Turn right in there,' and we got room to cut in.... We was coming up on the main street (probably Bay Street) and they had a policeman standing there directing traffic. Just as we run up there and I was fixing to jump out and throw my pistol down on him, he stuck out his hand to stop the other cars and told us to come on ... the policeman didn't know what had happened back there.

After hiding the car and the money bags in their rented garage, Willis and Jess returned to their hotel while Joe and Doc went to a movie. They knew there would be a dragnet and roadblocks, so they decided to lay low for a couple of days and act like tourists. They hadn't been masked, but they were confident that nobody would have gotten good descriptions in all the excitement.

The Newtons had escaped from the scene of the crime, but they were shaken. They hadn't expected a shootout. Willis admitted years later that the Toronto bank-messenger robbery was one of the few times in his life that he'd been "boogered" (frightened).

The whole drama at the intersection of Jordan and Melinda had played out in less than two minutes. Toronto police arrived on the scene about a minute after the gang drove off. Duck, Harris, Campbell, and Lord

Artist's sketch of the Newton Gang's bank-messenger robbery in Toronto on July 23, 1923. This crime was dramatized in the 1998 film The Newton Boys, *starring Matthew McConaughey and Ethan Hawke.* THE *GLOBE AND MAIL.*

were rushed to hospitals. Only Campbell, with his punctured lung, had a life-threatening injury. His wife and son stayed at his bedside while he lay in critical condition. "I hope they get those blackguards," Mrs. Campbell told the press. "They are beasts and have no conscience whatever." Happily, Campbell recovered.

The gang had pulled off what was, up to that date, the biggest robbery in Toronto history. The swag was about $84,000. The violence shocked the citizenry. After all, this was Toronto the Good, not Chicago. The *Star* reported, "It seemed less like a scene in orderly Toronto than like a climax in a sensational moving picture show."

The robbers left confusion in their wake. Witnesses thought there had been as many as six or seven bandits. They also thought that one of the bandits had been shot. One witness was sure that the driver of the getaway car had been a "coloured man." In Willis and Joe's account, only the brothers were in on the job and none of them were injured.

The only potential clue the bandits left behind was the shotgun Willis dropped, and police had no way of even tracing where it came from.

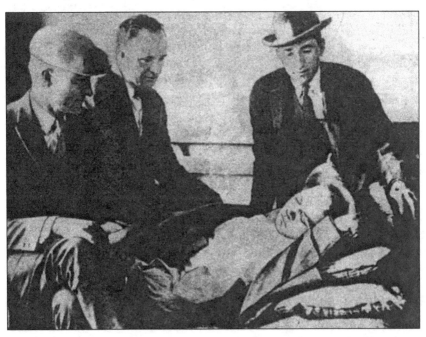

Willis, Jess, and Joe Newton in court with Doc (foreground) who had been wounded during a train robbery.
CLAUDE STANUSH AND DAVID MIDDLETON.

The press speculated that the bandits were "U.S. Jailbirds." The day after the robbery, police found the burned-out hulk of the Studebaker near Fort Erie. It seemed that the robbers had fled across the border with the loot.

Actually, the Newtons had buried most of the money in what Willis called "sandy country" about thirty miles from Toronto. Then they went to Niagara Falls and took a ferry to the American side. Each brother had about five thousand dollars under his shirt, sewn into a vest made of "ducking material." They took a train to Chicago and stayed there a week. Then they went back to Canada to recover the loot. The gang drove across the border at Niagara Falls in a car that had money stuffed under all the seats. Then, through connections in the Detroit underworld, Willis exchanged the Canadian money for American greenbacks.

Years later, Willis claimed that the Newtons returned to Toronto, thinking of pulling another robbery. They were disappointed to see that the foot messengers were gone. All of the money was now transferred by car and there were even well-armed policemen on horseback. That killed any plans of a repeat raid. They went back to Chicago, but still hadn't given up on the idea of another heist in Canada. Willis and Jess went to Winnipeg, which also had a currency clearing house. But the situation was the same as in Toronto. The money was too heavily guarded to be easy pickings. Willis said, "And I think it was because of what we'd done in Toronto."

In spite of their long string of successes, Willis wanted the Newtons to make one big haul that would set them all up for life and enable them to get out of the outlaw "business" for good. On June 12, 1924, the Newton boys and a partner named Brent Glasscock robbed a train at Rondout, Illinois. They plundered the mail cars for more than 3 million dollars in cash and bonds, making it the biggest train robbery in American history. However, in the course of the holdup, Glasscock panicked and shot Doc by mistake. The gang made a clean getaway with the loot, but their subsequent search for a doctor to tend to Doc put the police on their trail. Soon they were all in jail.

Through plea-bargaining and helping the police recover much of the stolen money, the Newton brothers received amazingly light sentences. None of them spent more than a few years in prison for the Rondout robbery. Nor were any of them ever charged with the robbery of the Toronto bank messengers. Not until the 1994 publication of *The Newton Boys: Portrait of an Outlaw Gang*, a book based on extensive interviews with Willis and Joe in their later years, did people know that the Texas outlaws were responsible for the morning on which, in the words of the Toronto *Globe*, "Cold-blooded and calculated villainy stalked abroad in the streets of Toronto."

CHAPTER 5

VERNE SANKEY:
Kidnapper

Public Enemy Number One! During the crime-ridden early years of the Great Depression, that dubious honour fell to some of the most notorious bandits in American history. Outlaws like John Dillinger and Pretty Boy Floyd didn't want it. Psychopath Baby Face Nelson gloried in it. But even though these and a few other "celebrity" criminals in turn topped the list of men most wanted by J. Edgar Hoover's fledgling Federal Bureau of Investigation (FBI), none of them was the first. That distinction went to an American-born naturalized Canadian citizen whose criminal career was somehow overlooked by the mythmakers of outlaw and gangster legends.

Verne Sankey was born in Avoca, Iowa, in 1891; the youngest son in a homesteading family. He grew up in a frontier environment and fell in love with the lore of railroading. While young Sankey worked as a farmhand, he dreamed of being an engineer.

Verne Sankey, the Canadian Pacific Railway engineer who became a kidnapper and America's first Public Enemy Number One.
COLORADO HISTORICAL SOCIETY.

In 1914, twenty-two-year-old Sankey married his boyhood sweetheart, nineteen-year-old Fern Young. He took his bride north to Canada, where railroading was booming because of a flood of immigration to the West. The couple settled in Melville, Saskatchewan. Sankey soon found a job with the Grand Trunk Pacific Railway.

Sankey started out as a watchman in the railyards, looking out for thieves and train-hopping hoboes. He was eventually promoted to fireman, shovelling the coal that kept the locomotive running. Then at last Sankey's childhood dream came true: he became an engineer.

Just like the riverboat pilots of Mark Twain's day, early twentieth-century railroad engineers had a special mystique. There was an aura of adventure about them that Sankey liked. Engineers were also relatively well-paid. That became especially important to Sankey when in 1919, Fern gave birth to a daughter whom the proud parents named Echo.

Life in Melville was good for the Sankeys. They owned an attractive home, and every year Verne bought a new Nash automobile. The family went on vacations that most of the neighbours couldn't afford. By the time the Grand Trunk Pacific Railway merged with the Canadian Pacific Railway in 1923, Verne had become a naturalized Canadian citizen.

Most of the people who knew Sankey found him friendly and outgoing. He enjoyed bowling and was a fan of the local hockey team, the Melville Millionaires. He was charming, intelligent, and a gifted storyteller. He could juggle and would perform for kids. He enjoyed a drink, but was never seen drunk. Sankey was of stocky build, and not tall — only five-foot-seven. But his boyish features, soft blue eyes, and winning smile complemented his pleasant personality. Not everyone, however, was won over. Some of Sankey's railway colleagues considered him a show-off and a braggart.

Sankey did indeed like to flash his money and be seen as a high roller. He and Fern both had expensive tastes. They dressed in fine clothes for social occasions and Verne often gave his wife gifts of expensive jewellery. But their love for the good life wasn't the biggest drain on the family finances. Sankey was a gambler!

Sankey would bet on almost any game of chance, but he was especially addicted to cards and dice. When Sankey was winning, he liked to tip generously and squander money like a big shot. When he lost, he was compelled to keep playing in the hope of hitting another hot streak. Sankey also liked to play the stock market, investing in commodities the same way that he bet on horses or the turn of a card. An engineer's pay couldn't support that kind of lifestyle. Like many other people looking for fast, easy money, Sankey became a bootlegger.

Prohibition had made the United States into a legally "dry" country, but it had done nothing to dry up the American thirst for alcoholic beverages. If anything, many people were drinking more simply because it was forbidden. Canadian beer and liquor flowed across the border, smuggled by anyone willing to take the risk of arrest. The potential profits were too great for a man like Sankey to ignore.

Sankey established an extensive bootlegging enterprise. He ran whiskey into Michigan, Minnestoa, Colorado, Wyoming, and North and South Dakota. Sometimes the booze was hidden in the boxcars of the trains he drove. Other times Sankey drove across the border in an old Tin Lizzie with cases of whiskey stowed in a secret compartment. He would pose as a railroad man visiting his home in the United States. He often took Echo along his rum-running trips. Sankey enjoyed the little girl's company and he thought that the border guards wouldn't suspect a man travelling with his young daughter of smuggling liquor.

As a bootlegger, Sankey was a sharp businessman. He dealt only in top-quality Canadian spirits. He undercut the prices of rival bootleggers, many of whom were peddling watered-down whiskey and home-brewed moonshine. Wherever Sankey went, he made a point of making friends with people in influential positions. Mayors, police chiefs, bank presidents, and the members of the social elite of communities like Denver were all listed in Sankey's book of contacts. He even sent them Christmas cards.

Sankey was also a careful operator. On one occasion he was in a diner in a North Dakota town, with a carload of booze parked out front. He spotted two men he thought were Prohibition agents watching him from across the street. Sankey finished his lunch and then went out the back door. He took a train out of town, abandoning the car and the liquor.

Bootlegging was so profitable for Sankey that he began to lose interest in railroading. He took long leaves of absence from his job with the CPR. He moved his family to Regina in 1930. From there he ran liquor over the border in two big Nash cars that were equipped with truck springs to carry the heavy loads. Amazingly, Sankey's criminal record for that period was almost spotless. He was arrested for bootlegging once, in Fergus Falls, Minnesota. He posted bail and then skipped.

Sankey's bootlegging was no secret. He often told friends colourful stories about close calls with the cops. Officials on both sides of the border turned a blind eye because they'd been bribed or because they disagreed with the whole idea of Prohibition. However, when the wild decade of the Roaring Twenties went out with a whimper and the crushing Dirty Thirties began, Sankey's bootlegging business faltered.

The slide began with powerful crime syndicates that didn't like competition from freelancers. The syndicates were run by ruthless criminals who operated on a corporate scale. One crossed them at one's own peril. In one American city after another, Sankey was literally run out of town.

The Great Depression made things even worse. Many people no longer had money to spend on illegal booze. Prohibition would be in effect until 1933, but most of the criminals who profited from it could see in advance that their cash cow wasn't going to last and they'd have to find other ways of making a dishonest living. Verne Sankey decided to gamble on bank robbery.

Sankey was an avid reader of true crime magazines. He concluded that most criminals got caught because they were stupid. He believed that a smart man, like himself, could commit a felony and get away with it simply by planning carefully.

On February 28, 1931, Sankey was the engineer on a train that took the Melville Millionaires to Regina for a hockey game. That morning Sankey and another man, masked and armed, robbed the Royal Bank of Canada at the corner of Albert Street and Thirteenth Avenue. They forced manager Douglas Melklejohn to open the vault at gunpoint, and then tied up him and teller David Slinn, covering their eyes and mouths with tape. The bandits looted the vault of $12,000 and made their getaway in a car. According to one story, the bag containing the stolen money was among the bags of hockey gear loaded onto the train for the team's trip home.

A month after the Regina holdup, Sankey took his last leave of absence from the CPR. He never returned. The lure of easy money taken at the point of a gun overwhelmed his love of railroading.

By this time the Sankey family included a son, Orville, born in 1929. Sankey bought 320 acres of farmland in Buffalo County, South Dakota, eleven miles from the village of Gann Valley. He put the title to the land in Fern's name. Sankey built a three-room clapboard house with an unusually elaborate basement. Then he set himself up as a farmer, raising corn, cattle, and turkeys.

But the farm was really a well-planned robber's lair. It was remote. The only way in from the road was by a mile-long grassy path. No one could approach the house unnoticed. The door was at the back, which meant the occupants could slip out into a ravine, unseen by anyone coming in from the road.

As always, Sankey made friends with his neighbours, the nearest of whom were three miles away. He pitched in when they needed help with farm work. His winning ways made him popular in Gann Valley and the nearby town of Kimball. Nonetheless, there were oddities about Verne Sankey that raised some of his new neighbours' suspicions.

Where, in the middle of the Depression, did he get the money to buy the farm? Why was he always flush with cash when everyone else was broke? Where did he go on his frequent trips away from home? How could he afford a brand-new 1932 Ford Model 18 V8 sedan?

Other things made some of the South Dakota farmers uneasy about the newcomer. He associated with men whom the police knew to be shady characters. Planes occasionally landed on his land in the dead of night. There was an incident in which Sankey shot and wounded an alleged intruder. He said the man was a turkey thief, but then, strangely, didn't press charges. Meanwhile, Sankey was still bootlegging, though not on as big a scale as he had done previously.

On October 4, 1932, three men robbed a bank in Vayland, a town near Gann Valley. They escaped in a car after grabbing a paltry $900. One day later, a bank in the nearby community of Winner was robbed, possibly by the same gang. Suspicion eventually fell on Verne Sankey as the leader of the robbers, but nothing was ever proven. However, if Sankey was involved in the South Dakota robberies, it's possible that one of his accomplices — who might also have been the other man in the Regina stickup — was a Canadian named Gordon Alcorn.

Born in Welwyn, Saskatchewan, in 1905, Alcorn came from a railroading family. He knew Verne Sankey from boyhood and grew up admiring the colourful engineer who told such wonderful stories and always had a wallet full of money. Alcorn even worked for the CPR as Sankey's fireman.

A tall, gangly youth, Alcorn was easygoing and shy. The only time he was ever in trouble with police in Canada was when he was fined two dollars for using abusive language. But Alcorn was easily led and Sankey took advantage of that. Whether or not Alcorn was in fact involved in armed robbery, he would be a key participant in the events that made Verne Sankey notorious.

One of the most highly publicized crimes in twentieth-century America was the kidnapping on March 1, 1932, of aviation hero Charles Lindbergh's baby son. The snatching of an innocent child for ransom outraged the nation. Even convicted gangster Al Capone, from his prison cell, offered his services in getting the little boy home safely. The child was eventually found dead. More than two years later, a man named Bruno Richard Hauptmann was arrested and charged. He was tried, convicted, and executed. But before the Lindbergh kidnapping case was finally stamped CLOSED, it created a logistical nightmare for American law-enforcement agencies. It also opened a new door to fast money for criminals.

At the time, American legal jurisdiction was divided among federal, state, and municipal authorities. The various law enforcement agencies jealously guarded their own turf. Communication among them was poor and co-operation sometimes non-existent. The Bureau of Investigation, a branch of the Department of Justice, and the forerunner of the Federal Bureau of Investigation (FBI), was a small, almost insignificant agency with extremely limited authority. Its new director, J. Edgar Hoover, was an ambitious, publicity-hungry autocrat who would use any means, fair or foul, to extend his department's power. He was delighted when the American government passed the Lindbergh Law, which made kidnapping a federal crime. During the early 1930s, Hoover would capitalize on other sensational crimes in his quest for power and glory.

The Lindbergh kidnapping touched off a rash of abductions in the United States. The victims were nearly all very wealthy men. The whole nation sympathized with the Lindberghs, especially after the discovery of the decomposed little body. But many people in Depression-stricken America felt little empathy for rich adult males. They and their families, living in opulence while others lost their homes and went hungry, were hardly touched by the Depression. Some of the wheelers and dealers among them had even profited from the misfortunes of others. Criminals saw them as fair game. Holding a rich man for ransom could be much more lucrative than armed robbery, and not nearly as dangerous.

By April 1932, Gordon Alcorn had joined the ranks of the unemployed, having been laid off by the CPR. He was in Winnipeg, living hand-to-mouth while he looked for work. Alcorn had made friends with a man named Arthur Youngberg, a Minnesota native of Swedish background. He was over six feet tall and powerfully built, but, like Alcorn, naive in the ways of the world. Youngberg had worked for the CPR for thirteen years and had even known Verne Sankey. He, too, had been laid off.

Sankey looked up Alcorn while he was in Winnipeg on bootlegging business. Inspired by the Lindberg case, he wanted Alcorn to help him kidnap some wealthy Winnipeg citizen and hold him for ransom. Sankey had even made inquiries about renting a house where the victim could be held. Alcorn would have none of it. But he was still unemployed and broke a few weeks later when he received a letter from Sankey inviting him and Youngberg to go to South Dakota and work for him on the farm. Both young men liked that idea. Sankey went to Winnipeg to pick them up and they arrived at his farm on November 11, 1932. Alcorn and Youngberg happily began their work as farmhands, not suspecting that Sankey had other plans for them.

Shortly after Christmas, Sankey told his two workers that he was taking his family to Denver for the winter because Fern couldn't stand the prairie cold. Alcorn and Youngberg were to look after things while he was away. In fact, Sankey was going to Denver to lay plans and recruit yet another member for the "gang" he was clandestinely assembling.

Carl Pearce of Colorado had served with the American army in the First World War. He had suffered shell shock and had never recovered. Pearce had been in and out of psychiatric hospitals. He had a nervous twitch and his hands often shook. He couldn't hold down a job. When his wife left him, he began to drink heavily. He associated with bad characters and once spent ninety days in jail for passing bogus cheques. It was through his descent into the underworld that Pearce met Sankey, and then Fern's sister Ruth Kohler, who had been recently widowed. Carl and Ruth were both lonely, lost souls, and they fell for each other.

Sankey rented a house in Denver and invited Carl and Ruth to stay with him, Fern, and the kids. The house was also home to some of Sankey's bootlegging friends. It was ideal for Pearce. He had a woman who was willing to look after him and easy access to the booze he needed.

When Sankey visited the farm, he found Alcorn suffering because of a vicious fight he'd had with Youngberg. The big Swede had knocked most of Alcorn's teeth out. A legitimate farmer might have dismissed both of them, but Sankey wasn't about to let a little fracas get in the way of his grand plan. Leaving Youngberg to look after the farm, he took Alcorn to Denver for medical attention.

At the house in Denver, Sankey once again brought up the subject of kidnapping. This time Alcorn was receptive. Sankey had made a detailed study of the best prospects. He had finally decided on Charlie Boettcher. They would demand $100,000. Alcorn thought that was too much and suggested $25, 000. They compromised on $60,000. Carl Pearce typed out the ransom letter.

Charles Boettcher II, age thirty-two, belonged to one of the wealthiest families in Colorado. His paternal grandfather, also named Charles, had become rich in the hardware, sugar beet, and cement industries. His father, Claude, had enhanced the Boettcher fortune through shrewd investments. They were an influential and politically powerful family.

Charlie was a good-natured man who liked to party, gamble, tell jokes, and sometimes drink too much. He was also a dedicated baseball fan. He and his beautiful wife, Anna Lou, and little daughter, Ann, lived in Denver's exclusive Capitol Hill district in an elegant twenty-one-room chateau Claude had built as a wedding present. Charlie had named the house *Les Trois Tours* for its three towers. Charles Lindbergh was one of the many celebrities who visited there. To the Boettchers, the Great Depression was just a passing storm to be weathered. It didn't interfere with their opulent lifestyle. Then one night the Sankey gang came calling.

On the evening of February 12, 1933, Charlie and Anna Lou's car pulled into the driveway of *Les Trois Tours* and stopped in front of the garage. When Charlie got out, Verne Sankey's voice came from the darkness. "Come here, Charlie, and stick up your hands."

Charlie, who was slightly intoxicated, was startled. Anna Lou, eight months pregnant, told him, "This is a holdup. Don't resist."

Then Sankey said, "Do what you're told, and everything will be all right."

He handed an envelope to Anna Lou, who was still in the car, and politely said, "Mrs. Boettcher, open that envelope, please."

She did so, and a smaller envelope fell out. Sankey took back the first envelope and said, "Now open that one."

As Anna Lou tore open the second envelope and unfolded the note inside, Sankey withdrew. He forced Charlie into a car driven by Alcorn and they sped away. The typed message in Anna Lou's shaking hands said:

> Do not notify the police. If you do, and they start making it hot for us, you will never see ___ alive again. We are holding ___ for Sixty Thousand Dollars. We are asking you to get this money in Ten and Twenty dollar bills and they must be old bills only. When you get the money ready and are willing to pay as above for the safe return of ___, then insert the following add in the Denver Post, personal items ...
>
> (Please write, I am ready to return) SIGN (Mabel) ...
>
> We will not stand for any stalling thru advise [sic] that police may give you. You are smart enough to know what the results will be if you try that. You know what happened to little Charles Lindbergh through his father calling the police. He would be alive today if his father had followed instructions given him. You are to choose one of these to [sic] courses. Either insert add and be prepared to pay ransome [sic], Or forget it all.

Anna Lou's first phone call was to Charlie's father. In spite of the threat in the note, Claude immediately called the police. A patrol car arrived at the scene of the crime within three minutes and was quickly followed by more. Five minutes after Claude's call, police were swarming through Denver with orders to stop and search any small black sedan — a description that fit thousands of cars. Anna Lou hadn't seen the licence-plate number.

In fact, Anna Lou could give the police few clues. Sankey had been masked. She could only report that the kidnapper was white, short, and stocky, and had unusually round eyes.

Denver police Chief Albert T. Clark was certain that Charlie had been abducted by professional criminals and announced that he would be safely returned to the bosom of his family within forty-eight hours. Clark's dragnet scooped up plenty of suspects, including several well-known gangsters. There was no evidence connecting any of them to the kidnapping. The mention of the name "Lindbergh" in the ransom note had investigators wondering if Charlie had been taken by the still-at-large kidnappers of the Lindbergh baby.

The Denver police put *Les Trois Tours* and Claude's gated mansion under armed guard. Some of the officers even toted machine guns. But their biggest problem was keeping the hordes of newspaper reporters, photographers, and curious gawkers at bay.

Meanwhile, by the evening after his abduction, Charlie was sitting blindfolded and miserable in the basement of the Sankey farmhouse. When the masked men had him in their car, they'd tied his hands and taped his eyes closed, and then put sunglasses on him. He'd endured a ride of over 570 miles of back roads in complete darkness. When the kidnappers had to stop for gas, they told him he'd be okay as long as he behaved himself.

Arthur Youngberg was taken completely by surprise when Sankey and Alcorn arrived at the farm with a man who was obviously a prisoner. When Sankey told him to take care of the "new boarder," Youngberg replied that they'd better take Charlie back where they found him or they'd all wind up in jail. However, after the smooth-talking Sankey assured Youngberg that they wouldn't get caught and he'd have a "nice fat share of the proceeds," Youngberg agreed to go along with the plan. His job was to be Charlie's keeper.

Charlie's basement prison was a damp room with a cot, a coal-oil lamp, a table, and a couple of chairs. Youngberg brought his meals, coffee, and cigarettes, but was always careful not to let Charlie see his face. He occasionally gave Charlie a shave. Sometimes Youngberg stood behind the prisoner and took off the blindfold so he could read a magazine. He warned Charlie not to look around if he didn't want to be "bumped off." Charlie would talk to his captor about his wife and family, whom he said were surely concerned about his safety.

On February 15, Claude placed the ad in the Denver *Post*, as the ransom note had instructed. The days since his son's abductions had been confusing. He and Anna Lou had been swamped with phone calls, most of them from cranks looking for money. Sankey himself had added to the confusion when he made Charlie write letters to Claude and Anna Lou, and then delivered them via the Boettchers' pastor, the Reverend B.D. Dagwell. The letter to Claude admonished him for not following directions, and told him, "Charles is very nerves [sic] and frightened. He often asks if we will release him if you pay and I keep telling him we will, but he lives in fear of being bumped off."

Claude desperately wanted his son back alive and unharmed. But he was a hard-dealing businessman who wasn't used to being pushed around. He wasn't going to pay a cent until he saw Charlie safe and sound. On February 20, Claude had an open letter to the kidnappers published in the *Rocky Mountain News*:

> I have received many ransom notes, through the mail and otherwise — most of them obviously spurious. Some of the notes received, however, I am convinced, by certain inclosures, among other things, came from the persons who have my son in custody.
>
> The contents of these notes I have not divulged to the police or the press. The conditions and method of payment of ransom contained in these notes were such that they cannot under any circumstances be carried out. Furthermore, no assurance was given of the safe return of my son when the ransom was paid....
>
> Obviously the police, the press, myself and family are each actuated by different motives — the police primarily to apprehend the culprits, the press to print all the news, myself and family to accomplish the safe return of my son. I appreciate and am confident of the sincere motives of both the police and the press, but in this situation I feel that I must and will act independently if the opportunity is presented. Claude K. Boettcher

Sankey responded to Claude's letter with one of his own. He accused Claude of trying to set a police trap. He warned him that if instructions weren't followed, he'd raise the ransom to $100,000. Moreover, if any of the kidnappers should be killed by police while trying to collect, others would "even the score." The letter had a postscript: "Charles is suffering as we keep his eyes taped all the time and at times he is in a very bad condition."

Claude replied on February 21 in a "night extra" of the Denver *Post*. He said he had received many ransom notes, all of which told him to call off the police and drop the ransom money at some remote location. None of them assured Charlie's safe return. As Claude's letter stated:

> It is very obvious that I am powerless to call off the police and under present conditions it would be absolutely impossible for me to go to any designated place alone without being followed by the police and representatives of the press, even if I was willing to do so. Hence, I am powerless to act on the instructions received up to this time.

The Boettcher kidnapping became international news. England's London *Daily Mirror* conducted an exclusive telephone interview with Anna Lou via the transatlantic cable. The beleaguered woman, virtually a prisoner in her own house, and due to deliver almost any minute, was a physical and emotional wreck. She couldn't sleep and spent the late night-hours doing jigsaw puzzles, which were the rage of the day.

While Anna Lou fretted and Claude fumed, back in South Dakota, Sankey planned further kidnappings. He sometimes discussed his ideas with Alcorn and in Charlie's presence. Sankey told Alcorn that the farm was a perfect kidnappers' lair and would never be found. Charlie heard him say, "Miles make no difference to us. When we want someone, we get them, and when we get them, we will collect."

Claude's patience reached the breaking point on February 23. He issued an ultimatum, insisting that Charlie be released by midnight of the twenty-fifth. He personally guaranteed payment of $60,000. Then he angrily told reporters that if Charlie suffered the slightest harm, he'd spend ten times the ransom fee to have the kidnappers brought to justice.

In a letter that was hand-delivered to Claude, Sankey flatly stated again that he wanted the money first. Claude refused. He wrote, "I feel if

I paid that money before I got my boy, I would be signing his death warrant. Men who kidnap will murder."

Sankey finally decided that he had to get Charlie out of the farmhouse before any neighbours became suspicious. Local folks had a habit of dropping in unexpectedly. He sent Claude a letter agreeing to his terms. Then he contacted Pearce and made arrangements to move Charlie to the house in Denver in case plans went awry. Pearce had already been kept busy typing Sankey's handwritten notes and arranging for their delivery to Claude.

Early on the morning of March 1, Sankey and Alcorn put Charlie in a car, still bound and blindfolded, and drove to Denver. At a secret location they met Pearce, who had a note from Claude promising payment with no police interference once Charlie was released. At 7:45 p.m., the kidnappers let Charlie out of the car and drove away. Charlie peeled the bandages from his eyes and saw that he was on a street about three miles from his home. He went into a drugstore and phoned his father.

Sankey and Alcorn drove to a place outside the city not far from the arranged site where the ransom was to be dropped off. They watched from a hiding place for a car whose lights had been fixed in a manner that identified it as the money car. The car appeared around 8:30. It stopped on a bridge, and one of the occupants dropped a package into the dry creek bed below. After the car drove away, Sankey waited a while to be sure it wasn't being followed. Then he climbed down to the creek bed to retrieve the package. Worried that Claude might have double-crossed them with a bundle of old newspapers, he and Alcorn quickly tore the package open. Inside was $60,000 in ten- and twenty-dollar bills. As they congratulated each other on pulling the perfect crime, Sankey and Alcorn were unaware that Secret Service agents had marked all of the bills with indelible ink.

Charlie's release made headline news. He gave the Denver *Post* a detailed account of his harrowing sixteen days of captivity in a dank basement. "Where I was held and by whom I do not know ... I am thankful that they treated me as gentlemanly as possible under the circumstances.... Desperadoes? Undoubtedly."

When reporters piled onto the doorstep of Claude's mansion, he chased them away at gunpoint. Then he swore that he would get the men who had kidnapped his son if it took the rest of his life. Now that Charlie was safe, the hunt was on.

As soon as the Denver police heard that Charlie had been released, they set up roadblocks all around the city. They had been informed of the drop-off location, but a miscue in police communications allowed Sankey and Alcorn to slip through the first line of the dragnet. However, police had in fact been watching the drop-off car and had seen the kidnappers' car. Now posses were patrolling in and around Denver, trying to intercept it. Twice, they almost caught the fleeing kidnappers. But like gangsters in a James Cagney movie, Sankey and Alcorn roared through the roadblocks with guns blazing. There were no casualties, but Sankey's car was perforated with bullet holes.

Travelling by the roughest back roads, and with no lights on, Sankey made it to Greeley, Colorado. It was there that Alcorn, unnerved by the shootouts and certain that Sankey was going to drive them right into the arms of the police, got out of the car, dropped his gun on the street, and ran. After a close call with the Greeley police, Sankey returned to the back roads and eventually arrived at the farm.

Claude offered a twenty-five-thousand-dollar reward for information leading to the kidnappers' capture. Police pumped Charlie for every scrap of information he could give them. During the drive to Denver, Charlie had briefly slipped the bandages from his eyes and got a glimpse of the outside. He'd seen the word "Torrington," the name of a small Wyoming town, on a gas station sign. That detail told police the direction he'd come from. When they worked the time Charlie had spent in the car into the equation, they concluded that the kidnappers' hideout was somewhere in the Dakotas.

After fleeing from Sankey, Alcorn spent a few days wandering through Colorado, Wyoming, and Nebraska, travelling by foot, bus and freight train. He checked newspapers, certain of seeing front page stories about Sankey's arrest. When it was finally clear to Alcorn that Sankey had given the cops the slip, he made his way back to the farm. Sankey, Alcorn and Youngberg all thought they were now in the clear. Back in Denver, however, the lure of Claude's reward money began to produce results.

On one of his benders, Pearce had been overheard boasting that he was being paid $2,000 for typing the ransom letters delivered to Claude Boettcher. An informant told the police. On March 5, officers went to Sankey's Denver house and picked up Pearce, Fern Sankey, Ruth Kohler, and Ruth's sixteen-year-old daughter Merelyn for questioning. A search of the house turned up $1,400 in cash and handwritten drafts of the ransom letters.

Fern, Ruth, and Merelyn denied knowing anything at all about the kidnapping, but Pearce talked. He gave the police the names of Sankey, Alcorn, and Youngberg, as well as the location of the farm in South Dakota. He claimed that Sankey had talked him into typing the ransom letters because he was the only one who knew how to use a typewriter.

The police were satisfied that Merelyn was innocent of any criminal involvement, but they didn't believe Fern or Ruth. Realizing that she could face a long prison sentence if she were convicted of being an accomplice, Fern hired a Denver attorney named Ben Laska. He was a high-priced lawyer known for taking on sensational cases.

While Pearce and the women were still being interrogated in Denver, a trio of officers the press would dub the "Three Georges" headed for the Sankey farm. They were George Carroll, the sheriff of Cheyenne, Wyoming; George Smith, Wyoming's law enforcement commissioner; and Detective George O'Donnell of the Denver Police Department. Not wishing to alert the suspects with a direct approach, the officers set out by car from the town of Mitchell, Nebraska, about sixty-five miles south of the farm. They were caught in a wicked March blizzard that buried the road in four-foot snow drifts. Forced to abandon their car, they proceeded on snowshoes.

At the town of O'Neill, Nebraska, the Three Georges boarded a train for Chamberlain, about twenty miles southwest of the farm. There they enlisted deputy sheriff Charles Farnsworth. He called Sheriff Lars Rasmassan of Buffalo County, South Dakota, and asked him to join the posse at Kimball. Rasmassan brought along his deputy, Armour Schlegel. The Three Georges weren't aware that Deputy Schlegel was a good friend of Verne Sankey. He'd helped build the farmhouse and had even looked after the turkeys.

Armed with pistols, rifles, and machine guns, the posse set out for the isolated farm on March 6. En route, they stopped at the ranch of Sankey's nearest neighbour. To their surprise, Arthur Youngberg was there, helping the owners butcher cattle. He quietly submitted to arrest.

The three Georges expected a gun battle when they reached the farm. Instead, they found the place deserted. The suspects had been tipped off.

The officers could only confirm, from information Charlie had provided, that this was indeed the place where he'd been held. On his first night in jail, Youngberg made a failed attempt at suicide by slashing his wrists and throat with a razor blade. Sankey had told him that if he were captured, death would be better than prison.

Charlie recognized Youngberg's voice and accent, and fingered him as one of the kidnappers. Youngberg swore that he'd never seen Charlie before in his life. He refused to co-operate with the police. Then he received a telegram from an older brother in Winnipeg, chastising him for being led astray by Sankey and urging him to tell the truth. Moved by his brother's concern, Youngberg told the police all he knew about the Sankey gang.

People who knew Verne Sankey were stunned when they saw his name in the newspapers. Even those who had known him as a bootlegger had never for a moment thought he would stoop to kidnapping. The publicity the case was getting was irresistible to J. Edgar Hoover. Even though his bureau had played no part whatsoever in the arrests of Pearce and Youngberg and the discovery of the other kidnappers' identities, Hoover shamelessly authorized a press release in which he took credit for playing a "vital role" in the Boettcher case. His agents, he said, were hot on the trail of Sankey and Alcorn.

One week after Charlie's release, Anna Lou gave birth to a healthy baby girl. The IRS decided that the $60,000 Claude had paid to the kidnappers fell under the category of "gift," on which Claude was obliged to pay a tax. Neither J. Edgar Hoover nor anyone else in law enforcement knew where Sankey and Alcorn were.

While Sankey, Alcorn, and Youngberg were still at the farm, Sankey had divided up the loot. The original agreement had been that Sankey would get $30,000, Alcorn $18,000, and Youngberg $12,000. However, Sankey deducted $1,000 each from the other men's shares. He said $500 was for Pearce and the rest was to cover his own expenses. The three men buried most of the cash at various locations on the farm, keeping just a few thousand for travelling money. When Youngberg was arrested, he knew where the hiding places were, but that was one bit of information he didn't share with the police. He hoped it would be a trump card he could play in negotiating a deal.

When Sankey and Alcorn left the farm, they went to the Twin Cities of Minneapolis–St. Paul. After almost being trapped by the police following the money pickup, Sankey had guessed that the bills were probably marked. The Twin Cities were known as "safe" territory for outlaws because corrupt officials protected them from police — for a price. It was a good place to launder hot money. While staying at a first-class Minneapolis hotel, Sankey wrote a letter to Fern, unaware that she was in custody. The Denver police intercepted it. But by that time the news of Youngberg's arrest was splashed all over newspaper front pages. Sankey and Alcorn immediately fled to Chicago where they took rooms under assumed names.

Sankey was afraid that Youngberg would lead the police to the buried loot. He had always been a gambler and now decided to take a big risk. He took a train to Council Bluffs, Iowa, where he bought a used car. Travelling by night along back roads with the lights off, he drove to a spot a few miles from the farm. He parked the car and went the rest of the way on foot.

Police had occupied the farm ever since the first raid, hoping the kidnappers would return. They had searched everywhere for stashed money, but without success. Officers armed with machine guns patrolled the property to keep away would-be treasure hunters and unwelcome newspapermen. Watching from the darkness, Sankey could see policemen inside the well-lit farmhouse.

Crawling on his hands and knees, Sankey went to a spot where most of his and Alcorn's money was buried in tin cans. With only a pocket knife, he began digging in the frozen ground. When the knife snapped in two, he continued digging with his bare hands. A police car passed by, forcing Sankey to duck behind a tree. When the officers got out and went into the house, he resumed digging. Sankey at last crept away into the night with $40,000. The next morning the police found the holes, the tin cans, and a broken pocket knife. A few thousand dollars of Youngberg's share still lay hidden, and Youngberg still hoped that would be enough to help him cut a deal with the police.

For weeks, the police tried without success to pick up the kidnappers' trail. Fern, on the advice of Ben Laska, insisted that she knew nothing of her husband's criminal activities. She played on the prevailing chauvinistic attitude that a wife's duty was to look after the home and not question where her husband got his money. "Is it any wonder we are surprised when something unusual happens?" she said in wide-eyed innocence to a Denver *Post* reporter. Then, in April, an arrest in a remote hamlet in Manitoba provided police with a break and gave Fern considerable cause for worry.

Back on June 30, 1932, twenty-year-old Haskell Bohn, son of a wealthy St. Paul family, had been the victim of an abduction that now looked like a rehearsal for the Boettcher kidnapping. Bohn had just pulled into the garage of his home when two armed men forced him into a car. They taped his eyes shut and drove him to a house where he was kept in the basement. Ransom notes sent to Bohn's father made frequent references to the Lindbergh kidnapping as a means of scaring him into paying up. The initial demand had been for $35,000. Bohn was released after one week, upon payment of $12,000.

Police investigating the Bohn kidnapping eventually came up with the name of Ray Robinson. He was a Canadian who was an old railway pal of Sankey and Alcorn. American officials contacted the Royal Canadian Mounted Police, who found that Robinson had deposited $10,000 in a Winnipeg bank shortly after the Bohn payoff. The Mounties finally located Robinson in the little community of Rorketon, two hundred miles northwest of Winnipeg. Unable to explain where the money had come from, Robinson confessed to the Bohn kidnapping. He said he had pulled the job with Verne Sankey and that they were both drunk when they did it. Moreover, Robinson claimed that Fern was in on the crime. Bohn had been kept blindfolded most of the time that he was a prisoner, but he said that a woman had brought him his meals. He was able to identify a house in Minneapolis as the place where he'd been held. The house had been rented by Verne Sankey.

Now sought for both the Boettcher and Bohn kidnappings, Verne Sankey was the most hunted fugitive in the United States. He was wanted on a long list of indictments for violations of the Lindbergh Law. J. Edgar Hoover didn't like the idea of publishing a federal list of "Public Enemies." He thought it would only serve to feed criminal egos. But his superiors in government disagreed. When the first list was compiled, Verne Sankey's name was at the top as Public Enemy Number One. Gordon Alcorn's name was next.

Sankey kept a low profile in Chicago. To anyone who asked, he was William E. Clark, a successful businessman. Alcorn, going by the alias

Walter B. Thomas, met a young divorcée named Angeline "Birdie" Christopherson Paul. They fell in love and were married in May. But any dreams Birdie might have had of wedded bliss were soon shattered.

When Sankey had returned from his clandestine visit to the farm, he and Alcorn agreed that it wouldn't be wise to keep large amounts of cash in their apartments. They buried most of the money at an isolated spot outside the city. Alcorn was resentful of the manner in which Sankey had chiselled him out of part of his share, so later he went back and dug up the loot. Then he and his bride quietly moved to a new address.

Sankey's gambling habit took him to the racetrack almost daily. Soon he needed cash and was furious when he found the cache had been cleaned out. It didn't take Sankey long to track Alcorn down. He was on the street outside Alcorn and Birdie's new apartment building when they approached on the sidewalk. To Birdie's horror, Sankey pulled a gun and said, "Stick 'em up!"

With Birdie about to become hysterical, Alcorn calmly said, "Don't scream." Then he told Sankey, "Put that gun in your pocket. I'll talk to you."

Sankey agreed to go inside and talk, but he kept the gun on Alcorn. When they were in the apartment, Alcorn explained that he had been worried that someone might find the money, so he'd taken it for safekeeping. Sankey didn't buy the story and told Alcorn to produce the money. Alcorn gave him a club bag stuffed with cash. Sankey took most of it, leaving Alcorn a few thousand dollars. Then he shook his former partner's hand, wished him and Birdie good luck, and left. The two kidnappers never spoke to each other again.

Back in Denver, Arthur Youngberg was finally convinced to help the police find some of the ransom loot. Claude told him he would be allowed to keep 10 percent of any recovered money as a finder's fee. Having failed to swing a deal with the police, Youngberg disclosed the location at the foot of a fencepost where a can containing $9,630 was buried. True to his word, Claude paid Youngberg $900. A few days later, Sankey made another secret night visit to the farm, hoping to retrieve Youngberg's stash. It was his turn to be disappointed at finding an empty hole.

The search for Sankey and Alcorn reached as far south as the Mexican border and north into Canada. In late May, a Chicago policeman spotted someone he thought was Sankey at a soccer game. He gave chase, but the suspect lost himself in the crowd. It seemed that Sankey was a phantom who could vanish at will.

Then on June 15, 1933, William Hamm, the wealthy president of the Hamm Brewing Company, was kidnapped in St. Paul. The abduction was soon followed by a ransom note demanding $100,000, which had been signed by Hamm. Police investigation would eventually reveal that Hamm had been grabbed by the notorious Barker gang and their Canadian partner Alvin Karpis. But at the time, police were certain that the elusive Verne Sankey had struck again. Sankey was also the number-one suspect in the July 22 kidnapping of wealthy Oklahoma oil man Charles F. Urschel, who had actually been grabbed by George "Machine Gun" Kelly. A search of the South Dakota farmhouse turned up papers that indicated Sankey had been planning to kidnap baseball star Babe Ruth and former world heavyweight boxing champion Jack Dempsey. When the Babe learned of this he quipped, "I don't want him coming my way unless I can get my hands on a bat."

In what seemed to be an open season on the rich and the famous, top law-enforcement officials like J. Edgar Hoover were under pressure to catch the criminals quickly. In fact, Hoover said the villains should be "exterminated." One of the agents he put on the Sankey case was Melvin Purvis, who would soon gain international fame as the cop who killed John Dillinger.

But in the summer of 1933, Claude Boettcher wasn't satisfied with the efforts of the police to catch Charlie's kidnappers. He had at least a dozen private detectives chasing down leads all over the United States and in Canada. These investigators were provided with money to hire assistants, drivers, airplane pilots, and to pay informants. Claude also received reports of investigations conducted by Canadian National Railway detectives. Claude accumulated a thick file on Sankey's and Alcorn's personal backgrounds and on Sankey's bootlegging activities, but no clues as to where the fugitives could be hiding.

On January 17, 1934, kidnappers abducted banker Edward G. Bremer of St. Paul and demanded $200,000 ransom. This would turn out to be yet another crime of the Barker-Karpis gang, but Sankey was again the first suspect. Actually, at the time of the Bremer kidnapping, Sankey was on a bus from Chicago to Detroit. Gambling and bad commodity investments were draining his money fast. He was going to Detroit to look into the purchase of a delicatessen. The deal didn't work out and he returned to Chicago.

Because of Claude's offer of a hefty reward, police had been swamped with "tips" from people hoping to cash in. Most of the information was useless. But on January 26, Melvin Purvis was contacted by Mrs. Carrie Fischer of Chicago. She had seen Verne Sankey's picture in the newspaper and she recognized him as a man she'd often seen in her neighbourhood. He was a regular customer of a barber named John Mueller.

Mrs. Fischer's information was pure gold for Purvis. He had already learned that Sankey was going under the alias of Clark. Purvis questioned John Mueller, who identified a photo of Sankey as "Mr. Clark," and said that he often came into the barbershop for a haircut and shave.

Purvis soon located Sankey's Chicago residence, an apartment he shared with a twenty-eight-year-old woman named Helen Mattern. Youngberg had told police that Sankey had resolved never to be taken alive. Purvis therefore decided against a raid on the apartment. That would almost certainly result in a gunfight, putting the lives of officers and Helen Mattern at risk. Instead, he would move against Sankey when he was off-guard and vulnerable — sitting in a barber's chair.

Purvis placed men in and around Mueller's barbershop. He knew that J. Edgar Hoover hated sharing glory with other law-enforcement agencies, but he had to bring the Chicago police department in on the stakeout. Federal agents still weren't permitted to carry guns, and Sankey was likely to be armed.

For two days Purvis and his men waited, but Sankey didn't show. The police weren't aware that Sankey had recently had three prominent moles on his face surgically removed. The incisions were too tender for shaving. However, on the third day of the police vigil, Sankey felt that his face had healed well enough for him to endure a shave.

Sankey suspected nothing when he entered the barbershop that afternoon and settled into the chair. Mueller dropped the sheet over him. Suddenly policemen emerged from a back room with guns in their hands. Two of them shoved the muzzles against Sankey's head. Sergeant Thomas Curtain said, "Don't move, Verne. We're police officers. You're under arrest."

Sankey tried to jump from the chair, but the officers shoved him back, warning him not to put up a fight. Sankey said he wasn't trying to fight, he was trying to run so they'd shoot. "You might as well kill me, anyway," he said.

Sankey wasn't armed. But in the hem of his coat the police found some pills. He'd been prepared to take poison rather than go to prison.

In Sankey's apartment police found guns, ammunition, and $3,450 in cash. A weeping Helen Mattern insisted that she had no idea her boyfriend was a wanted criminal. The building manager backed her story. "They were really model tenants, never made any fuss and nobody saw much of them … when the federal agents came, I almost fainted, I was so shocked."

The capture of Public Enemy Number One was headline news across the country. J. Edgar Hoover played it for all it was worth, even inferring that his agents had prevented Sankey from committing suicide with the lethal pills. But if the news-hungry public that had been following the case expected a sensational trial, they were in for a stunning disappointment.

Melvin Purvis personally took charge of Sankey's police interrogation. Sankey admitted he had kidnapped Haskell Bohn and Charlie Boettcher. He was bitter about the "dishonourable" way Claude had called in the police after he and Alcorn, in good faith, had released Charlie unharmed. Sankey denied any involvement in the other kidnappings of which he was a suspect. When Purvis asked if he'd been involved in the kidnapping of the Lindbergh baby, Sankey became angry. "I am a man," he snapped indignantly. "I would kidnap a man. I would never kidnap a child."

Sankey was taken under heavy guard to Sioux Falls, South Dakota. He was lodged in the state penitentiary where security was stronger than that of the county jail. Aside from a single day he'd spent locked up because of bootlegging, Sankey had never before been behind bars.

Meanwhile, police had tracked down Alcorn. Helen Mattern, who knew him only as Walter Thomas, gave them information about a used car he'd bought in Chicago. Purvis's agents questioned automobile dealers until they found one who had sold a car to one Walter Thomas. He had the buyer's address. The day after Sankey's arrest, police burst into Alcorn's residence at 11:00 p.m. He was in bed and offered no resistance. The only gun on the premises was a .25-calibre pistol hidden under a sofa cushion. Birdie denied knowing anything about her husband's criminal activities.

At the time of his arrest, Alcorn had eleven dollars to his name. He confessed to his part in the Boettcher kidnapping. When Charlie was told that both Sankey and Alcorn had been caught, he exclaimed, "That's great! Now they've got 'em all."

Alcorn actually seemed relieved that his run from the law was over. "I had a swell time with my share of the ransom," he said. "I bet I made all of the night clubs in Chicago. The money's all gone now, every cent of it, and I'm ready to take the consequences. I never was cut out for this kidnapping racket anyhow."

Alcorn was locked in a cell a few doors down from Sankey. It's unlikely that they so much as had a glimpse of each other. Sankey evidently did feel regret for dragging the young man into his web. "Alcorn is a swell fellow," he said. "He used to fire for me up in Canada when I was a railroad engineer. He was never in trouble before in his life."

Ben Laska flew to Sioux Falls to be Sankey's legal counsel. Sankey was more concerned about his family than he was about himself. He told Laska to look after Fern and the children. Of himself, he said, "Don't worry. I'll never do a day for this rap."

That was the morning of February 7. Sankey made it clear to Laska that he couldn't stand the humiliation of having his wife and children seeing him in prison. The next day, Sankey stuffed a handkerchief into his mouth, made a noose with a necktie that nobody had the foresight to take away from him, and hanged himself in his cell. Sankey had spoken his last words to Harold Alcorn, who had come from Canada to visit his brother, and had stopped for a moment in front of Sankey's cell. "Tell my gambling friends up there I have been paid twenty years in advance, and am now working it out."

The press denounced Sankey as a coward for taking the easy way out. J. Edgar Hoover was disappointed that his justice department would be denied the publicity that would have come with Sankey's conviction and incarceration in the federal penitentiary at Leavenworth, Kansas. He was determined that the rest of the gang would feel the wrath of the law.

Federal prosecutors tried very hard to have Fern and Ruth convicted as Sankey's accomplices. In one of the longest trials in South Dakota history, the charges against Ruth were eventually dropped due to a lack of evidence. Ben Laska succeeded in winning an acquittal for Fern. Ironically, Laska was prosecuted for accepting ransom money for his legal fees and served a term in prison.

Carl Pearce and Arthur Youngberg were both sentenced to long prison terms. Youngberg was paroled for good behaviour in 1943. Pearce, who suffered from psychoneurosis, was paroled on a medical recommendation for clemency in 1944.

Gordon Alcorn was sentenced to life imprisonment. He was sent first to Leavenworth, and then to the new maximum-security prison in San Francisco Bay — Alcatraz! Although he boasted of making friends with such notorious inmates as Machine Gun Kelly and Al Capone, Alcorn was a model prisoner. He often expressed remorse for his crimes. The prison staff liked him. Nonetheless, he feared for his life among the hard cases in Alcatraz. Alcorn had never been a tough guy.

In 1936, Alcorn's family in Canada began a campaign to have him released and deported. They even gained the support of the Boettcher family. During the trial of Fern and Ruth, at which Alcorn and Charlie had both testified, Alcorn had personally apologized to Charlie.

The American government was reluctant to grant Alcorn any kind of reprieve, concerned that it might send the wrong message to other would-be kidnappers. But Alcorn's family persevered, especially after Sankey's other Canadian henchman, Ray Robinson, was quietly released from Stillwater Penitentiary and deported in 1940. Unfortunately for Alcorn, the authorities seemed determined to make him pay in the absence of the deceased Sankey.

It wasn't until 1949 that Gordon Alcorn was finally let out of prison and deported to Canada. He wrote to Claude, thanking him for his kindness in recommending his release. For the rest of his life, Alcorn was a hardworking, honest citizen. But he couldn't shake the guilt from his brief career as a kidnapper. He died alone in a Vancouver rooming house in 1982. As a young railroader, Alcorn had admired smooth-talking Verne Sankey. In the end he was, in a way, the last victim of America's first Public Enemy Number One.

CHAPTER 6
SYDNEY LASS AND JACK O'BRIEN:
Mysterious Pat Norton

The two men had been loitering for hours in front of the Durable Waterproof Company at 646 Adelaide Street West in Toronto. It was Friday, September 19, 1930, and the Great Depression that had started less than a year earlier had already cast its grim shadow over the city. The streets were full of unemployed men with nothing to do, and vagrants had become a common sight. These two, however, weren't victims of the

Jack O'Brien (left) and Sydney Lass (right) robbed the payroll of the Durable Waterproof Company in Toronto.
TORONTO *STAR.*

massive layoffs that had followed the stock market crash of October 1929. They were thieves who had chosen to live on the wrong side of the law, and they were waiting in ambush.

At 2:45 p.m. a car pulled up. In it was Albert Hattin, age eighteen, an employee of the Durable Waterproof Company. He was returning from a bank where he'd picked up three bundles of cash — the company's weekly payroll. Riding with him as guard was a bank messenger. The bandits struck before Hattin could even get out of the car; opening the door and grabbing at the money satchel. Several witnesses later gave accounts of the robbery. One was six-year-old Johnnie Brooks, who'd been sitting on a baker's wagon and saw the whole thing.

"There was a fat guy and a little skinny guy," said Johnnie. "The fat guy carried the bag out to the sidewalk and dropped it. He stuffed a large package and papers into his pockets. I saw him get into a green car, then he jumped out again ... and ran away along Adelaide Street."

Charles Arrowsmith, the driver of the Canada Bread Company delivery wagon, provided a more detailed account:

> I had noticed one rather stout man sitting on the railing. He jumped off and ran toward the door of the factory and then I heard a cry and witnessed three men fighting. One of them apparently had driven up to the factory with the payroll. He was carrying it in a leather satchel.
>
> The stout man had a gun. They struggled for a few seconds and secured hold of the satchel and started to run for the motor car in which I think the employee of the company had driven up to the factory with the money. In running towards the car they dropped the money satchel and three packages fell out. They stopped and picked up a large and small package.
>
> The stout man climbed into the driver's seat of the car and the other fellow ran around to climb in the other side. He could not get the door open. They both jumped out. The fat man ran east on Macdonnell Square ... the other chap ran south around the square ... It all happened so sudden. The employee of the company ran into

the building after the satchel had been snatched from his hands and he had been knocked down.

The thieves got away with $1,021. Police Chief Dennis Draper confidently predicted an arrest within twenty-four hours. There had been other holdups in the city, which the police believed had all been committed by the same robbers. The chief said his men were about to close in on the bandits. However, none of the suspects the constables hauled in for questioning had been involved in the payroll heist.

It wasn't until a week later that Toronto police detectives finally got a lead on the two bandits. In Orillia, a man known as Jack O'Brien got drunk and boasted about the robbery. He also said his real name was Pat Norton. That name immediately got the attention of Chief Draper and every cop on his force.

At the time, Pat Norton was an elusive phantom to Ontario police. A man who went by that name had been with Bill and Sid Murrell on April 11, 1921, when they killed a man while robbing a bank in Melbourne, Ontario. Sid had been hanged, Bill was sentenced to life in the Kingston Penitentiary, but Norton had vanished. Canadian police had no records of a Pat Norton, but believed the man they were looking for was an escaped murderer from the Michigan State Penitentiary, who used a string of aliases, including John Price, "Honest" John Morten, Ernest George Norton, "Two Gun" Jack O'Brien, and Babe O'Brien. In 1928, during the much-publicized hunt for Orval Shaw, the eccentric small-time criminal known as "The Mystery Man of Skunk's Misery," there had been false rumours that the trickster Shaw had hooked up with the much more dangerous Norton.

Depending on which story he told, O'Brien was born in either Detroit or Scotland. He would have been about thirty years old at the time of the Toronto robbery. Of average height and build, he could have been the "skinny guy" Johnny Brooks had seen.

O'Brien had been living in Orillia for about a year and a half and was friends with a local man named John Ainsworth. He worked as a painter, and occasionally made trips to Toronto. At about the time of the Durable robbery, Ainsworth was arrested in Toronto for car theft. The Toronto police learned that he was wanted in Orillia as the principal suspect in the burglary of the town's Central Hardware Store. Thieves had made off with rifles, shotguns, and ammunition, which police believed were to be used for holdups. Then came O'Brien's drunken claim that he was Pat Norton.

Toronto detectives also learned that O'Brien had been keeping company with Sydney "Sunny" Lass, who sometimes went by the alias Sam Levy. They'd been seen together in Orillia and in the Lido Restaurant on Temperance Street, a known hangout for Toronto hoodlums. With his short, stocky frame, Lass could have been the "stout man" with a gun who Charles Arrowsmith had seen.

Although the Toronto *Star* referred to Lass as a "well-known Torontonian" (that is, well-known to the police), he was originally from Greenwood, British Columbia. Lass was twenty-seven years old at the time of the Durable holdup. He first got in trouble with the law in 1910 when, at the age of seven, he was arrested for theft. The case was remanded and then apparently dropped. In 1913, ten-year-old Lass was again charged with theft and this time put on probation. The next year he was in court again, facing three charges of theft, and was once more put on probation. Young Sydney's incorrigible ways finally caught up to him in 1915, when the twelve-year-old was found guilty on three more charges of theft and sent to the Victoria Industrial School for an indefinite period.

Five years later, Lass was arrested in Detroit' for robbing a pawn shop. He was sentenced to ten-to-twenty-five years in the Michigan State Penitentiary, with the judge recommending that he serve at least fifteen years. It was 1920, and Sunny Lass was still a teenager.

The purpose of prisons at that time was simply to administer harsh punishment. The concept of educating and rehabilitating inmates was still in its infancy. Wayward, impressionable youths were tossed into a brutal environment with hardened criminals. Prisons were little more than schools for crime. Lass no doubt considered himself lucky when he was paroled after ten years, and sent back to Canada. But he hadn't changed much from the seven-year-old boy who'd been caught stealing.

An escort of six detectives and constables took Ainsworth to Orillia for a preliminary inquest into the hardware store burglary. The senior officer carried warrants for the arrest of O'Brien and Lass. He took along the extra manpower because there had been reports that O'Brien and Lass might try to rescue Ainsworth or kill him to shut him up. A large crowd of Orillians hung around the courthouse "to see what would happen." However, the suspected bandits were nowhere to be seen, and the police were told they'd fled to Montreal. The police doubted the truth of that information. After Ainsworth had been committed for trial, they took him back to Toronto over a secret route that involved criss-crossing secondary roads to hide the movements of the police cars in order to foil anyone who might be following or lying in wait.

On October 1, while Toronto police staked out the haunts frequented by the likes of O'Brien and Lass, The OPP began a province-wide search. They thought they had a lead when the manager of the liquor store in Lindsay reported to local police that a woman had tried to purchase more alcohol than was allowed by the strict regulations of the time. She'd presented a permit for purchasing liquor made out to John Ainsworth. After being refused, she'd left in a car with two men. It took the police a day or so to locate the woman's residence. The house was empty. Neighbours said there had been two men staying there, but they'd gone to Detroit. The police didn't know if the strangers were O'Brien and Lass.

The search suddenly shifted back to Orillia with the report of a missing girl. Anna Bryson, age seventeen, had been an "admirer" of O'Brien, and police had questioned her. Anna quit her job without notice and then disappeared.

Meanwhile, O'Brien and Lass had been seen in a restaurant between Orillia and Barrie. A waitress recognized them from photographs in the newspapers. Anna had given those pictures to the police. The waitress phoned the OPP detachment in Barrie. She said that when the men left, they drove toward Orillia.

Police feared that O'Brien and Lass were after Anna because of the pictures. The girl might have been thinking the same thing and had gone into hiding. She no doubt would have been terrified to learn that the man she knew as Jack O'Brien might really be Pat Norton, a convicted killer.

Police raided Anna's home, but it was deserted. A squad of officers searched the swampland near Orillia, but found nothing. Then on October 2, officers tracked Anna down as she was attempting to get some extra clothing before fleeing Orillia. They wouldn't say where they found her or where they had taken her for safekeeping. A police spokesman would say only that Anna lived in fear of O'Brien.

Certain that O'Brien and Lass were in the Orillia area, police threw out a wide net, expecting to snare them as they drew it tighter. But if the two were indeed in the district, they managed to slip through the cordon. On the night of October 3, Toronto police responded to a report that O'Brien and Lass had been spotted in the city's west end. Police cars and motorcycles sped to the location and prowled the surrounding streets. After a few hours of fruitless searching, they gave up. "Just another rumour," an officer told a reporter.

Police still had no real evidence to support O'Brien's drunken boast that he was Pat Norton. Even though Norton had been known to use the alias Jack O'Brien, it was almost as common a name as John Smith. Police had very little concrete information on the Pat Norton who'd been a member of the Murrell gang. But now, thanks to Anna Bryson, they had a photograph.

Chief Draper personally went to the Kingston Penitentiary to talk to Bill Murrell. Bill had been in prison for over nine years and hadn't set eyes on Pat Norton since the day of the Melbourne bank robbery. Nonetheless, he identified the man in Anna's photograph as Pat Norton.

Toronto police and the OPP searched for O'Brien and Lass for several weeks without finding a trace. Then they received information that the fugitives were in New York City, and two Toronto police detectives, Walter McConnell and Archie McCathie, were sent there. On Saturday, November 1, the Canadian officers accompanied by a squad of New York police caught O'Brien and Lass in Pennsylvania Station as they were about to board a train. McConnell said, "We want you O'Brien, and you too, Lass."

Lass had a revolver in his pocket, but with four police guns pointed at him, he didn't try to draw it. The pair had arranged passage on a ship to Europe, and were on their way to the harbour when they were arrested. In a West 34th Street apartment where O'Brien and Lass had been staying, police found guns and burglar tools.

According to American police records, Jack O'Brien couldn't have been the Pat Norton who'd been in on the Melbourne bank robbery, because he was in jail at the time. His real name, the Americans said, was Elmer J. Giller. He was indeed an escapee from the Michigan State Penitentiary, but he'd been doing time for armed robbery, not murder. Even so, the New York police said that O'Brien was one of the most "hard boiled" gunmen they had ever encountered.

"The only thing I would go back to Toronto for would be to shoot up a bunch of their dicks and people there," O'Brien snarled to New York police. "Youse'll never get me to Toronto or anywhere else in Canada."

The New York police sent photographs of O'Brien and Lass to Toronto and witnesses there identified them as the Durable bandits. A New York magistrate dismissed the local charges against the pair to smooth the extradition process. Evidently, Michigan authorities hadn't requested that O'Brien be extradited to that state to complete his prison term.

O'Brien and Lass were held without bail in a New York City jail. Both initially decided that they would fight extradition. Lass's mother, Ethel "Fanny" Lass, went to New York and was in the courtroom for the bail hearing. She broke down in tears when federal marshals wouldn't allow her to approach her son. Later, she obtained a pass to visit him in the detention cell for half an hour.

O'Brien attempted to escape when he was being taken from the court building back to jail. He tripped one of the officers escorting him and ran from the building. Three police officers fired at him as he ran down the street. None of the shots hit O'Brien, but two officers caught up with him before he got very far. They beat him into submission with blackjacks.

Back in Ontario, information provided by Ainsworth led police to the guns that had been stolen from the hardware store. Some had been buried near Orillia, and others had been tossed into the Don River. After a judicial hearing held in Orillia, County Crown Attorney F.G. Evans told the Toronto *Star*, "If we can show evidence from this hearing to the New York court which would convict the pair there, we shall get them back to Canada to stand trial."

The extradition process ran into delays in the office of the British consul-general in New York. The attorney for the consul-general requested an adjournment until December 1 to allow time for the attorney general of Ontario to forward official depositions. At that time, Canadian foreign affairs were still overseen by the British government. It wouldn't be until December 1931, with the passage of the Statute of Westminster, that the final strings of colonialism were cut and Canada became fully independent of Mother England.

Lass finally decided that it might be in his best interests to waive extradition and voluntarily return to Canada. Things might go easier for him in court, he thought, if he didn't put the Canadian government through a lot of trouble. O'Brien was still determined not to be sent back to Canada.

Ainsworth was sentenced to three years in the Kingston Pen. In Toronto, Chief Draper cancelled the Lido Restaurant's licence, effectively shutting down the hoodlum hangout. The proprietors eventually went to jail on convictions of perjury.

In spite of Lass's reluctant agreement to return to Canada without a legal fight, O'Brien's extradition proceeding had to run its course. It was mid-December before the New York court ruled against him and turned both men over to Canadian police. Once the pair were lodged in Toronto's Don Jail, they had to wait for the next assize to have their day in court.

O'Brien and Lass went to trial for armed robbery on February 17, 1931. The Crown presented witnesses who positively identified them as the men who had robbed the Durable payroll. Then the trial took a dramatic turn when Ethel Lass was on the stand. She told the court that she hadn't known the whereabouts of her son between 1921 and 1926. She also said Sydney was married and that before the holdup he'd been living in Toronto with his father-in-law. Ethel insisted that Sydney couldn't have been involved in the robbery, because he'd left Toronto more than a week before it occurred. Asked why Lass's wife wasn't in the courtroom, Ethel replied, "She's sick in bed."

As Ethel was being cross-examined by Crown prosecutor Charles W. Bell, K.C., she suddenly swooned on the stand. She swayed sideways and then collapsed into the arms of a court matron. Two constables carried her out of the room. Lass put his hand over his eyes.

Shortly after, as Ethel was returning to the courtroom, she slumped to the floor. There was a cry for "a doctor in the house." A physician named Laxton, who was among the spectators, went to Ethel's aid. Later he spoke to the presiding magistrate, Mr. Justice Jeffrey. The judge told the press, "It has been stated to me that she is in a state of hysteria; that she could throw it off, but that she does not appear to want to help herself."

Ethel's hysterics didn't win any sympathy for the defendants. They were each sentenced to twenty years in Kingston. In passing sentence, Mr. Justice Jeffrey said to Lass and O'Brien, "I am going to teach you, and by your example, others like you, that the criminal does not break the law. He breaks himself against the law."

Before being shipped off to the pen, O'Brien spoke at length to a Toronto *Star* reporter. He admitted to leading a life of crime and said he'd broken out of American prisons twice. He said he would rather have been sent back to the Michigan State Penitentiary because he'd heard that Canadian prisons were "too tough."

"I might as well have got thirty years," O'Brien said. "Long terms make criminals. Look at me. At eighteen I was put away for a long sentence and I was educated to be a criminal in that prison.... Society has done nothing to help the criminal. True, we break the law and the law sees that we are punished, but we are sent to prison and herded together. No one sees that first offenders are kept separate from the hardened type. I wish I had it all to live over again, that's all. It has paid me poor dividends."

O'Brien said his mother was dead and his father was living in Detroit. "I have no one to worry over, anyway." He strenuously denied being a violent, notorious character.

"I never shot a man in my life. The Toronto police thought I was Pat Norton, wanted for murder and bank robbery. They painted me black. They knew I wasn't Norton. I was in prison when the Murrells and Norton committed that crime at Melbourne."

Oddly enough, O'Brien claimed to have known the Murrell brothers in their hometown. "I met them in London," he said. "Sidney was quite a boxer." O'Brien said he was honestly employed with a boat-building company in Orillia when he drunkenly announced that he was Pat Norton.

O'Brien told the reporters it was a letter Sydney Lass had written to his wife in Toronto that sent the Canadian police to New York City. He also claimed to have come close to escaping from the New York jail. "I gave it up. I was nearly away there."

O'Brien closed the interview with a statement that would have pleased Chief Draper and the Canadian public in general. "Your courts are different ... Your whole procedure of law is different. No fooling with the Canadian police or law courts — they mean business. I watched my chance [to escape] in Toronto, but I didn't get one."

O'Brien's claim to have been associated with the Murrell brothers in London raises questions, especially since, while intoxicated, he'd blurted out that he was Pat Norton. The Murrells began running afoul of the law soon after they returned home from military service in the First

World War. Then, in April 1921, they were involved with Pat Norton in the tragic Melbourne bank robbery. O'Brien said he was in prison at the time. So when did he meet the Murrells in London?

Bill Murrell identified Anna Bryson's photograph of O'Brien as a picture of Pat Norton. Of course, time could have clouded his memory. Then Michigan authorities had said that O'Brien was really escaped bank robber Elmer Giller. O'Brien went along with that to the extent that he tried to have himself sent to the Michigan State Penitentiary instead of Kingston. But was that really because he was concerned about the "tough" Canadian prison?

The science of criminal investigation was still primitive by today's standards. Communications and information sharing among police forces and various other law enforcement agencies was often poor. Criminals were sometimes known only by their aliases, and could be registered into prisons under false names. If a convict had never before had a mug shot taken or been fingerprinted, authorities would be unaware of the deception. It could be possible that O'Brien really *was* Pat Norton, and wanted to avoid a long incarceration in Canada in case Canadian authorities discovered his real identity.

Whatever the bandit's name was, he was registered into the Kingston Pen as John O'Brien, prisoner #2119. He was lodged in cell 7-1-H, and worked as an orderly in the prison's hospital and dental office. He once lost his smoking privilege for a week for refusing to unload potatoes for the officers' mess. O'Brien was released on April 27, 1946, and disappeared from official record. He was most likely deported to the United States.

Sydney Lass (prisoner #2125, cell 2-4-F) was put to work in the prison tailor shop. His record shows that he was not as well-behaved an inmate as O'Brien. He was reprimanded for such offences as refusing to obey guards' orders, refusing to cut stone, having contraband in his cell, insolence to an officer, and fighting in the tailor shop. In January 1935, Lass was transferred to the Collins Bay Penitentiary.

Even though he hadn't been a model prisoner, Lass was released on a ticket-of-leave in December 1942. Two years later he was back in the Kingston Pen, convicted on charges of shop-breaking and receiving stolen property. He'd served about a year of his most recent sentence when his name came up in a police investigation into a robbery that had taken place in Brantford while he was out of jail. Lass would have to be sent to Brantford to stand trial for that crime. On December 9, 1945, guards searched Lass before putting him on a train. In the lining of his coat they found a dagger that had been made from a prison mess hall table knife, and a small bag of pepper. Lass intended to use the pepper and the blade in a hare-brained escape plan once he was on the train.

Lass escaped conviction on the Brantford robbery charge. He was released from prison on May 5, 1946. Like O'Brien, he slipped into obscurity. No criminal who could be identified as Pat Norton of the Murrell gang was ever taken into custody.

CHAPTER 7
THE HYSLOP GANG:
Suicide and the Hangman

In the decade known as the Dirty Thirties, Canada, like the rest of the world, was in the grip of the Great Depression. In the United States, the early years of the 1930s had seen a brief but spectacular era of banditry brought about by such notorious criminals as John Dillinger, Pretty Boy Floyd, Baby Face Nelson, and Bonnie and Clyde. There had been a rise in the crime rate in Canada, too, as desperate unemployed men decided to steal what they could no longer earn through honest labour. And while Canada didn't experience the so-called "Golden Age" of gun-toting, bank-robbing desperadoes, there were nonetheless dramatic criminal exploits that caught the public's attention, and more often than not ended in tragedy. One such story began with a bungled robbery in New Westminster, British Columbia.

On the morning of December 18, 1935, the store windows of downtown New Westminster glittered with all the trappings of Christmas. However, the mood of the people in those grim "Hard Times" was probably more accurately represented by the thick fog that rolled through the city streets. At 8:45, two armed men entered Philip Spurgeon's jewellery shop on Columbia Street and announced, "This is a stickup; no fooling!"

The bandits ordered Spurgeon and his employee, Rene Winston, to the back of the store at gunpoint. Before they could grab any merchandise, Miss Winston began to scream. Startled, the robbers ran out the front door. Spurgeon pursued them, shouting for the police.

Constable Danny Gunn of the New Westminster Police Department had just come off night duty. He was standing at a corner waiting for a streetcar when Spurgeon's cries caught his attention. He saw two men run across Columbia Street. They shot at Spurgeon, who was hot on their heels.

Immediately Constable Gunn drew his revolver and took up the chase. He engaged the stickup men in a running gunfight as they raced up Lorne Street to Clarkson Street. There, a confederate awaited them in a car with the engine running. The gunmen jumped in and the car roared away with Gunn's bullets whistling after it.

Visibility was poor in the dense fog. At the intersection of Second and Durham Streets, the bandit car collided with a milk-delivery truck. The dazed milkman stumbled out of his vehicle and saw three men flee the scene of the accident on foot and disappear into the fog. An examination of the car showed that Dunn had hit it twice. The occupants had been very lucky, because one of the constable's bullets had pierced the back window and shattered the rear-view mirror above the driver's seat.

The getaway car was registered to a local man, John Roy Godbolt, age twenty-five. Godbolt had a criminal record and had only recently been released from prison. He was soon identified as the driver. Police issued a warrant for his arrest on a number of charges, including the attempted murder of Constable Gunn.

At 11:35 on the morning of December 23, the same two gunmen who had tried to rob the jewellery store burst into the Royal Bank of Canada on Commercial Drive. One of them said, "This is a stickup!" While they made the three clerks and six customers line up against a wall, another bandit entered the bank. All were armed with automatic pistols.

Branch manager J.W. Logan was in his office with the door locked, unaware of what was happening. He heard a pounding on his door. He had only partially opened it when he saw a gun in the hand of the man on the other side. Logan tried to slam the door shut, but the robber threw himself against it, sending the manager sprawling. Logan then tried to kick the door shut, but the gunman smashed the glass with the butt of his pistol. Logan made no further resistance. This wasn't the first time his bank had been robbed. He joined the rest of the staff at the wall.

The bandits cleaned out the drawers of one teller's cage of about $2,000. The second teller's cage was locked and they wasted no time trying to open it. They backed out of the bank and made their escape in a taxi driven by a fourth member of the gang. He had circled the block while his companions robbed the bank.

Twenty minutes later, the taxi was found parked on a side street. On the floor of the back seat, with his hands tied behind his back and adhesive tape over his mouth, was cab driver Bill Perry. He told police that two men had walked into the Star Cabs office and hired him to drive them to Stanley Park. Along the way they had hijacked his cab at gunpoint and bound him. En route to the bank, they'd picked up two more men. The driver, he said, wore horn-rimmed glasses.

The robbers had not been masked. They all wore dark overcoats and fedoras pulled down to hide their eyes. Even so, witnesses could see that one rather tall man had red hair and freckles. The robbers all appeared to be in their late twenties. The Vancouver police had the witnesses go through stacks of mug shots and wanted posters, but apparently to no avail. Several known underworld characters were picked up for questioning, and then released.

Vancouver's first bank robbery of 1936 took place at 10:45 a.m. on January 13. Two bandits, one of them a tall redhead, strode into the Bank of Montreal at Prior and Main Streets and told the five people within to "Stick 'em up!" Each bandit wielded two pistols. While one covered the people with his guns, the other rifled the teller's cage of about $1,000. Then he told manager G.W. Richardson to open the vault.

Like Mr. Logan at the Royal Bank, Richardson had been the victim of bank robbers before. On that occasion, the thieves had locked him in the vault. This time, he said he couldn't open the safe. With no further words, the robbers fled, taking with them a .38 revolver that was in a teller's drawer. The bandits wore mufflers to partially conceal their faces, but several times during the holdup the mufflers slipped, allowing witnesses to provide police with good descriptions. The day after the robbery, British Columbia Provincial Police arrested two suspects in Port Coquitlam and sent them to Vancouver. They were interrogated and placed in a police lineup, but finally proved to be the wrong men. Within twenty-four hours, the real culprits struck again and this time the raid was bloody.

So far, there had been no casualties in the holdups pulled by the still-unidentified hoodlums. Witnesses had even commented on the relatively quiet manner in which they had gone about the business of armed robbery. That changed when just before noon on January 15, the gang hit the Canadian Bank of Commerce at the corner of Powell Street and Victoria Drive in Vancouver.

Hugh Gibson, one of just two customers in the bank, was cashing a cheque at William Hobbs's teller's cage when three armed men dashed in through the front door. One of them yelled, "This is a holdup!" A bandit shoved Gibson aside, levelled a pistol at Hobbs, and barked, "Stick 'em up!"

Before Hobbs could make a move, the bandit shot him in the throat. Hobbs collapsed with blood pouring from the bullet hole. Another bandit fired a shot at manager Thomas Winsby, but missed. Winsby rushed to the vault and grabbed an automatic pistol. He managed to get off a couple of wild shots before a bandit's bullet pierced his arm and shoulder, knocking him out of action.

The bandits ordered the ledger keeper, D.A. McRae, to open the cage. McRae obeyed, and the bandits stepped over the prone figure of Hobbs, who lay in a spreading pool of blood. They cleaned out the cash drawers of about $1,200. Then they exited the bank to the street, where a taxi driven by a fourth gang member picked them up. McRae immediately phoned the police, who arrived within minutes. They found Hobbs on the floor with Gibson crouched beside him, holding up the wounded man's head in an attempt to slow the flow of blood.

"I thought it was a joke," Gibson told a Vancouver *Province* reporter after an ambulance had whisked Hobbs and Winsby to a hospital. "But when I saw the gun in the man's hand, I knew it was a holdup all right. I was watching the bandit and I don't know if Hobbs did put up his hands, but almost at once he fired. As I looked up I saw Hobbs fall. It was a dirty low trick. He didn't give the poor fellow a chance."

Some men in a beer parlour across the street from the bank had been drawn to the doorway by the sound of gunshots. They had seen the bandits come out of the bank. One of them, a tall red-haired man, put his gun in his pocket and then calmly lit a cigarette. When he noticed the men at the tavern door, he pulled the gun out again. The men ducked back inside and didn't see the thieves make their getaway in the cab. A man named L.P. Gordy had just come out of the nearby Hamilton Café. He saw the bandit wave his gun at the men and heard one of the other bandits say, "Shoot the son of a bitch." When the taxi arrived and the robbers climbed in, he heard one of them tell the driver, "We had to shoot a guy."

A motorist coming down Powell Street had seen men come out of the bank with guns in their hands and get into the cab. Realizing at once what was happening, he followed the cab to a location on Clark Street where the gunmen jumped out and ran around a corner. The man knew better than to try following them further. He hurried to the nearest telephone and called the police. Radio squad cars arrived quickly, but the robbers were gone. No doubt they'd had another getaway car parked nearby. While officers were questioning people in the bank and scouring the downtown area for any sign of the hoodlums, Vancouver police headquarters had a phone call from Daniel Warnock, the taxi driver whose car the bandits had used.

At about a quarter past eleven that morning, Warnock had stepped out of his cab company office and found three men sitting in his taxi. They said they wanted to be driven to Coal Harbour. Thinking them to be legitimate passengers, Warnock got behind the wheel. As they neared the destination, one of the men stuck a gun in Warnock's side and growled, "Keep driving."

The hoodlums made him stop on Pipeline Road, about a quarter of a mile from the Vancouver Police Department's horse stables. They ordered him out of the car, bound his hands and feet with tape, slapped tape across his mouth, and dumped him in the bushes. Then they drove off in his cab. One of them wore horn-rimmed glasses.

Warnock managed to struggle to his feet and hop to a tree. He rubbed his face against the trunk to get the tape off his mouth. Then he hobbled to the road. He was rescued by a passing driver who freed him from his bonds and then took him to the police stables where he phoned to report the theft of his cab.

Thomas Winsby's wounds were not life-threatening. But the bullet that had torn through Hobbs's throat had struck the top of his spine. Even if he survived, he'd be paralyzed. Hobbs spent the last night of his life in an oxygen tent in Vancouver's General Hospital, fighting for every breath. At 8:45 on the morning of January 16, twenty-five-year-old William Hobbs died. Now the fugitives were wanted for murder. Only one bandit had shot Hobbs, but under Canadian law at that time, if two or more people set out with the intention of perpetrating a criminal act, and one of them committed murder, all were held equally responsible.

At a special meeting of Vancouver's City Council, Mayor Gerald McGeer speculated that the bank robberies and murder had been the work of American criminals "of the most dangerous and vicious type" who had been driven out of their country. In the United States, McGeer said, the forces of law and order co-operated in a crackdown on bandit gangs. But in British Columbia, the provincial police and the various municipal police departments lacked the funding and the organization required to be effective. McGeer said the situation left Vancouver's city police "under handicaps that work to the advantage of the criminal element … It should be fairly clear to everyone that we cannot prevent the operations of twentieth-century criminals with nineteenth-century police methods."

Vancouver Police Chief William W. Foster assured City Council and the press that everything possible was being done to apprehend the culprits. Suspects were being rounded up and questioned. Routine police work had been set aside so officers could concentrate on the manhunt. Roadblocks had been set up throughout Vancouver and the Lower Mainland. Police were watching the bus terminals and train stations. No motor launch could leave the docks without inspection. Police in Alberta and the states bordering British Columbia had been alerted. The Canadian Bankers Association posted a $5,000 reward for information leading to the arrest and conviction of the bandits.

Meanwhile, the press reported that William Hobbs's shocked and grieving parents were en route to Vancouver by train from Edmonton. Reporters had learned that Hobbs had briefly regained consciousness in hospital. He'd managed to gasp to detectives, "He did not give me a chance to put up my hands. He fired first thing."

What the press didn't know yet, and Chief Foster was keeping quiet for the sake of the investigation, was that the Vancouver police already had some strong leads. Witnesses from the bank robberies had in fact pointed out three faces in the Vancouver Police Department's "Rogues Gallery" of photographs: George "Blackie" Lawson, age thirty-five; Charles Russell, age twenty-five; and Jack "Red" Hyslop, age twenty-three.

These men all belonged to a pack of thieves and troublemakers the Vancouver police had labelled "the Hyslop Gang" because the tough young redhead appeared to be the leader. Although Lawson was much older, he had only recently slipped into a life of crime. A native of Melita, Manitoba, he had worked for several years in the logging camps of Vancouver Island. Men who had known Lawson there recalled him as a hard worker who was friendly and well liked. It was a mystery to most of them why he had suddenly gone bad. Others suspected it was because he had caught what newspapers of the time discreetly called a "social disease," which affected his mind.

Jack Hyslop was born in Scotland in 1914. His family immigrated to Vancouver when he was ten years old. Jack's father fell ill with chronic asthma and couldn't work. His mother's only income was a small pension. Jack had to quit elementary school and take a job as a delivery boy. He gave his pay to his mother. Jack was known as a good, honest kid who attended church and Sunday school. But like many youngsters growing up in poverty, he made some bad choices.

The trouble started with some minor brushes with the law. Then early in 1933, Hyslop was sent to the Oakalla prison farm for three months for being

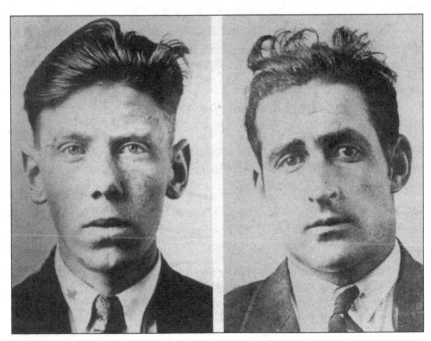

Jack "Red" Hyslop (left) and George "Blackie" Lawson (right): Vancouver bandits who started out as honest kids but made some bad choices.
VANCOUVER PUBLIC LIBRARY.

in possession of a stolen car. He hadn't been out of jail for long when he participated in an armed robbery. He was caught and sentenced to two years in prison. By the time Hyslop was released, he'd become embittered toward society in general. He had a bad temper, and police had him marked as a "dangerous character." There had been several incidents in which he'd been arrested for allegedly shooting at people without provocation. Investigating officers had found witnesses unwilling to testify against him, and had therefore been obliged to release him. Hyslop had supposedly said on several occasions that he would "shoot to kill" before he'd go back to prison.

Detectives were told to keep a lookout for two other members of the Hyslop Gang: William Davies, age thirty-one; and Earl Dunbar, age thirty-two. They learned that Dunbar had a room in a boarding house on Cambie Street. A pair of detectives watched the place for a while, but when Dunbar didn't show up they searched his room. They found a handgun and a mask. There was also a postcard from a western American city. From it, detectives gleaned a clue that implicated James Lawler, age twenty-six; and David Anderson, age twenty, in the botched jewellery store heist. Both men were known Hyslop associates.

Then police had received a tip from a woman who, after hearing about the robbery and shooting, remembered seeing two men walk away from a car parked in a back lane. The car was still there. Detectives found the key in the ignition. The car was registered to a man named Donald McNeill, who had reported it stolen several hours after the robbery.

Two detectives went to McNeill's home to question him. He seemed nervous and his answers weren't at all satisfactory. When the detectives pressed him to tell the truth, McNeill changed his story. He said some friends who lived in a house on East Tenth Avenue had borrowed his car. When they didn't return it at the agreed time, he went to their house to see them. They told him they'd had some trouble and the police were looking for the car, which they'd left in a lane two blocks away. That evening, McNeill said he'd read about the robbery and shooting in the newspaper. That's when he phoned the police and reported his car as stolen. The detectives were sure McNeill wasn't telling them everything. They took him to police headquarters for further questioning.

McNeill had given the police an address, but they didn't want to just barge in and risk triggering a gun battle. They also had to be sure McNeill was telling the truth. Plainclothes detectives discreetly questioned neighbours. People told them several men and two women had been going in and out of the house for about two weeks. One day, two men were seen carrying in what appeared to be a heavy club bag. The day after the robbery and murder, two of the men had thoroughly scrubbed down the verandah, even though there had just been a heavy rain. It looked as though they were trying to cleanse the place of evidence. Neighbours didn't connect the suspicious behaviour with the bank robberies. They thought the strangers were bootleggers.

The local grocery store owner told police the women did all of the shopping for the people in the house. They were very frugal at first and paid for their purchases with handfuls of change, as though they didn't have much money. After the first bank robbery, the women suddenly had plenty of paper currency. They bought large quantities of food and cigarettes. Police searched for the house's owner, a forty-one-year-old taxi driver named Fred Healy. He had disappeared.

At ten o'clock on the night of January 16, police cars converged on the house on East Tenth Avenue. Chief Foster personally directed the raid. Twenty-four officers surrounded the house, which was in darkness. Superintendent Harold Darling and Detective Inspector Gordon Grant took the considerable risk of going to the front door and ringing the bell.

William Davies answered the door, opening it just a crack. The officers shoved their way in and one of them pressed the muzzle of a revolver against Davies's stomach before he could bolt. Quietly, Grant ordered the bewildered Davies to lead him through the house and not make a sound. If at all possible, the officers wanted to pull off the raid without a gunfight. As it turned out, there was no fight in this bandit gang.

Officers swept through the house and met no resistance at all. Davies claimed he was just a visitor. Earl Dunbar was trying to hide behind the living-room door. When he saw a gun in an officer's hand, he threw up his hands and cried, "You don't need to use that!" Charles Russell was hiding under a bed. He meekly surrendered without trying to use the three pistols he had on him.

A search of the house turned up several hundred dollars from the bank robberies. Among a cache of guns and ammunition was the revolver that had been stolen from the Bank of Commerce. A roll of tape of the same type that had been used to bind and gag the unfortunate taxi drivers was added to the mounting evidence. Dunbar and Russell were charged with murder, and Davies as an accessory to murder.

At a luncheon the next day, Mayor McGeer congratulated Chief Foster on the success of the raid. He was confident that the rest of the gang would soon be in custody. Foster told the press that officers not directly assigned to the manhunt were "scouring the city for all undesirables and underworld characters with a view to placing them in jail or driving them from the city."

The police learned that most of the gang members had rooms in boarding houses and had been using the Tenth Avenue house as a hide-out. Fred Healy had evidently rented it to them, knowing that they were plotting and carrying out bank robberies. The morning after the raid, Healy walked into the police station with his lawyer and gave himself up. He was charged with being an accessory to murder.

At a coroner's inquest held on January 20, five witnesses identified Charles Russell as the bandit who had gunned down William Hobbs. Earl Dunbar was identified as the one who had shot Thomas Winsby. Throughout the four-hour hearing, Russell, who was known to have a taste for fine clothes and was nattily dressed, seemed amused at the proceedings. According to the *Daily Province*, he was "ice cold." Dunbar, on the other hand, frowned often and "showed decided reaction to the evidence."

For the next few days, newspaper headlines across Canada were dominated by news of the death of King George V and the accession of King Edward VIII. But in Vancouver, reports on the hunt for Hyslop and Lawson still merited front-page space. In the hours after the raid, police kept watch on the robbers' lair, hoping the unsuspecting fugitives might return. Questioning of the captured bandits revealed that hours before the police closed in, Hyslop and Lawson had left in the company of two women, now identified as Mary Gorry and Frances Morton, both twenty-eight.

The vigil at the house proved futile. Then a rumour spread that Hyslop and Lawson had engaged police officers in a gunfight, but Chief Foster quickly dismissed that as false. Citizens were encouraged to keep providing the police with tips, which had been coming in at a record rate, but were cautioned not to approach the suspects, who were considered armed and dangerous.

Some of the tips the police received led them on wild goose chases to locations in Vancouver and nearby communities. Officers raided scores of rooming houses, only to come away empty-handed. One man the police picked up bore such a resemblance to Lawson that he could have been a double, but he was able to prove his identity. Chief Foster told the citizens of Vancouver, who were nervous about two potentially deadly criminals on the loose, "It is just a matter of time."

A big tip finally paid off on January 21. It led the police to a West Pender Street apartment that Frances Morten had rented under an assumed name. She and Mary Gorry were taken into custody. In the apartment, detectives found men's clothing and papers bearing Lawson's name, including his birth certificate. They also found two boxes of bullets.

The net was tightening around the fugitives. They had little money. The loss of Frances Morten's apartment had left them with no safe refuge. They were — in the parlance of the underworld — so "hot," that nobody would take the risk of helping them. The only ammunition they had were the bullets in their guns. Detectives who had an ear to the underworld grapevine heard whispers that the pair had been talking about pulling another bank robbery. Every bank in Vancouver was placed on alert, but no robbery was attempted. Word on the grapevine also had it that Lawson was badly in need of medication for his "social disease," and that Hyslop might be willing to give himself up if he could escape prosecution for murder.

A good lawyer might well have been able to save Hyslop and Lawson from the hangman. Neither had fired the fatal shot, and in similar cases the Canadian government had sometimes granted clemency and commuted death sentences to life imprisonment. But Jack Hyslop, who'd foolishly sought an escape from poverty through crime; and George Lawson, whose mental state might well have been affected by the ravages of syphilis, chose in the end to take their own way out.

It was yet another tip that drew the attention of the police to a rooming house called the Oaks Rooms on East Hastings Street in the city's east end. Chief Foster was once again in charge as more than forty constables and detectives surrounded the building at 7:30 on the evening of January 23. Extra guards were placed at the entrances and at the foot of the fire escape. Beams from police flashlights probed the shadows as officers armed with revolvers, riot guns, and tear-gas guns took up positions.

The police had been told only that Hyslop and Lawson were inside; they didn't know which room. Therefore, they had to undertake a coordinated room-by-room search. As one group of officers began on the first floor, Sergeant A. Hann climbed the stairs to the second floor. A detective was already at a desk at the end of the corridor, looking through the second-floor register. Hann decided to go up and begin a search of the third floor. He'd ascended just a few steps when the usual night sounds of a working-class rooming house — conversation, laughter, arguments, radio music — were shattered by two gunshots fired almost simultaneously. Sergeant Hann dashed back down to the second floor. A startled lodger stuck his head out of his door and said, "There is something wrong in that room." He pointed at room number 40.

Hann pounded on the door and called, "Open up in there! Police!" There was no answer. He put his shoulder to the door and the flimsy lock gave way. Gun in hand, the sergeant burst into a room that was dark, silent, and reeking of gunsmoke. He saw at once that there would be no need for the riot guns and tear gas.

Jack Hyslop and George Lawson lay on the floor almost at right angles to each other, their feet nearly touching. Each had a bullet hole in the left side of the head. Hyslop's left hand clutched a .38 Smith and Wesson. Inches from Lawson's left hand was a .38 Iver Johnson. Other police officers poured into the room. One constable opened the window and called down to the police below, "They are shot. Both dead."

Hyslop was actually still alive, but unconscious. He would die hours later in Vancouver General Hospital with his family around him. His father, who was a patient in the hospital, was brought to his dying son's side in a wheelchair.

"If I knew that Jack was in the Oaks Rooms last night, he would have come out for me without any shooting," his mother lamented. But as she was led away from his body she said, "It was better that it should have ended this way." Perhaps she was thinking of the possibility of Jack being hanged.

Evidently Hyslop and Lawson realized the police had found them. Rather than face arrest, trial, and death on the gallows, they had stood face to face and committed suicide. Police and forensic experts dismissed a story that said they had shot each other, which would have been almost impossible.

Detectives found $135 in the bandits' pockets. They had no spare ammunition. The seedy room in which they had reached the end of the line was sparsely furnished. The only items police found in it that belonged to the dead men were a felt hat, a pair of gloves, and a pair of horn-rimmed glasses.

The Hyslop Gang was finished, but two members were still wanted for robbery. Thanks to postcards and letters that James Lawler and David Anderson mailed to their friends in Vancouver, the police learned they were travelling with two women on a leisurely tour of the western United States. Because American media rarely reported on events in Canada, Lawler and Anderson were unaware that Hyslop and Lawson were dead, and the rest of the gang in jail. They wrote that they were heading for Chicago where Lawler, using the name Mitchell, would check for mail at the general delivery window of the post office.

Vancouver police passed the information on to the Chicago police, advising them that the Canadian fugitives were probably armed. On January 27, Lawler was arrested in the Chicago post office. Shortly after, Chicago police officers broke down an apartment door, taking Anderson and the women completely by surprise. There was a gun on the kitchen table, and another one in a dresser drawer, but Anderson was seized and handcuffed before he could reach for either weapon.

The women said they had met the men in British Columbia and had no idea they were criminals. They were deported back to Canada. Lawler and Anderson were held in a Chicago jail until Vancouver police detectives arrived to take custody of them.

Lawler and Anderson were tried for the botched jewellery store robbery and the Royal Bank stickup, and were sentenced to twenty years in prison. John Godbolt got ten years for his part as a getaway car driver. Frances Morton and Mary Gorry were released. That left the gang members who were charged with murder and accessory to murder in the death of William Hobbs. The trial was held in April before Chief Justice Aulay Morrison.

The chief suspects, James Russell and Earl Dunbar, had backgrounds in petty crime, auto theft, and bootlegging, and had done time in jail. Dunbar admitted to participation in the bank robberies, but said he had been the driver and therefore wasn't in the bank when Hobbs was shot. Moreover, he claimed that he had gone along on the robberies out of fear of Jack Hyslop. He said Hyslop had threatened to blow his and Russell's brains out if they didn't help him rob some banks. Hyslop, said Dunbar, had once told him he would "bump off a fellow who took a roll of money off him."

Russell denied any involvement in the crimes at all. He said he'd been out shopping at the time of the murder and knew nothing about it until he heard the news on the radio. Russell's lawyer, T.F. Hurley, argued that the gun that killed Hobbs had discharged accidentally. He also suggested that bank manager Winsby fired first and that the bandits shot back in self-defence.

Russell seemed impassive throughout the trial, smiling occasionally. Once, when a witness made a statement that struck most of the people in the courtroom as funny, he joined in the outburst of laughter. Dunbar was the opposite; sullen, and constantly licking his lips in nervous anxiety.

The testimony of the accused men and the arguments of their defence counsel didn't stand up to the evidence. Eyewitnesses again identified Russell as the "iron-nerved" bandit who had killed Hobbs and Dunbar as the robber who had shot Winsby. The jury took only ninety minutes to reach a guilty verdict.

Chief Justice Morrison sentenced Russell and Dunbar to death. Upon hearing the terrible words, "To be hanged by the neck until you are dead," Russell hardly flinched. Dunbar almost collapsed. "He is weak," Russell later told a guard.

Fred Healy was convicted of being an accessory after the fact and sentenced to fifteen years. Walter Davies was also charged with being an accessory, but the Crown withdrew the charge due to lack of evidence. The judge advised him to follow the example of the Greek philosopher Socrates who "made a practice of never looking into a tavern or getting himself mixed up with tumultuous or ill-considered people." Davies was released, along with Mary Gorry and Frances Morten.

Charles Russell went to the gallows in the Oakalla prison at 6:45 on the morning of November 6, 1936. He approached the scaffold smoking a cigarette, which he tossed aside before his arms were pinioned and the hood was pulled over his head. Earl Dunbar, whose execution was postponed due to an appeal, followed Russell to the gallows on November 27. Suicide and the hangman ended the short and sordid tale of the Hyslop Gang.

CHAPTER 8
THE POLKA DOT GANG:
"A Strange Fraternity of Men"

The idea of a bandit gang using a specific article of clothing as a badge of identity may seem like the stuff of adolescent comic book fiction. Surely, any "professional" criminal would realize that anonymity is a key factor in avoiding arrest. For a bandit to advertise himself with a trademark would be foolish. Nonetheless, there have been robber gangs who, out of a desire to be flamboyant or a juvenile need for attention, have accessorized so as to make their mark for the media and the public. For example, John "Red" Hamilton, the Canadian member of the John Dillinger gang in the 1930s, was in his youth associated with a band of hoodlums whose leader wanted them all to wear white hats when they pulled robberies, so the world would know them as the White Hat gang. In Chicago, over a period of a few months in 1942, a gang of young gunmen who wore blue polka-dot bandanas gained national notoriety as the Polka Dot Gang. Whether by coincidence or deliberate imitation, polka-dot bandanas gave a name to a robber gang that plagued southern Ontario around the end of the Second World War.

The robberies began in the spring of 1945. Nazi Germany had been defeated and the newspaper front pages were full of information on the trials and executions of Vichy traitors in France and speculation on how the war with Japan would be brought to a close. A series of armed holdups in cities like London, Guelph, and Hamilton caught the attention of the press when it became apparent that the same gang was responsible for all of them.

The Guelph robbery was typical of the gang's methods. Early on the morning of June 25, four bandits forced open a back window of the

Wellington meat-packing plant on the eastern outskirts of the city. The thieves quietly made their way to the office. They had likely been watching the place for a few nights, because they seemed to know the routine of the watchman, sixty-eight-year-old J. Forestell. He had just done his rounds and had sat down in the lobby for a smoke when they broke in.

Forestell heard a noise and went to investigate. When he opened the office door, he was confronted by the intruders. One of them said, "This is a holdup." Then another one slugged the unarmed watchman over the head with a wooden stick that was used for hanging meat.

The blow knocked Forestell out cold. Twice he stirred and began to come to, and both times he was bludgeoned back into unconsciousness. The robbers put him in a chair and tied him up.

The bandits went to work on the safe with a sledgehammer and other tools. Investigators later determined that these criminals were experienced in cracking safes. Once they had the double doors open, they scooped out over a thousand dollars in cash and bonds. They scattered the rest of the contents around the office. Then, instead of hightailing it, the robbers pulled up a table and sat down to a snack. They broke into the smoked meat room from which they filched a cooked ham and helped themselves to some chocolate milk and soft drinks staff had left in the office icebox.

After the bandits left, it took Forestell an hour to wriggle loose from the chair and call for help. It was about 4:00 a.m. when the phone rang in the Guelph police station. Constables who responded to the call sent the battered old night watchman to St. Joseph's Hospital where he was treated for severe lacerations to the head and a broken jaw.

(L–R): Kenneth Green, Hubert Hiscox, Bruce Kay, George Constantine, and George Dobbie were the core members of the Polka Dot Gang that terrorized postwar southern Ontario.
TORONTO *STAR.*

Another victim whom the gang handled roughly was Norman Bowman, engineer of the Duff & Sons packing plant in Hamilton. In the early hours of August 27, five bandits broke in and stole $14,000 in cash, Victory bonds, and war savings certificates. Bowman was subjected to a pistol-whipping. "They jumped on me when I was in the engine room," Bowman said. "I was hit in the face twice. I was told to lie down on my face. I obeyed. I told the fellow who hit me, 'You didn't have to do that.' He replied, 'Shut up or I'll put a bullet through you.' Then they tied me up."

Bowman suffered a broken nose and cuts to his face. The night watchman, Frank L. Tomlinson, was also beaten and tied up. Help didn't come until after 4:00 a.m., when Tomlinson failed to punch in his regular signal to a security company.

From witnesses' accounts, police concluded that no more than five men made up the gang, and not all of them participated in all of the robberies. This was later proven to be only partially correct. Victims described the leader as a six-foot-tall, well-dressed youth. They were armed with revolvers and machine guns and they all masked the lower parts of their faces with red polka-dot bandanas. War news was soon sharing space in Ontario newspapers with stories of the depredations of the "Polka Dot Machine Gun Gang." The name would soon be shortened to the Polka Dot Gang as the robbers struck again and again.

The gang's favourite targets were the offices of dairies, creameries, packing plants, and flour mills. The safes in those businesses were full of cash for payrolls and daily operations. Such places were easy pickings because they lacked the security measures used by banks. On some occasions the bandits even robbed employees of any money they had in their pockets.

Emboldened by their successes, the Polka Dot Gang turned their attention to the big city. Their first known attempt at a robbery in Toronto came on the night of August 24. Four of them were attempting to break into the office of Urquhart Motors on Dufferin Street, when they were interrupted by Constable Walter McGowan of the York Township police. They fled after exchanging shots with the officer. McGowan was later able to identify two of the suspects in court.

The gang had better luck on September 16, when they broke into the Lake of the Woods Milling Company on Dupont Street. The robbery was carried out with the violence that had become as much the gang's trademark as the polka-dot bandanas. The victim was the night watchman, William Cunliffe.

"I had just reached the shipping room on the main floor when three men appeared," Cunliffe recalled later. "One man had a small machine gun, the others two revolvers. The man with the machine gun hit me four times on the head with some part of it. I crumpled to the floor."

The robbers wrapped a towel around Cunliffe's bleeding head and tied him up. Then they dragged him along with them as they went from room to room. "They seemed perturbed about the clocks," Cunliffe said. "They kept asking me how they operated." The robbers were concerned that the plant might have a signal system that was connected to the clocks.

In the office, the thieves left Cunliffe tied up on the floor while they hammered away at the safe. "It sounded like a boiler shop," he said. The robbers got away with over $1,200. Cunliffe was found seven hours later. His injuries kept him hospitalized for two weeks.

The Roselawn Farm Dairy on Dufferin Street was the next target. The office safe contained $7,000, and in a storage vault was $17,000 worth of furs. Early in the morning of October 8, the gang forced their way into the building. They took night watchman William Bartie and employee George Bradley by surprise, beating and kicking them into unconsciousness. Bartie said later, "They slugged me on the back of the head so hard, it broke my false teeth." The bandits took $150 that Bartie had in his wallet. They bound both men's hands and feet and threw a cover over Bartie's face to muffle his groans.

The robbers were working on the safe when two employees, Roy Downing and Lloyd Kearney, arrived at the dairy. Two bandits armed with a machine gun and a revolver met them on the stairs that led to the second floor office. "One move and you've had it!" a gunman snarled, and ordered them up the stairs. "Going upstairs, he jabbed the gun in my back and made me put my hands up," Downing said. "He acted like he meant business, so I put them up … It was a gruesome sight to see Bill (Bartie) lying on the floor in what looked like a pool of blood. Bradley was lying there too. I thought they were both dead."

Downing and Kearney were both made to lie face down on the floor while the thieves resumed their sledgehammer attack on the safe. They were still at it when they were suddenly startled by a sharp ringing noise.

"It's a burglar alarm!" one bandit cried. In an instant they all dropped their tools and ran for the stairs.

The "alarm" was actually the telephone. It rang because a twenty-year-old shipping department employee named Lew Ireland, who had arrived at work early and had no idea a robbery was in progress, tried to call the office. That attempted phone call brought young Ireland within a hair's breadth of losing his life.

When nobody answered the phone, Ireland suspected something was wrong. He jumped into a truck and drove around the building to the front entrance. His truck almost collided with the bandits' getaway car and was blocking their escape. Ireland wasn't alarmed at the sight of a strange car. "At first I thought they were pranksters," he said later. "Strangers often park on our lot."

Then a machine-gun barrel poked out of one of the car's windows and fired a quick burst of eight bullets. Ireland immediately backed out of the way and the bandits roared off. "There was a steady flame from the barrel of the gun, but none of the shots hit me," Ireland told a reporter. "It must have been my lucky day."

Inside the building, a groggy William Bartie heard the shooting. He told the press, "When I heard the eight shots, I thought somebody was killed. They were desperate men, all in their early twenties. The big man gave the orders, and only when the telephone rang did any of the others speak. He was frightened and the mention of a burglar alarm made the others scared, too. All wore red-and-white polka-dot bandana handkerchiefs over their faces."

The newspapers praised Lew Ireland for accidentally thwarting a major robbery. The fact that Lew's sister Kay was the current Miss Toronto added to the story's appeal. But the papers were hardly off the presses when the Polka Dot Gang struck again.

At 4:00 a.m. on October 9, night mechanic Howard Segee was in the grease pit under a bus in the garage of the West York and District Bus Lines on St. Clair Avenue West. It was the first time in many nights that he was alone at work. The Polka Dot raid was sudden and swift.

"There was a terrific crash when they smashed down the front door," Segee said. "Then the five of them were on top of me. They all had their guns on me. One got out some sash cord and bound my wrists and ankles.

Another held a gun over me. They made me look away from the front office where the others were rolling the safe out."

This time the gang didn't waste time trying to open the safe on the premises. They loaded it onto a truck they had stolen for the job. Less than twenty minutes after they'd first burst in, the bandits drove away.

Fortunate to have escaped the beating the Polka Dot Gang gave other victims, Segee wiggled over to the desk and knocked the telephone to the floor. He managed to use one finger to dial the operator and tell her to call the police. Two detectives arrived within minutes. Police found the stolen truck and the smashed safe on a side street. The raid had netted the gang $400 in cash, a $100 Victory bond, and $350 worth of bus tickets. They'd overlooked $3,000 in cheques on the office manager's desk.

Probably disappointed with the scanty swag, especially after the failure of the Roselawn Dairy raid, the Polka Dot Gang swooped down on Hall's Dairy on Christie Street just two nights later. The prize was a safe containing $4,000. That night's events might almost have been taken from a comedy sketch, had it not been for the real danger to which employees James Morgan and Basil Kirkey were exposed.

Morgan was the company's stableman. "I had just cleaned up the stable and was preparing to feed the horses, when they [the bandits] came into the harness room," he said later. "The big fellow, who didn't have a gun, came up and struck me a blow on the nose."

Kirkey, who'd been working outdoors, had just stepped inside to take shelter from a rainfall. He was sitting on a milk case when the "big fellow" who had assaulted Morgan took him by surprise with a hard blow.

"They all had red polka-dot handkerchiefs over their faces," Morgan said. "They ordered us into the stable. First they told me to hold my hands behind my back and they tied them with clothesline rope they had with them. They made me go on my hands and knees and laid me at the rear hoofs of a horse. They tied Kirkey the same way, threw him on the floor and put an old blanket over him. Then they went upstairs."

Once again, the robbers planned to steal the safe and break it open later. They tossed two bales of hay from the loft to serve as a cushion when they dropped it from the second floor to the ground. But moving the extremely heavy mass of iron and steel from the office to the loft door was time-consuming and required the efforts of all five men.

Down below, Morgan and Kirkey had no intention of waiting for the robbers to come back. Bound as he was, Kirkey turned somersaults across the stable floor, out through the open door, and down the driveway. He was trying to reach Christie Street where he could call for help.

Morgan, whose nose bled steadily from the blow he'd received, struggled for twenty-five minutes to get his hands free. Then he untied his feet and ran from the building. Four blocks away, at the corner of Dupont Street, he came to a restaurant, the nearest place with a telephone. To his frustration, a soldier in a wheelchair was using the phone and wouldn't give it up. Morgan was reluctant to take the phone away from a disabled war veteran. Ten minutes passed before he was finally able to call the police.

Back at the dairy, the bandits laboriously hauled the safe to the loft door. Then one of them went downstairs to check on Morgan and Kirkey. They were gone! Instantly alarmed, the gang abandoned the safe and fled. As they sped away in their vehicle, they passed Kirkey lying in the darkness by a pool of water, just a few feet short of Christie Street.

Morgan's call brought squads of constables and detectives to the dairy, "ready for a gunfight." But even through the robbery had been thwarted, they arrived too late to nab the Polka Dot Gang. The uncooperative war vet had given the bandits the time they needed to escape.

The gang hadn't done very well in Toronto, so they immediately headed out of the city to look for prey in smaller communities. While Toronto was still buzzing over the failed Hall's Dairy heist, the Polka Dot Gang drove to Stratford. Their target was the Swift Canadian meat-packing plant.

At eleven o'clock on the night of October 12, Viola Taylor, the company's cleaning lady, had just finished her duties. She'd been assisted by her sons Ernest, fifteen; and Don, eleven. Joseph Miller, the night engineer, opened the door to let them out. They were suddenly confronted by five men wearing polka-dot bandanas and armed with machine guns and revolvers. The intruders pushed their way in and one announced, "This is a stickup!"

The robbers ordered Miller, Taylor, and her frightened sons into the office. They tied up Miller and the boys, but only told Taylor to lie face down on the floor and not move or make a sound.

"The only thing they said was that they were not here to kill us," Miller later told reporters. "One said, 'We were trained in the army only to kill the enemy.' They said they wouldn't hurt us if we did what they told us."

The four prisoners could only lie still and listen while the bandits hammered open one of the two safes in the office. Miller saw one of them pilfer a flashlight, which he would eventually identify in court. Startled by a ringing telephone, the gang hauled the smaller safe out to their vehicle and drove away. It was found smashed open a day later on a side road near Tavistock. The gang's take was $3,216.

After the bandits left the office, young Don Taylor wriggled out of the ropes that bound his hands and feet. Before untying the others, he barred the office door because he was afraid the robbers would come back. The phone call that had frightened the gang off had come from the Stratford police station, where a sergeant was making his regular check with the night engineer. When no one answered, constables were sent to the plant, but arrived minutes after the bandits had fled into the night.

Then on October 17, two men armed with revolvers and wearing polka-dot bandanas hit the Canadian Bank of Commerce on King Street in Toronto. They ordered the three staff members and five customers, all of them women, to line up facing a wall with their hands in the air. One of the customers, Laura Rolling, was checking her safety deposit box when the bandits burst in. She described the robbery for the Toronto *Star*:

> At first I thought some men had come in for repair work, then I saw a man at the door with a polka-dotted hand-kerchief over his face. I knew it was a holdup. "Don't look at us," he said. Then he pointed a silver revolver at Hilliard Brian, the bank manager, and said, "You open the vault." As he stood in the doorway of the manager's office, I risked another look. He said, "If you keep looking at me, I'll give you something."
>
> The way he said it made me think he meant it, and I was pretty careful after that. Then he came into the man-ager's office and marched Mr. Brian and I out into the main part of the bank ... "Don't look at me and face the

wall," he told us. "There's no danger. Nobody's going to get hurt. Just don't look at me."

Another customer, Mrs. E. Patton, had her little daughter in the bank with her. The toddler had wandered away from her mother when the bandits charged in. Mrs. Patton saw the guns and cried, "Oh, my baby!" The gunman nearest to her said, "Oh, that's all right. We won't hurt her." He let the frightened mother pick up the child and then ordered her to join the others facing the wall.

Hilliard Brian opened the vault as ordered, but he stalled for time as he did it. By the time the door finally swung open, the robbers knew they had been in the bank too long. They snapped up $2,000 in bundled bills that they stuffed into their pockets, but they left $1,000 in bonds. Then they ordered the staff and customers into the vault.

Brian begged the robbers not to shut and lock the door. In that airtight space, the prisoners could suffocate before help came. One of the bandits said, "I won't set the lock. I'll just close the door and set a chair against it. But don't you open it right away." Brian waited less than a minute before he pushed the door open, but the robbers were gone.

Police were unsure if the robbery was a Polka Dot Gang job, or the work of other criminals wearing the now infamous bandanas to mislead investigators. These men had struck in the daytime and hadn't shown the kind of callous brutality that had accompanied other Polka Dot holdups. Nonetheless, police officials declared that the Polka Dot Gang now topped the list of "Public Enemies" in Ontario. They believed the gang had a hideout somewhere in the Toronto suburbs and wasn't likely to give up without a fight.

There was no report of Polka Dot Gang activity for days after the bank robbery. Police said the gang had gone into hiding because with every cop in Ontario on the lookout for them, the situation had become "too hot" for them to risk venturing out into the open. A Toronto *Star* editor, making a bad pun on the word "polka," wrote, "Those polka dot hold-up men who are waltzing around the country naturally lead the police in a dance."

Whether or not the police were amused, they were certainly determined to have the last laugh. In fact, they already had several suspects under surveillance. These men all had criminal records, and in spite of the polka-dot masks, they had certain physical features that matched up with descriptions given by witnesses. Toronto police detectives who had been quietly running down leads were almost certain they knew the identity of the six-foot-tall gang leader who had a taste for expensive clothes.

On October 26, the suspects drove through Toronto, making stops in front of large bakeries and dairies. There were unaware that police were tailing them. It seemed to the detectives that the five men were "casing" potential targets. The suspects were outside the Acme Dairy on Spadina Road when the police moved in.

Realizing they had been spotted, the suspects made a run for it. Their car sped through downtown traffic at speeds of up to fifty miles an hour, with the cops in hot pursuit. Seven police cars full of constables closed in to cut off their escape. At the intersection of Dufferin and Van Horn Streets, Sergeant Keith Sisson and Cadet Earl Snider intercepted the fugitives with their patrol car, forcing them to stop. Cadet Snider jumped out and covered the suspects with a shot gun. Sergeant Sisson placed them under arrest as more police cars, with sirens wailing, arrived on the scene. The suspects were not armed and no polka-dot bandanas were found on them or in their car. Nonetheless, the police had good reason to believe they had captured the Polka Dot Gang. The men were held without bail on charges of vagrancy while detectives continued their investigation. Within a week, the police had enough evidence to lay serious charges.

On November 2, the prisoners were taken to police court and their pictures appeared in the Toronto *Star* that same day. For the first time, Canadians saw the faces of the Polka Dot Gang: George Constantine (also known as Constantino), twenty-two; George Dobbie, twenty-nine; Bruce Kay, twenty-five; Hubert Hiscox, twenty-six; and the tall man believed to be the leader, Kenneth Green, twenty-two.

Ken Green, nicknamed Budger, was born in Toronto. His alcoholic father often disappeared from home for long periods, leaving Green's mother, who had a speech impediment, to raise four children. She took in boarders, but still had such a difficult time making ends meet that she had to periodically send the children to stay with relatives. At one point, the young Greens were placed in a children's centre. As a boy, Ken was clever and fun-loving. But he was hot-tempered and could explode at the slightest provocation. He had a deep resentment for discipline and the law that led him into delinquency and two terms in reformatories. Toronto police came to know Ken Green as a tough, brutal criminal.

Curiously, two days before the arrest, police had picked Green up in Markham for public drunkenness. He'd put up a fight, giving one officer a broken nose and a black eye. A day later he was out on bail. Perhaps he'd been the key in leading detectives to the rest of the gang. At the time of the gang's arrest, Green had allegedly threatened to blow Sergeant Sisson's stomach out.

The men faced six charges of armed robbery, two charges of assaulting night watchmen, and one charge of firing a gun at Constable Walter McGowan with intent to maim. Magistrate R.J. Browne warned defence counsel Harold Chaplin, "Don't take up my time talking about bail."

With charges officially laid, the case was remanded to a later date. Over the next few weeks, while the Polka Dot Gang members sat in jail, several petty robberies were pulled by imitators wearing polka -dot bandanas. On victim had his skull fractured by a "polka dot hoodlum" who robbed him of thirteen dollars. Newspaper editors were still mining the name for silly puns. "Criminals, it is claimed, can be reformed," wrote one. "Can the Polka Dot gang change its spots?"

On November 7, George Constantine pleaded guilty to a charge of breaking and entering. On the night of July 29, he'd been caught in a solo attempt to burglarize a gas station on Queen Street West. Police had not yet connected him with the Polka Dot robberies, and he'd been granted bail. Now that he faced those charges, Constantine no doubt thought it best to own up to the break-in, and present himself as a repentant criminal.

"He wants to go straight," said Harold Chaplin. "He told me there's nothing in the game." Constantine was sentenced to two years in prison for burglary. He would face additional time if convicted on any of the Polka Dot charges.

On December 10, all of the gang members pleaded not guilty to all of the charges and chose trial by judge without jury. Constantine, already under sentence, was ineligible for bail. Magistrate Browne again denied bail for the other four. On December 27 there came the surprising news that Chaplin had convinced Judge James Parker to release George Dobbie and Bruce Kay on $20,000 bail. The principal condition was that they appear in court on a specified date in January 1946. Dobbie and Kay had no intention of keeping that appointment. They fled to the United States. However, their freedom was short-lived.

On January 17, Detroit police stopped a car for a traffic violation. The car was registered to Kay's wife, Mary. In it were Kay, Dobbie, and another Toronto hoodlum named Albert Hall. The car's trunk was full of burglary tools. It didn't take the Detroit police long to learn that two of the men had jumped bail in Toronto. The three Canadians were arrested and locked up in a Detroit jail. A judge set their bail at $25,000 each. Nobody was willing to post it.

The apprehension of Kay and Dobbie, whose names were now notorious, touched off an international legal dispute. Officials in Ontario wanted the pair back in Toronto to stand trial for their Polka Dot crimes. Michigan authorities wanted to prosecute them for possession of burglary tools. In May 1946, Inspector John Nimmo of the Toronto Police Department went to Detroit to testify at Kay and Dobbie's trial. He was to give evidence about the pair's criminal activities in Canada.

Theodore Rogers, a Detroit lawyer who was representing Kay and Dobbie, accused the Toronto police of trying to "frame" his clients for crimes in Canada for which they had not yet been tried, let alone convicted. Inspector Nimmo's intent, said Rogers, was to "pull the chestnuts out of the fire for the Toronto police," by giving prejudiced testimony that would have Dobbie and Kay convicted in an American court and sent to an American prison, so they wouldn't be available to testify in Toronto at the trials of their alleged confederates.

"I think there is animus in this case," Rogers argued. "I did not come prepared to combat the police of the Dominion of Canada. We might as well send them down the river now if we are going to allow the Toronto police and everybody else stick their noses in ... I have never tried a case so unfair, where everyone cooperated to convict the accused."

The jury didn't agree with Rogers and neither did Judge William McKay Skillman. Upon hearing the jury's verdict of guilty, he sentenced Dobbie and Kay to four to ten years in prison, and Hall to three to ten years. "We have enough customers of this type in our own country without importing them from Canada," Judge Skillman said.

By skipping bail in Toronto, Dobbie and Kay had betrayed the trust of four women who had risked their money and property to secure the bond that got them out of jail. One was Bruce Kay's mother, Catharine. The others were Mary Hoffman, who was Dobbie's former landlady, and two friends she had convinced to put up almost $6,000. A Toronto court ruled that the bail money would not be forfeited, but would be held until Dobbie and Kay were deported back to Canada, however many years that might be. The Polka Dot Gang case brought the very question of bail in Canada under scrutiny, especially as to how it was starting to resemble the American system. The Toronto *Star* reported:

> It is not clear ... that the law and practice regarding bail are susceptible of improvement. The professional bail bondsman should have no place in Canada. He has been in evidence in Ontario as well as in Quebec. The law should provide for the forfeiting of bail whenever a prisoner moves out of Canada without official permission. In these days of gangsterism, it is a question of whether there is sufficient reason for treating armed robbery and shooting with intent as less heinous crimes than piracy and treason and other rare offences for which bail is forbidden.

The Toronto trial of George Constantine, Kenneth Green, and Hubert Hiscox couldn't begin until after the Detroit court had finished with Dobbie and Kay. It finally began on June 11, 1946, and lasted a week. The prisoners in the dock were handcuffed together to discourage any attempt to escape.

Investigation had led police detectives to a building they called a "cottage" in a rural part of Richmond Hill. It was actually a dilapidated shack with two rooms and a loft, owned by Mary Clay, whose husband John was serving a term in the Kingston Penitentiary on a weapons conviction. Among the items the police found in the cottage and presented in court were two polka-dot bandanas. A considerable body of circumstantial evidence pointed to the cottage as the Polka Dot Gang's hideout.

Detectives had also located a garage on St. Clarens Avenue in Toronto that the gang used for storing a car registered to Kay. In the car were another polka-dot bandana and the flashlight stolen during the Stratford robbery. Several articles of clothing found in the garage: shirts, overalls, coats, and jackets, were identified by witnesses as garments worn by the robbers. There was also a hat with George Dobbie's initials in it. Searches of various addresses connected with the gang turned up what the Toronto *Globe & Mail* called "a formidable assortment of guns". In a field outside Hamilton where one of the smashed safes was found, police even picked up a cast-off milk bottle from a dairy many miles away that had been hit by the Polka Dot Gang. Dobbie was known to drink milk constantly for relief from a stomach ulcer.

The defendants all presented alibis to account for their whereabouts at the times the robberies took place. For Green and Constantine, the flimsy stories didn't stand up against the evidence. They were convicted on several charges of armed robbery, assault, and shooting at a police officer. Judge James Parker sentenced them each to fourteen years in the Kingston Penitentiary.

In the case of Hubert Hiscox, the police had been able to connect him with only one Polka Dot crime, the Lake of the Woods Milling Company robbery. The evidence they had on him wasn't strong enough to gain a conviction. Hiscox was acquitted and walked out of the courtroom a free man.

Hiscox had a checkered past. He was in the Kingston Pen doing time for armed robbery when the Second World War broke out. Hiscox got out of prison by volunteering to join the Canadian Army. He was first in his class with a pistol and a machine gun. Hiscox saw action at Kiska in the Aleutian Islands, and Italy, where he was a member of the famous Devil's Brigade. However, even as a Canadian war hero, Hiscox had his hands in crime. Wherever he was stationed, robberies occurred. When Hiscox returned to Canada and civilian life, he took his pistol and machine gun with him. After his acquittal, Hiscox would certainly have considered himself lucky not to be heading back to prison with Constantine and Green. But he had been drawn to the wrong side of the law and fate would soon catch up with him.

The prospect of fourteen years in the Kingston Pen didn't sit well with Kenneth Green. Rather than wait until he was confined in the prison fortress, he began planning a breakout from Toronto's Don Jail, where he and the others had been held since their arrest. Constantine was one of the prisoners brought in on the plot.

On June 27, thirty-one prisoners were in the exercise yard when Green, Constantine, and several others suddenly jumped the two guards on duty. They pulled strips of torn bedsheets from under their shirts and trousers and used them to bind the guards' hands and feet. One guard managed to cry out before he was gagged.

The prisoners who were in on the breakout rushed to a twenty-foot wall and quickly formed a human pyramid against it. Green was the first to climb up, with Constantine right behind. Unfortunately for them, the Don Jail's administration had a policy of putting an armed guard in the lane on the other side of the wall whenever prisoners who were considered extremely dangerous were in the exercise yard. The Polka Dot Gang members had earned that distinction. The guard in the lane heard his colleague's shout and drew his gun. When Green's head popped up over the wall, the guard ordered him to get down or he would blow it off.

Green obeyed instantly and the pyramid of prisoners disassembled before more guards poured into the exercise yard. The guards who had been bound — but were otherwise unhurt — were able to identify only five prisoners, besides Green and Constantine, who had participated in the failed breakout. But, as jail officials told the press, it required a good number of them to form the pyramid.

Two weeks later, when the seven prisoners were taken to court to be charged with attempting to escape custody, police armed with machine guns patrolled the route from the Don Jail to City Hall. Two cars full of heavily armed detectives followed the paddy wagon. Extra officers were on duty in the courtroom. These were precautionary measures in case underworld friends of the Polka Dot Gang tried to liberate Green and Constantine. No such attempt was made and a trial was set for late July.

With the exception of Hubert Hiscox, who was laying low after his acquittal, all of the Polka Dot Gang members were in jail. But their well-publicized criminal exploits, highlighted by the polka-dot "trademark," had made them almost legendary. In Toronto and other southern Ontario cities, burglars, muggers, and armed robbers were wearing polka-dot bandanas as though they had become the underworld's fashionable attire. Unfortunately for their victims, many of the criminals also copied the Polka Dot Gang's use of unnecessary brutality.

It remains uncertain just how many hoodlums were actually members of the Polka Dot Gang. Of the five who were arrested on October 26, 1945, not all had been present at all of the holdups for which the gang was held responsible. However, a man named Bruce Rodden, who may well have been involved with most of the gang's robberies, was not with the others when they were arrested, and so escaped the glare of publicity. The law finally caught up with him in 1948 and he was packed off to prison to serve a ten-to-twelve-year stretch. The police at that time referred to Rodden as a former member of the Polka Dot Gang. Robert Simpson, who was wounded by a police officer while resisting arrest after he was caught burglarizing a tobacco warehouse in 1948, was also considered to be a former gang member. Criminals associated with known Polka Dots, like John Clay and Albert Hall, could have been in on some of the gang's robberies. Green and Constantine blamed Toronto *Star* writer Gwyn "Jocko" Thomas for tagging them with the Polka Dot name, and said it caused bias against them in court.

Rumours began to circulate in Toronto about buried Polka Dot Gang loot. The total amount of stolen money the gang had accumulated was estimated to be about $25,000, and not all of it had been recovered. After the bandits' arrest, a woman named Iska Stone moved into the cottage in Richmond Hill. Knowing that the somewhat isolated building had been the hideout of the infamous Polka Dot Gang, Mrs. Stone and her friends had gone on "treasure hunts." They searched the ten-acre property and the cottage itself, even removing some of the bricks from the fireplace. They found nothing.

Then in the last week of July, two men showed up at the cottage and paid Mrs. Stone $10 to let them search for buried money. She followed them behind the cottage and watched as they dug in a spot marked by a scratch on the back wall. The men turned over just two shovelfuls of earth and uncovered a bundle of rags. From that they pulled out a glove that had $400 rolled up in it.

Mrs. Stone immediately told the strangers she wanted more than $10. She said she needed money for groceries. The men took a soggy $50 bill from the roll, dried it on the engine of their car, and then drove her to a grocery store. After she made her purchases, they drove her back home.

Over the next few nights, Mrs. Stone heard what she thought were prowlers outside the cottage. She became nervous and reported it all to the police. The two men were soon picked up for questioning. Police wouldn't give their names to the press, but said only that they were thought to be relatives or criminal associates of the Polka Dot Gang.

The newspaper stories about the $400 brought treasure hunters armed with spades, looking for buried loot. Mrs. Stone called the police, who subjected all of them to interrogation before letting them go. The Polka Dot treasure story fizzled out after the Toronto police announced they would be ploughing up the grounds in the unlikely possibility that more stolen cash might still be buried there.

Meanwhile, On July 30, the seven would-be escapees were taken to court to be tried for their attempted breakout. In the midst of the proceedings, the magistrate had the court cleared. Police said there were too many known friends of the Polka Dot Gang among the spectators. Six of the accused, including Green and Constantine, were found guilty.

Not until October 11 were the prisoners taken back to city hall court to be sentenced. They were kept in the court cells while they awaited their turn to go before the magistrate. Almost an hour passed before they were finally escorted to the courtroom.

Arthur Maloney, a lawyer representing three of the defendants, tried to explain why his clients had failed to report the escape plot to the Don Jail guards:

> This is a strange fraternity of men," he said. "The unwritten law that governs their lives is stricter and harsher than the law with which your honour and I have to deal. I do not condone men perjuring themselves in the witness box, but to admit and divulge a plot to escape is too much to expect. Heaven would be more understanding of the sin of perjury than the men in this strange fraternity would be of informers.

In spite of Maloney's eloquence, Green, Constantine, and the other escape plotters each had eighteen months added to their prison time. According to the usual routine, the prisoners should then have been returned to their court cell to await transport back to the Don Jail. But the desperate men had seized an opportunity to make another attempt at escape.

While the prisoners were in the courtroom, a pair of sharp-eyed city hall guards looked into the empty cell and spotted a tiny pile of metallic dust on the floor beneath the window. Closer inspection showed that the steel padlock that secured the frame of the bars in the window had been almost cut through. It was a hopeless bid for freedom, because even if the prisoners had succeeded in opening the barred window, they'd have found themselves facing a fifty-foot drop in view of busy Bay Street, with no way of getting down safely. The fact that they were all chained together added to the futility of the plan. The men had obviously used a hacksaw blade on the padlock, but it was never found, in spite of a close search of the cell and the courtroom.

Green and Constantine were finally put on a train to Kingston. They passed through the gates of the prison known as the "Canadian Alcatraz," and were lodged in the narrow cells that would be home for many years. The only member of the Polka Dot Gang still on the streets of Toronto was Hubert Hiscox. For months nothing was heard of him. When his name finally made the newspapers again, it did so with all the melodrama of a Hollywood gangster movie.

In the early morning of February 28, 1948, Hiscox broke into the office of the McKay-Muldoon Construction Company on Lascelles Boulevard in North Toronto. A storm was raging. Over the previous fourteen months, thieves had taken advantage of blizzards and thunderstorms to muffle the noise made by explosives they used to crack open safes in a series of late-night robberies. Whether or not Hiscox was involved in any of the burglaries would never be proven. But on this night there would be no doubt that the robber was the man the newspapers claimed was the "machine-gunner of the notorious Polka-Dot gang."

The first charge of nitroglycerine Hiscox used blew the bottom hinges off the safe's door. At the same time, it set off an alarm in the North Toronto police station. Patrol Sergeant Albert Russell and constables George Forest and William Vanson responded. When they arrived on the scene, they saw a single set of footprints in the snow. Sergeant Russell followed the tracks around to the back of the building while the two constables stood guard at the front door.

Russell found an open window and climbed in. Peering through the darkness, he saw a man standing by the safe. For a moment the man seemed preoccupied with whatever he was doing. Then he realized someone else was in the room and began to walk toward the window. Russell ordered him to "Stick 'em up!" The man stopped and raised his hands.

Russell later reported:

> As I stepped toward him, he suddenly wheeled and raced through the darkness to the front of the office. I went after him and saw him crouching behind a desk on which he had piled a filing cabinet. He had evidently seen the men at the front door.
>
> I yelled at him four or five times to get his hands up and then I could see him fumbling with something at the bottom of the desk. For a moment I thought he was trying to aim at me. Suddenly there was a terrific explosion and I thought somebody's gun had gone off. I returned fire, but apparently did not hit him. We found the bullet later.
>
> I was dazed for a moment and then I saw the man topple over on his left side. Then he told me he had no gun. He also told me his name. I could see he was badly hurt, so I shouted to the others to get an ambulance.

Sergeant Russell was fortunate to be alive and not even seriously injured. The explosion had cracked the plaster on the walls and blown out all of the windows. The constables outside said they thought the whole building was coming down. It's possible that the desk protected the sergeant from the full force of the blast.

An ambulance rushed Hubert Hiscox to St. Michael's Hospital. Part of his face was blown away, he was blinded in both eyes, his right hand had been blasted off, and the fingers of his left hand were pulverized. Three hours after he was wheeled into the emergency ward, Hiscox died.

At first it appeared that the explosion had been accidental. Investigators found a pair of wires leading from a spot under the desk to a set of batteries. From there, more wires stretched to the front of the safe where there were several detonated blasting caps. But it wasn't the charges Hiscox had set to blow the safe that had killed him. The nitro-soaked cotton batten he had packed around the safe door was still intact and had to be removed by a police-explosives expert.

Forensic evidence revealed that Hiscox had deliberately detonated a bottle of nitroglycerine. The Polka Dot Gang "machine gunner," who had beaten the rap while his companions went to prison, had committed suicide. Police detectives who kept an ear to Toronto's underworld grapevine learned that Hiscox had often told his friends that if he ever found himself cornered by the police, he would kill himself rather than go back to the Kingston Pen.

A month and a half after Hiscox's dramatic demise, Green and Constantine were involved in yet another plot to break out of prison. The Toronto *Star* reported on May 19, 1948, that the attempt was made "within the past few days." Other inmates who were in on the scheme were Allan Baldwin, serving thirty-four years for bank robbery and manslaughter; and Lawrence Burns and Albert Stoutley, sentenced to fifteen and twelve years respectively for armed robbery. Stoutley had been part of the failed human pyramid escape attempt at the Don Jail.

The atmosphere in the Kingston Penitentiary had been volatile due to a crackdown following the escape of three inmates in August of 1947. Long-term prisoners had allegedly been stirring up trouble among the other inmates. Increased security in the form of additional guards and stricter enforcement of regulations only stoked unrest and resentment.

Constantine, Baldwin, Burns, and Stoutley had somehow procured tools that they used to cut through the bars of a door and get into a corridor that would lead them to freedom. Three of them hid in a recess and then jumped a passing guard and tied him up. They were on their way out of the cell block when another guard confronted them with his revolver. He held them at gunpoint until help arrived. The four men were all tossed into the "hole," the Kingston Pen's dreaded solitary confinement dungeon. Green followed them when prison authorities learned that he had helped plan the escape.

That was the last attempt by any of the Polka Dot Gang to escape custody. Kenneth Green was not fated to leave prison alive. Late in June 1954, he fell ill with viral meningitis. He was taken to the penitentiary hospital while a section of the prison was placed under quarantine. Green died on

July 4 with his father and two brothers at his bedside. He was twenty-nine years old.

By the time of Green's death, Bruce Kay had been released and his whereabouts were unknown. American authorities had deported George Dobbie, not to Canada, but to his native Scotland. Only George Constantine remained behind bars.

Constantine served out his sentence and was released, but it wasn't long before he was once again treading on the wrong side of the law. In July 1958, he was arrested in Minden, Ontario, for passing counterfeit U.S. twenty-dollar bills. That landed him right back in the Pen. Constantine had been out on probation less than a year when in March 1969 he was arrested for breaking into a Toronto department store. Doing what a judge called "the thing he knows best" earned Constantine yet another prison term, this time for three and a half years.

Throughout the 1950s, armed robbers — most of them small-time hoodlums — carried on in the dubious tradition of the Polka Dot Gang by disguising themselves with polka-dot bandanas. Some even copied the original gang's practice of senselessly beating up night watchmen. In the autumn of 1960, the urban legend of Polka Dot Gang loot buried in the ground near the site of their old hideout in Richmond Hill arose again. As often happens with tales of outlaw booty, the amount of the swag had grown from $25,000 to $250,000! Treasure hunters equipped with a metal detector went over property that development had radically altered since 1945. They dug one shallow hole, found nothing, and gave up the search. In time the legend was forgotten. The gang that had been the terror of southern Ontario slipped into obscurity.

CHAPTER 9
STANLEY BUCKOWSKI:
The Long Road to the Gas Chamber

July 30, 1949 would go down in the annals of the Toronto Police Department as the beginning of one of the most horrific chapters in the city's history. The story opened with an armed robbery, and ended in an American gas chamber. In between lay a series of murders. Three of the victims were Canadians, as was the killer.

On that Saturday afternoon, a man walked into the Loblaw Groceteria on Parliament Street in Toronto. Dozens of shoppers were in the store and no one paid him any attention. When he passed by employees Agnes Tustin and Lucy Clark, he smiled graciously and said hello as he headed for the stairs leading to the office of the store's manager, Adam Stoddart. The two women thought he was making a business call and didn't even catch the scent of the belt of whiskey the man had downed just minutes earlier.

When the visitor entered the office he pulled a revolver and ordered Stoddart to open the safe and then lie down on the floor. Stoddart had no choice but to obey. The robber stuffed his pockets with money, warning the manager to be still, or "You'll get it."

While the gunman was robbing the grocery store, not far away on Gifford Street, twenty-four-year-old Alfred Layng had just finished repairing some screens for his house. A Second World War vet who had served in the RCAF, Layng was married to his boyhood sweetheart, Shirley. They had a daughter named Patricia, age four. With the screen repair done, Alfred and Shirley took Patricia for a walk down Parliament Street to treat her to a soda. They stopped at a shop where Shirley bought a piece of cloth and then continued on their way.

In the grocery store, the bandit fled from the manager's office with about a thousand dollars in a money pouch. Stoddart shouted for help. A clerk named Ron Barrett dove for the thief's ankles, but wasn't able to hold him. However, another clerk, nineteen-year-old Leonard Leftly, tackled him around the waist as he reached the front door. The man dragged Leftly out to the sidewalk and then shot him in the leg. Leftly fell to the ground, but the robber dropped the money pouch. The Layngs were just then approaching the corner of Parliament and Carlton Streets. "That's when it all happened," Shirley said later.

They could see a commotion in front of the grocery store and a man running toward them. Somebody shouted, "Stop that man!"

Alfred pushed little Patricia into a doorway and then stood in the man's path with his arms opened wide. The thief ran right into them. The two men grappled and fell to the pavement. "I stood there terrified, watching the struggle," said Shirley afterward. "Other people stood around with their mouths open, just gaping. I shouted for help, but there wasn't any help from any of the spectators at all. They just stood there."

Suddenly two shots rang out. The thief scrambled to his feet and ran down Carlton Street. No one else tried to stop him.

Shirley saw Alfred slowly get to his feet while Patricia cried, "Daddy! Daddy!" He reached toward his wife, took a couple of steps, and said, "Don't worry, I'm all right, hon." Then he fell dead at Shirley's feet. Alfred had been shot in the stomach and the heart.

"No person came forward to help me even then," Shirley told a Toronto *Star* reporter. "I had to leave him there and run into a store to phone for help. When I came out of the store, people were just standing around repeating the words, 'He's dead, he's dead.'"

Toronto Chief of Police John Chisholm quickly dispatched every available constable to the vicinity of Parliament and Carlton. Off-duty officers were called in to help search the neighbourhoods. But the robber-turned-killer was moving faster than word of mouth could spread news of the crime through the streets.

At first he tried to lose himself in the crowds on Carlton Street. But when he drew attention, he took to alleyways and backyards, leaping over fences and desperately looking for places to hide. A woman went into her garage, opened her car door, and was startled to see a man crouching on the floor. Threatening her with a gun, he got out, shoved her against the wall, and fled.

John Vancott of Seaton Street hurried into his kitchen when he heard his six-year-old daughter call out that a man was in the house. Vancott, who didn't know about the robbery and shooting, confronted a stranger who was sweating and breathing hard. He took the man for a lost drunk.

"I asked him what he was doing in my house and he replied he was just trying to get through to the street. I told him to get out…. Just as he disappeared from my sight, a police cruiser rounded Carlton and Seaton and came up to me. They raced back to find this chap, but he had gone from sight."

The police did find a bullet the fugitive had dropped in Vancott's house, but there were no fingerprints on it.

Albert Hailes of Ontario Street was washing his car when a stranger suddenly stuck a gun in his face and demanded the keys. Hailes handed them over, but when the man tried to start the engine, it wouldn't turn over. The gunman told Hailes to get behind the wheel and drive. Hailes refused, and the man dashed away on foot.

Somehow the fugitive managed to evade the police patrols and escape. Chief Chisholm called in every off-duty detective and put them to work chasing down leads. They questioned suspects from as far away as Niagara Falls. Chisholm replaced the detectives' .38 service revolvers with more powerful .45s. Police posted a reward of $2,000 for information leading to the killer's arrest. The Loblaw Company offered an additional $1,000. Telephone tips were coming into police headquarters at the rate of twenty-five an hour.

In the neighbourhoods through which the suspect had fled, Detective Sergeant Adolphus Payne literally crawled on his hands and knees in search of clues. He looked under porches and back steps, and at a house on Sherbourne Street his perseverance paid off. In a hasty attempt to change his appearance, the fugitive had taken off his suit jacket, fedora, and tie, and stuffed them under a rear stoop. The jacket's label had been removed, but in the pocket Payne found a pair of white gloves and two .38 cartridges. Under the back step of a neighbouring yard the detective found a pair of gold-rimmed reading glasses.

Initially, these items gave no clue as to the fugitive's identity. But Payne believed they could be crucial in leading police to the man. He had the hat, coat, and tie put on a mannequin and placed in the window of a store near the murder scene in hope that someone might recognize them. A police detective was on hand to take down any information anyone might have. Meanwhile, Payne went to work tracking down the makers of the jacket and the glasses.

Dozens of witnesses had seen the suspect's face. They went through stacks of mug shots, but to no avail. However, the descriptions they provided enabled a police artist, Detective Maurice Inglis, to draw a likeness that was sent to the newspapers for publication. The uncanny accuracy of the pencil sketch was to have dramatic results. But more than two years would pass before the Toronto police would finally locate Alfred Layng's killer. By that time, he had added to his score in homicide.

The man the police were looking for was Stanley Buckowski, age twenty-three. He was born in a remote part of Saskatchewan to Polish-Canadian parents. While still a boy, he moved to Toronto where he attended Essex Street Public School. Young Stanley fell in with bad company and started hanging out on street corners, particularly at the intersection of Bloor and Bathurst Streets, which at that time was a tough part of town. His first crimes were break-ins. He had an interest in chemistry and stole electrical devices.

At the age of fifteen, Buckowski pulled his first "armed" robbery. Using a cap gun, he stole a car from a motorist in High Park. He was caught and sent to juvenile court. Instead of handing Buckowski a stint in reform school, the judge released him to the custody of his father, with instructions that the elder Buckowski give the boy a sound thrashing. Stanley got that thrashing, but it didn't do any good.

Newspaper artist's sketch of the suspect in the Alfred Layng murder. The accuracy of the likeness caused Buckowski to panic.
THE *GLOBE & MAIL.*

Buckowski continued to mix with bad characters. He had developed the attitude that working for a living was for suckers. He and a partner held up a gas station. This time Buckowski had a real gun, but no bullets. They got away with it, so Buckowski decided to hold up a clothing store on Bloor St. The proprietor resisted and Buckowski struck him on the head with his empty gun. The man still put up a fight and the struggle took them right out the front door to the sidewalk. Buckowski was arrested and sentenced to two and a half years in prison. He was still only fifteen years old.

By the time Buckowski was released, he was a hardened criminal and considered himself a big shot. He went back to the gangs that hung out at Bloor and Bathurst. Burglary was his main source of income. Buckowski did, however, make one attempt to turn his life around.

When Canada declared war on Germany, thousands of young Canadian men enlisted to fight Hitler's Nazis. Buckowski joined the RCAF and was posted to a base in Saskatchewan. Instead of redeeming himself, though, he took a personal turn for the worse when he discovered narcotics and became addicted. He convinced a nurse to supply him with drugs and took advantage of his relationship with her to steal from the dispensary. He had learned that he could make easy money selling drugs.

Buckowski was transferred back to Toronto. He was still in the Air Force when he got married. After he left the RCAF, Buckowski and his wife Jean settled into an apartment in Toronto. Jean worked as a waitress and Stanley burglarized homes. He still didn't like the idea of getting a job himself, and he had an expensive drug habit.

The police were soon on to Buckowski. One night in April 1945, they picked him up while he was walking along Yonge Street. They searched his home and found a stash of jewellery, cameras, and seven bottles of whiskey that had been stolen from a house on Castle Frank Drive. Buckowski was convicted on two charges of burglary and sentenced to eighteen months at the Burwash Industrial Farm, a provincial correctional institution near Sudbury.

"I didn't get along very well there," Buckowski recalled later. "Out in the woods you had cold dinners in twenty degrees below zero. The warden was a tough guy. All he knew was the strap." According to Buckowski, Burwash made him "paranoiac."

Buckowski had trouble with a hip injury he'd received as a boy and Burwash didn't have the medical facilities to treat it. Jean made frequent trips to the parole board on his behalf. He was finally released on the condition that he check into Toronto's Christie Street Veterans' Hospital.

Buckowski's stay at Burwash had cured him of his drug dependency, but the series of operations he underwent on his hip increased his emotional problems. When he got out of the hospital he resolved to stay away from his old hang-outs and "the boys." Jean tried to make him stay home in the evenings, but she was now doing shift work as a hotel switchboard operator, and couldn't always be there. Sitting alone, Buckowski would drink heavily. By his own admission, Buckowski "got nasty" when he was drinking, and would beat his dog.

Restlessness and booze finally got the better of him and Buckowski started hanging out with his old crowd. Soon he was robbing again. Among the plunder from his burglaries was a pair of pistols. He kept them in a locker at the College Street YMCA so Jean wouldn't know about them and they wouldn't be in his home if the police came snooping. Buckowski got the idea that with the guns he could make a lot of money fast, and then "retire."

Buckowski's first target was the Alhambra Theatre. He stuck up the manager and got away with his pockets stuffed with cash. It had been too easy! Not long after, one night while Jean was at work, Buckowski got drunk and then robbed the Downtown Theatre at gunpoint. He easily made his getaway in a cab, with more than $4,000.

Buckowski bought a new car. He had several thousand dollars in his bank account. A smart professional criminal might have lain low and enjoyed the swag. But the two successful robberies had gone to his head. Buckowski had seen how busy the Loblaw Groceteria was on a Saturday and thought a holdup would net him $4,000. On that fateful July afternoon, he picked up his guns from the YMCA locker, braced his nerves with a few shots of whiskey, and then headed for Parliament Street.

It was through sheer luck that Buckowski escaped the police after shooting Alfred Layng. When he got home that night, Jean was at work. Thoroughly shaken over what had happened, Buckowski drank until he passed out. Early the next morning he got into his new car and drove to Wasaga Beach and rented a cabin. He thought it would be a good place to hide out until things blew over.

While Buckowski was holed up in Wasaga Beach, a few miles away, Robert Smith McKay and his wife Gloria were enjoying a "working holiday." Twenty-five-year old Robert was an RCAF veteran who had served in India during the Second World War and was now employed as a mechanic and electrician. Gloria, twenty-three, worked in a financial office on Bay Street. Because they were saving up to make a down payment on a house, the young couple didn't go out much. However, on weekends they liked to drive up to the hamlet of Minesing, where Robert's uncle, Nicholas Langelaan, owned a farm. Mr. Langelaan had injured his back and was in a cast, so Robert did farm work for him. To the McKays, the weekend trips to the farm were a welcome opportunity to get away from the city for a couple of days.

On the evening of Friday, July 29, Robert and Gloria packed up their car, a black 1942 Dodge sedan, and drove away from their flat on Emerson Avenue in Toronto. As always, they took their little spaniel, Toby. On Saturday, while Robert did chores, Gloria went to nearby Barrie where she bought pink and blue cotton material to make dresses for herself and Mrs. Langelaan. She finished both dresses before it was time to go back to Toronto.

It was a long weekend, and neither Robert nor Gloria had to be back at work until Tuesday. On Monday they talked about playing hooky from work for a day and not driving home until Tuesday evening. However, by Monday night they had changed their minds and decided they'd better head for home so they could go to work Tuesday morning. They said goodbye to Robert's aunt and uncle, promising to return in a couple of weeks, and drove away at 9:00 p.m. Gloria was wearing the new dress she had just made. On the back seat next to Toby was a .22 rifle she had given Robert as a gift for their fifth wedding anniversary, coming up on August 5. The couple never saw that anniversary. They didn't even make it back to Emerson Avenue.

At about 4:00 p.m. on Tuesday, August 2, a bricklayer named Charles Edwards was working on a house near the end of Saguenay Avenue, a dead-end street near the intersection of Bathurst Street and Lawrence Avenue in the municipality of North York. He took a few minutes' break from his work to walk down a path into a wooded ravine at the bottom of the street. He hadn't gone very far when he almost stumbled over what he first thought was a sleeping man. Edwards said, "Pardon me." Then he saw the blood.

Edwards hurried back to the construction site and told his foreman there was a dead man in the ravine. The foreman called the police. Edwards later told a reporter, "He scared the life out of me. I can still see his wide, glassy eyes staring at me … It was an awful shock. I'll remember seeing the body lying there, more like a ghost than the body of a human."

The man had been shot three times. Police quickly determined that he had not been killed at the site where the body had been found. There was no blood on the surrounding ground or bushes, and the way the shirt was pulled up from the waist indicated that the body had been dragged there. A wallet police found near the body was empty and it was evident that someone had gone through the dead man's pockets. Then a local resident turned in a woman's purse he had found in the ravine that morning. In the purse was a driver's licence belonging to Gloria McKay. The dead man was soon identified as her husband Robert.

Police began a sweep of Toronto, looking for a black 1942 Dodge sedan. Two constables found it just after 1:00 on the morning of August 3 in the parking lot behind the Christie Street Veterans' Hospital. Wrapped in a blanket, and jammed into the floor space between the front and back seats, with a suitcase covering it, was the body of Gloria McKay. She had been shot twice. The .22 rifle was under her body. The front seat was soaked with blood and somebody had used Robert's jacket to sit on at the steering wheel to avoid getting their pants bloody. Toby was tied to a bumper, whimpering, but unharmed. The car had probably not been there very long, or somebody would have noticed the dog. A constable was heard to say that he wished the dog could talk.

Forensic examinations showed that Robert and Gloria had died at about the same time. That meant the killer had driven around Toronto with Gloria's body still in the car after he had dumped Robert's body. There was no evidence that Gloria had been sexually assaulted. Oddly, there was still money in her purse, while Robert's wallet had been cleaned out. It was all very intriguing to investigators. The one solid fact they had was that the McKays had been killed with .38 bullets, the same calibre as the slugs that had been removed from Alfred Layng's body. All of the bullets were sent to an RCMP lab for ballistics study.

While Layng was being buried with military honours and the families of the slain couple were making their own funeral arrangements, Toronto Mayor Hiram McCallum ordered an "all-out police drive" to find all unlicensed guns in the city. "Anyone with a gun is a potential murderer," he said. "Any gun is a potential murder weapon."

The McKays' car was thoroughly examined for fingerprints, but none that were found on it matched anything in police files. Investigators from the Toronto Police Department, the Ontario Provincial Police, and the RCMP were all working on the case. The only clue connecting the murders was the calibre of the bullets that had killed the victims, but the police strongly suspected they had all been fired by the same person.

Officers travelled the highway between Toronto and Minesing, stopping at every house and business to ask if anyone had seen the McKays or the black Dodge. They received conflicting reports. Witnesses in Bradford said they had seen three people in the Dodge. But a waitress in a restaurant in Newtonbrook on the outskirts of Toronto said the couple had stopped there at 11:15 Monday night and that they were alone. She said Robert had hot dogs and coffee, and Gloria had a hamburger and a Coke. She chatted with them for about fifteen minutes. They told her they were on their way to Toronto.

Asked why she remembered the couple out of all the people she had served that night, the waitress said she recalled Robert's red hair and Gloria's dimples. She'd also heard the barking of a small dog coming from their car, which was parked close to the front door. The waitress said the two seemed very weary. After eating, they left the restaurant and drove away. The waitress believed she was the last person, besides the killer, to see Robert and Gloria McKay alive.

The police had a tangle of clues, some of which made no sense. They heard rumours that the couple had picked up a hitchhiker. Could the hitchhiker have been the man who killed Layng? If so, why would he flee Toronto and then return? If he killed the McKays to get their car, why did he abandon it? Baffled, the police issued a strong warning to motorists not to pick up hitchhikers.

The investigation seemed to have reached a dead end, when the work of Sergeant Payne began to produce results. Payne could see that the suit jacket he'd found had been tailor-made. With samples of material in hand, Payne and his team of detectives visited tailor shops all over the city. After two weeks they found a tailor in Toronto's east end who had made the suit three years earlier for a client named Stanley Buckowski. Similar sleuthing revealed that the reading glasses had been prescribed for Jean Buckowski.

Police now had a name for the number-one suspect in the Layng murder, though as yet they had no solid evidence connecting him to the McKay slayings. Nor did they have any idea where Buckowski was. Information was sent to police departments across Canada and in the United States, but for the time being the trail was cold.

Buckowski had in fact fled to the United States, perhaps by way of Montreal. He went first to New York and then to New Orleans where Jean joined him. He was using narcotics again, and got money by armed robbery and burglary. In January of 1950, the fugitive couple arrived in Los Angeles where they rented an apartment.

On the evening of February 1, the Buckowskis were strolling down an L.A. street when Stanley spotted a darkened house that looked like a good prospect for a robbery. Leaving Jean to stand watch on the sidewalk, he went to the front entrance and rang the doorbell. Nobody answered, so Buckowski cut the telephone wire and then broke in through the back door.

The lone occupant was an eighty-year-old widow named Helen Edmunds. Evidently she was asleep and hadn't heard the doorbell, but was awakened by the sound of breaking glass when Buckowski smashed the window in the back door. Mrs. Edmunds surprised Buckowski as he was going through a desk in the living room and he shot her. Buckowski would later offer the excuse that in the darkness, he thought he'd been confronted by a man. "She had a voice like a cement mixer," he said.

Buckowski fled the house empty-handed. "I had to shoot," he told Jean. The next morning neighbours found Helen Edmunds's body. The killer had placed the dead or dying old woman on her bed.

Buckowski knew that the Los Angeles police had little to go on in the Edmunds murder case. He wasn't known to local authorities, and he had outsmarted police before. Los Angeles was lucrative territory for a stickup man and burglar, so why move on to another city? Buckowski continued stealing and his confidence that he'd never be caught was his undoing.

One night, at the scene of an aborted burglary, police found a broken rope dangling from a skylight. They deduced that the intruder had fallen and could have been hurt. They checked out hospital emergency wards and in one ward they found that a man calling himself Frank Miller had been there with a fractured ankle on the night of the break-in. He'd left with his foot in a walking cast. A few weeks later, acting on a tip, police arrested Buckowski when he was buying heroin in L.A.'s skid row district.

The police put Buckowski in a hospital room with an officer standing guard outside the door. His ankle still hadn't healed, and there was the possibility of him going into withdrawal. The room was on the ninth floor, so the police didn't think it likely that he'd try to escape.

They were wrong. Buckowski tied blankets together and hung the makeshift ladder out the window. He climbed down to the end, still about thirty feet from the ground. In spite of his injured ankle he dropped down and disappeared into the night.

For about two months the police found no trace of the "cat burglar" they knew as Frank Miller. Then in May, a sharp-eyed officer patrolling Sunset Boulevard spotted a man whose face resembled one on a wanted poster in his precinct house. The suspect was sitting in a car. As the officer approached, the man jumped out of the car and bolted into a nearby park. He tried to hide in a wooded area that was soon surrounded by police.

Called upon to come out with his hands up, Buckowski chose to shoot it out. He had five pistols. The gunfight lasted until Buckowski ran out of ammunition. Amazingly, no one was hit by all the flying lead. With his last shot spent and nowhere to run, Buckowski finally surrendered. This time he was locked up in jail. When police searched Buckowski's apartment, they found a small arsenal of firearms.

Strictly as a matter of routine, the Los Angeles police sent Buckowski's fingerprints to FBI headquarters in Washington, D.C. Months earlier, during the investigation into the Layng murder, the RCMP had at last found in their files a record of Buckowski's fingerprints from one of his earlier arrests and had sent a copy to the FBI. In those days before computers revolutionized detective work, many weeks passed before somebody in FBI headquarters matched the fingerprints from the Los Angeles police with the set from the RCMP. The American Feds informed the Mounties that Stanley Buckowski was in a Los Angeles jail. The Mounties passed that information on to the Toronto Police Department.

The Toronto police had three unsolved murders on their hands and were relieved at the news that Buckowski had been arrested in California. He could be extradited and tried for the murder of Alfred Layng. But they still needed evidence to support their belief that Buckowski was also responsible for the McKay murders. This brought about a strange twist in international police co-operation that brought the L.A. police back to the Helen Edmunds murder case.

The examination of the McKays' car had turned up a palm print that didn't match anything the Toronto police had on file. They asked the Los Angeles police to send them Buckowski's palm print. The request was granted; the print matched the one taken from the Dodge. Now Buckowski could be tied to the McKay murders. Canadian authorities wanted Stanley Buckowski back in Ontario as soon as extradition could be arranged. But upon learning that he was wanted for murder in Canada, the Americans thought it might be worthwhile to do some back-checking on the person they had in jail. They had a handful of charges against him, including burglary and escaping custody, but a character like that might have been responsible for even worse crimes during his time in the United States.

First, a ballistics test showed that a .38 pistol taken from Buckowski's apartment had fired the bullet that killed Helen Edmunds. The only fingerprints on it were his. Then the police found Buckowski's palm print on a large piece of broken glass from Mrs. Edmunds's back door. The Los Angeles authorities told the Toronto police they wouldn't be sending Stanley Buckowski back to Canada. He would be tried in California for the murder of Helen Edmunds.

Buckowski admitted he had committed many robberies in the United States, but denied ever being in the Edmunds house. He said it wasn't his practice to cut telephone wires and smash windows. He also claimed he'd acquired the .38 pistol a month after the death of Mrs. Edmunds. However, under questioning, Jean confessed she had stood watch in front of the house while Stanley broke in. She was placed under arrest and charged with accessory to murder.

Stanley and Jean were tried together in a Los Angeles courtroom in late November 1950. Jean was acquitted and deported to Canada. Stanley was found guilty and sentenced to death in the gas chamber. His defence counsel entered an appeal for a new trial based on the circumstantial nature of some of the state's evidence. A principal point was Buckowski's insistence that he had stolen the .38 in a burglary after the murder. But he wouldn't give any details as to exactly when and where he'd acquired the gun. The appeal went through the long, time-consuming process of legal channels and was finally denied by the Supreme Court of California. Buckowski's home for the next year and a half would be a cell on death row in California's notorious San Quentin Penitentiary.

Death row inmates usually sought every possible legal avenue to postpone the execution date in hope of having the sentence commuted to life imprisonment. A case could drag through the courts for years. Buckowski wanted none of that. As far as he was concerned, the sooner it was all over, the better. He was anything but contrite and subdued as he awaited his fate. He loudly cursed the guards and his death row neighbours. During the daily one-hour period the men had in the exercise yard, Buckowski picked fights and once knocked another prisoner's teeth out.

As a condemned man, Buckowski did not have to see any visitors he didn't want to see, not even police. An FBI agent went to San Quentin hoping to talk to Buckowski about a series of burglary-related murders that had occurred in New Orleans. Buckowski refused the agent's request for an interview. Two Toronto police inspectors also travelled all the way to San Quentin, only to be turned away. It was therefore a surprise to the prison administration when Buckowski agreed to be interviewed by a newspaper reporter from Toronto.

Gwyn (Jocko) Thomas was a veteran reporter who had been covering Toronto's crime beat for the *Daily Star* for many years. In October of 1951, he learned from reliable sources within the police department that they had tied Buckowski to the McKay murders, but couldn't get into San Quentin to question him. Thomas got permission from the *Star*'s president, Harry C. Hindmarsh, to fly to California on the chance that Buckowski might talk to him. He took along photographer Doug Cronk.

In an interview room watched over by a burly guard, Thomas came face to face with the killer who had eluded the Toronto police for so long. Buckowski had a terrible rash on his face and refused to have his picture taken. However, he didn't object to Cronk sitting in on the interview. Buckowski told Thomas, "You'd better take shorthand, because when I talk, I talk fast and it's hard to get me to stop. I'll give you a good human interest story, and in it will be everything I've done." Then, smoking the occasional cigarette, Buckowski spilled out his life story.

The condemned man told the reporter all about his boyhood, his early career as a burglar, his time in Burwash, and his enlistment in the

RCAF. Then came his marriage to Jean and his failure to break away from the street-corner gangs.

When Buckowski recalled the grocery-store robbery, he said of his shooting of Alfred Layng: "This fellow was putting his nose into something that wasn't his business. He grabbed me. I said, 'Let me go.' He didn't and I shot him in the leg. He still hung on and I shot him again and he dropped. I guess the bullet went through his heart. He didn't mind his own business, but he was a good citizen."

In Wasaga Beach on the Monday after the murder, Buckowski became alarmed when he saw the drawing of what he thought was his face in a newspaper. It was such a close likeness, he was sure he had been identified and the police were after him. Because he had lost the glasses he'd borrowed from Jean, he couldn't read the text that accompanied the picture. Otherwise he would have known the image was a sketch which the police believed resembled the suspect, whose identity was still unknown.

"I figured right then and there they knew I killed Layng," Buckowski told Thomas. "I was desperate. If they knew I killed Layng, they wouldn't have any trouble knowing I had a car. I had to get out of there fast. I left my car beside the cabin I had rented and started out for Toronto. I got as far as Elmvale. Everybody seemed to be looking at me. I knew the cops would be out in full force. I tried a couple of cars but no one would give me a lift."

What Buckowski told Thomas next was his own version of the McKay murders. Legally, it would never have stood as a confession. It was vague on some points and raised questions that would never be answered. There'd be no way of telling how much he embroidered the story, or what he left out. But his account held enough hard facts to leave little doubt of his guilt:

> At the side of the road I saw a parked car. A young couple were in the front seat. She was asleep on his shoulder. I got in the back seat. I woke them. I told them I wanted to be driven to Toronto. I pulled out my gun and told him to get going.
>
> He didn't give me any argument at first. I was in the back seat and I held the gun at his neck at first and told him not to try any funny stuff. He drove fast and I told him to

slow down because he was trying to get the cops to come after him. When we got to Toronto, I told him to turn off at certain streets. He wouldn't do what I told him even though I warned him he would get shot if he didn't. Once he said, "Go ahead, punk, kill me."

He seemed to get mad. He drove against red lights and was going sixty miles an hour. I couldn't make him slow down. He went against five more red lights. He turned along Eglinton Avenue, which wasn't where I wanted to go.

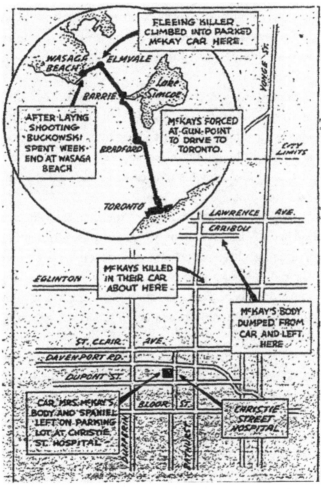

This map traces Buckowski's route from the time he left Wasaga Beach until he disposed of the McKays' bodies.
TORONTO *STAR*.

I hadn't told him what I had done. What I wanted was for him to go along a side street. Then I would take the car. But when he started to drive all over the street on Eglinton Avenue near Bathurst, I pulled the trigger. I kept pulling the trigger. She started to scream. I pulled the trigger on her.

This allegedly took place on one of downtown Toronto's busiest thoroughfares, with traffic heavy in both directions. Yet, nobody saw or heard anything. How exactly did the car come to a stop with a dead man at the wheel? Were there no blaring horns or curses from the vehicles behind the Dodge? Buckowski only said that no one seemed to realize that the man and woman slumped over the dashboard had just been shot.

I squeezed my way into the front seat and drove up a few streets until I found a lonely spot where I intended to leave them both. I mustn't forget to mention the dog. He was a little sandy-haired spaniel. He'd been very quiet until just after his master was dead and then he began howling.

I pulled the man's body out of the car. I knew he was dead because I got him many times. She was still groaning. Just after I got his body out and dragged it to a place where I figured it wouldn't be found, the dog started barking some more. There was commotion. Someone was coming and I had to get out of there quick. She was still groaning.

Buckowski said he dragged the woman over the front seat into the back and covered her with a rug. Then he drove to the Christie Street Hospital parking lot. "When I got there," he said, "I knew she was dead." He wiped the car down to remove his fingerprints. He said he couldn't bring himself to kill the dog because it reminded him of his own little spaniel, so he left Toby tied to a bumper.

Buckowski told Thomas he spent that night at the home of a friend. The next day he learned that the police had no idea who had killed Alfred Layng. "I'll tell you, I felt sick," he said to Thomas. "What a nightmare when I realized that what I saw of myself was not a police picture but a drawing." Buckowski said he regretted killing Robert and Gloria McKay, whom he called "a couple of sweet kids."

When Thomas asked Buckowski if he had any message for the youth of Toronto, he dismissed the question by saying, "I'm no grandstander or wise guy." At one point during the interview, Buckowski became a little nostalgic and asked Thomas about three of his old cronies from the hangout at Bloor and Bathurst: "Norm, Buster and Teddy." Thomas was familiar with all three because of their frequent appearances in police court. Before the guard took Buckowski back to his cell, he told Thomas, "My life is a nightmare that is soon to come to an end."

Jocko Thomas's death row interview with Stanley Buckowski was one of the biggest scoops of his long and distinguished career. It solved the mystery of the McKay murders and provided an insight into the life of a killer. The story won Thomas a National Newspaper Award. But it also had one unpleasant result Thomas would have preferred to avoid. The *Star* sent him back to San Quentin in May of 1952 to cover the execution.

Buckowski's lawyer, Ralph Rubin of San Francisco, had been hard at work on a petition that would have postponed his client's date with the gas chamber by at least a few months. However, he needed Buckowski's signature on it and Buckowski stubbornly refused to sign. The night before

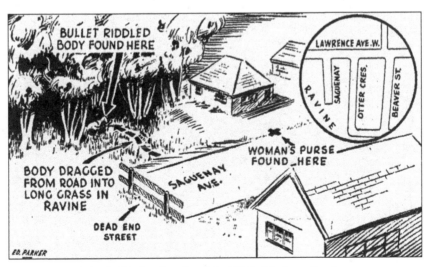

Newspaper artist's sketch of the location where Robert McKay's body was found.
TORONTO *STAR.*

the execution, Rubin pleaded with Buckowski one last time. Buckowski called the man who was trying to save his life a "shyster," and cried, "Leave me alone! Get out!" A Roman Catholic priest who came to offer spiritual comfort was treated just as scornfully. Buckowski said he just wanted to "die in peace."

Buckowski spent his last night listening to music from a stack of phonograph records. He'd been provided with headphones so as not to disturb the other death row inmates. At ten o'clock on the morning of May 9, he calmly walked to the "Green Monster," as the residents of San Quentin called the gas chamber, the latest "humane" device for administering capital punishment. Jocko Thomas, who witnessed the execution, called it "sickening." He watched Buckowski writhe in agony and froth at the mouth. The tough reporter had to turn his face away. The convulsions finally stopped after thirteen long minutes.

Stanley Buckowski's body was buried in an unmarked grave, mourned by no one. His wife Jean was in Vancouver, working as a waitress. His father, according to information given to Jocko Thomas, had died from a broken heart, refusing to believe his son was a murderer. When Robert McKay's widowed mother, Nancy, was told that her son's killer had been executed, she spoke the final words in the sordid tale of Stanley Buckowski. "This is the last chapter," she said. "Poor Bob … I've cried too much to cry anymore. I'm glad it's settled."

CHAPTER 10
JOSEPH MCAULIFFE:
Lethal Pursuit

At 2:45 p.m. on Wednesday, June 21, 1950, twenty-three-year-old Lavona Leedham was in her teller's cage in the Imperial Bank of Canada on the main street of Langton, population 250. It was the only bank in that community in the heart of southern Ontario's tobacco-farming country. Mrs. Leedham was serving the lone customer in the bank, Frank Hall, owner of a general store in nearby Cultus, when she happened to look through the bank's glass-panelled front doors and saw a black Ford Meteor pull up. The driver got out and entered the bank. Mrs. Leedham later reported:

> He was wearing a sun helmet and sun glasses, and was carrying what I thought was a cheque or a small piece of paper. As he stood near Mr. Hall he pulled a gun from under his coat and said, "Alright, back up everyone! In the corner and face the wall!"
>
> I remember him saying to me, "Back out of the cage." I didn't realize at first that it was a hold-up and he told me again to get out of the cage.
>
> There is a glass partition above the counter on the north side of the teller's cage and the man moved further towards the north wall. Before leaving the cage I tripped the burglar alarm. This alarm rings in Van Hooren's garage to indicate a hold-up. I left the cage and assembled with the others in the northeast corner. There were

five of us. The bank has a staff of six but the manager, Mr. A.S. Beattie, had gone upstairs to his apartment a few minutes before.

The bandit wearing the sun helmet and dark glasses was thirty-two-year-old Joseph Herbert McAuliffe. Originally from North Bay, Ontario, he'd been raised by an aunt in Windsor after his mother died. Prior to the Second World War, McAuliffe had been in trouble with the law over some petty burglaries and had used the alias Fred Walker. During the war he had been a sergeant in the Canadian army, and served as a military artificer, responsible for the maintenance of fire-arms. After the war, McAuliffe had returned to crime, operating princi-pally as a counterfeiter. He used his skills as a machinist to make bogus fifty-cent coins. Considering the buying power of a dollar in 1950, that wasn't quite as small-time as it might seem today. It was a need for cash to upgrade his equipment that compelled McAuliffe to plan a bank robbery.

Artist's sketch of the disguised bandit who held up the Bank of Canada in Langton, Ontario, on June 21, 1950.
TORONTO STAR.

The gun that Lavona Leedham had first seen in the bandit's hand was a .38 police service revolver. McAuliffe used it to force Frank Hall to assist him in the robbery. A grill and a locked gate separated the front area of the bank from the back, where the tellers' draw-ers and the vault were. McAuliffe climbed over the gate and then ordered Hall to follow. McAuliffe then pulled a folded paper shop-ping bag out of his coat and told Hall to fill it with money from the cash drawers. To discourage any hesitation or heroics, the robber drew a second gun: an automatic Colt pistol.

Meanwhile, the alarm Lavona Leedham had tripped went off in Lambert Van Hooren's Shell gas station and pool hall a short distance down the street from the bank. Van Hooren told his wife it looked like there was trouble at the bank. Cecil Aspden, the local school-bus driver and rural-route mailman, thought he overheard Van Hooren say there was a fire at the bank.

This wasn't the first time bandits had hit the Langton bank. On September 12, 1945, four gunmen had robbed it of over $30,000. They were eventually caught and packed off to prison. At that time an Ontario Provincial Police constable was stationed in Langton. However, in a departmental shuffle made in the autumn of 1949, OPP constables posted in small communities like Langston were moved to a detachment in Simcoe, twelve miles away. The absence of a police officer in Langton might well have been one of McAuliffe's reasons for choosing the bank there.

Instead of calling the police in Simcoe, Van Hooren went to investigate himself. There had been several false alarms at the bank in the past. McAuliffe saw him peering through the window and gestured menacingly with a gun for him to come inside. Van Hooren obeyed, afraid that harm might come to the gunman's prisoners if he didn't. Soon Van Hooren was with the other people who'd been herded into a corner and told to keep their backs turned. Cecil Aspden followed moments later. He protested that he couldn't climb the gate, but quickly responded when McAuliffe snarled, "Come on, climb over or something worse will happen to you."

While Hall was filling the shopping bag with cash, three more customers came in: an insurance salesman from Brantford named Richard Broad, a local tobacco farmer and insurance company owner named Arthur Lierman, and William Goddyn, who worked on Lierman's farm as a sharecropper. All were made to climb over the gate.

Hall found a small metal box in one of the cash drawers. The bandit said, "Open it, chum." The box contained some bills and rolls of coins. "Dump it in the bag," McAuliffe ordered.

Hall dropped the whole box into the shopping bag. It ripped right through the bottom. Cursing, McAuliffe pulled a second shopping bag from inside his coat. "Put the money in there, goddamn you!" he growled. "Not the cash box, you fool! Just the money!"

When all the money from the drawers was in the bag, McAuliffe told Hall to join the others. "Turn your back, chum," he said. "Then he asked, "Who has the combination for the safe?"

Henry W. Thompson, the bank's accountant, said that only the manager knew the combination and he wasn't in the bank. Thompson was playing for time, and McAuliffe knew it. "I'm not fooling," the gunman warned. "You go in and open up that safe, or you'll get a sore head."

The vault door was already open. The safe inside had a double set of doors with multiple locks. The lock for which only Mr. Beattie had the combination had already been thrown. Thompson and Mrs. Leedham each knew one of the other two combinations. Fearful for their own lives and the lives of the other people, they went into the vault to open the safe. McAuliffe kept one gun trained on them and the other on the rest of his captives. "If you do any talking about this after I'm gone," he threatened, "I'll come back and kill you, because I don't intend to get caught."

While Mrs. Leedham was taking her turn at the safe, Thompson had an opportunity to get a good look at the robber.

> He was about twenty-five to thirty years of age, about five feet eight inches tall, sallow complexion, weighing about 155 pounds, well built, not stocky or wide shoulders, a nicely built fellow. He wore a buff coloured sun helmet, dark green sun glasses, a dark blue suit coat, a dirty blue shirt, not a sport shirt, open at the neck and I believe it had thin stripes; dark pants and black shoes. He didn't wear gloves.

When the safe was opened, McAuliffe handed Thompson and Mrs. Leedham his loot bag and told them to fill it. He wanted everything, including the rolls of coins. He didn't enter the vault himself, because he had to keep an eye on the other people. A couple of times, while the robber was thus distracted, Thompson and Mrs. Leedham stuffed bundles of money behind some storage boxes. He caught them at it and cried, "Hey! None of that! Pick that up!"

"Pick what up?" Mrs. Leedham asked.

McAuliffe didn't press the issue. He was anxious to get away. Successful stickups never took more than a few minutes and he'd already been in there almost a quarter of an hour. Telling Thompson and Mrs. Leedham to get out of the vault, McAuliffe took the bag of money from them. Then he ordered all of the captives *into* the vault.

All this time, nobody outside knew what was happening in the bank. Not even Mr. Beattie in his upstairs apartment had any idea that his bank was being robbed. He was getting ready to play golf with a local physician, Dr. W.J. Nicholson. Beattie went down the stairs to a vestibule. On one side was a door to the outside. On the other was a door that opened into the bank area behind the gate. That door had a peephole in it. If Beattie had stopped to take a look, he would have seen a gunman herding his staff and customers into the vault, and could have slipped out to get help. Instead, he opened the door and walked right in on the robbery. *"You!"* McAuliffe snapped, "Get in the vault!"

The stunned manager did as he was told. The bandit still had guns in both his hands, so he told Frank Hall to pick up the shopping bag. Hall tried, but the weight of all the rolled coins made it so heavy that the handles tore loose. McAuliffe told him to lift up the bag and put it on the end of the counter, near the door Beattie had just come through. Then he ordered Hall back into the vault.

McAuliffe closed the vault door, but was unable to lock it. He pocketed his pistols, seized the loot bag in his arms, and fled from the bank. Before he reached the Meteor, the bottom of the bag broke through. Bundles of bills and rolls of coins spilled into the street. McAuliffe grabbed up as much money as he could and tossed it into the car. Then he jumped in and squealed away. McAuliffe's initial haul had been more than $22,000. But his greed in taking the heavy coins, which amounted to just a few hundred dollars, cost him much of the swag. He roared out of Langton with about $8,000.

At this point, on what had started out on a quiet summer day in a peaceful Ontario village, the worst crime to occur had been an armed robbery. Dramatic enough for any community! Nonetheless, in spite of all the potential for danger, nobody had been hurt. The situation was about to turn deadly.

After the vault door slammed shut, the prisoners didn't know whether or not the bandit was still in the bank. They waited two minutes before somebody tried the door and found it wasn't locked. Art Lierman and Bill Goddyn were the first ones out of the bank, with Lambert Van Hooren right behind. Curious people who had seen the black Meteor race out of town at high speed — and the spilled money on the sidewalk — were gathering in front of the bank. They asked what was going on, but the men were in too much of a hurry to respond. Concerned that the bandit would get away before police could arrive, they'd decided to go after him themselves.

Van Hooren wanted Lierman to go with him in his car. Instead, Lierman ran to his own blue Plymouth, in which he always kept a .22 rifle for shooting small game. As he got behind the wheel, Goddyn jumped in the passenger side. They sped off in pursuit of the Meteor, with Van Hooren not far behind.

At the intersection with the Twelfth Concession south of Langton, Lierman stopped, trying to guess which way the bandit had gone. A local man who'd been working on a church on the Twelfth Concession happened by, and Lierman asked him if he'd seen a black Meteor. The man pointed west and said the car had passed him at the church.

Lierman and Goddyn changed places in the Plymouth, with Goddyn taking the wheel and Lierman getting in the passenger side. He reached behind and grabbed his rifle off the back seat. Then they sped off.

Back in Langton, Van Hooren stopped at his father's house to tell him about the robbery. Archie Van Hooren, a taxi driver, jumped into his cab to join in the chase. At a gas station at the junction of the Twelfth Concession and Townline Road, the Van Hoorens learned that the black Meteor had screeched through the lot between the pumps and the building and then wheeled south onto the third concession road, almost smashing into a parked truck. Art Lierman's Plymouth was five hundred feet behind it, travelling fast with the horn blaring. Archie told Lambert to head for Glen Meyer, while he went to Frogmore. He couldn't be sure which back roads the bandit and the pursuers might take, but he thought that either he or his son might catch up with the Plymouth.

At Frogmore, Archie stopped to speak to Harry Carruthers, who was working at the roadside in front of his house. He said the Meteor had just passed by, with the Plymouth three hundred feet behind. Art Lierman had been holding a rifle out the window and the gun was pointed at the car in front. Both vehicles had turned onto the Kinglake

Road. Instead of following, Archie took a detour, thinking he might be able to head the bandit off at Kinglake. That decision might very well have saved his life.

When McAuliffe realized he was being pursued, he tore up and down the back roads, trying to lose the Plymouth, but it was gaining on him. On one of the concessions, the cars roared past the farm of Henry Menary, who later reported hearing gunshots. Mrs. Menary said she actually saw Art Lierman firing his rifle at the Meteor.

Kinglake Road was just a narrow, sandy track connecting the hamlets of Frogmore and Kinglake. It was suitable for plodding farm vehicles, not cars racing at full speed. Keeping control of a fast-moving car on the soft sand would have been extremely difficult. The Meteor threw up a cloud of sand and dust that would have been blinding to the driver behind.

At a spot about half a mile from Frogmore, the Meteor went off the road and came to a sudden stop in a three-foot deep ditch. McAuliffe might have lost control of the car because a lucky shot from Lierman's rifle punctured one of his rear tires. More likely it was because, in his rage, McAuliffe had taken one hand off the steering wheel to return fire; not

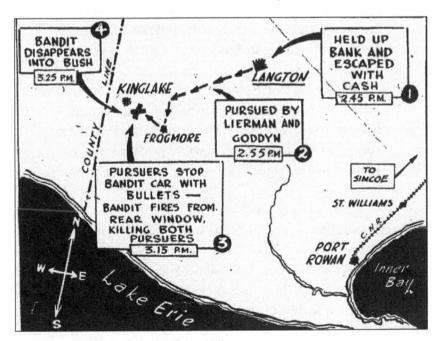

Map of the route taken by the bank robber and killer.
TORONTO *STAR.*

163

with a pistol, but with a Sten gun. A Sten was a submachine gun developed by the British during the Second World War. While the Meteor ploughed along the sandy lane, McAuliffe turned and fired a burst through his back window, peppering the Plymouth with slugs. The Plymouth rolled to a halt at the same time that the Meteor went into the ditch. No more than fifteen minutes had passed since McAuliffe had fled from the bank.

McAuliffe got out of the car. He'd been banged up when the car slammed into the ditch, but was otherwise unhurt. However, he was in a blind fury. His plans had been ruined! Sten gun in hand, McAuliffe walked back to the bullet-shattered Plymouth. He fired through the driver's side window, then he walked around to the passenger side and shot again. As he took to the bush to make his escape on foot, McAuliffe didn't know that witnesses to the murder were hiding just a few feet away. Bobby Nichols, sixteen, and Ray Pressey, eighteen, had seen the whole thing. Bobby described the scene to a reporter:

> Gosh, I was scared. We were hoeing tobacco when I heard a single shot and looked up. I saw the cars going by very fast and making a big cloud of dust. The leading car swayed and went into the ditch. I ducked flat on the ground and then I heard more shots as if they came from a pistol or a rifle.
>
> While I was looking I saw a man in the car on our side slump over. It was Art Lierman, who used to be our neighbour when we lived in North Middleton. When I was lying down, Ray saw someone run into the bush. I saw him too. He went south. I couldn't tell what he was wearing. I was too scared.

Bobby told another reporter he had seen the driver of the Meteor poke a gun in the window of the Plymouth and fire it. When the stranger was gone, Bobby ran to his house and told his father, who called the police. Ray went to Kinglake. There he met Archie Van Hooren and told him what he had seen. Archie drove down the road alone. Later he described the murder scene.

There was no one around. The Meteor was in the south ditch and Lierman's car on the road six feet behind, full of bullet holes. I went past the car, then backed up beside Lierman's car. I saw two bodies. I then drove to Frogmore to the store and told them to call the police. I picked up Harry Carruthers and went back to the scene.

There was still no one around, although a group of people had gathered at the Kinglake end of the road. I saw one bill blow across the road and Carruthers picked it up. It was a $20 bill; he later gave it to the police. I drove fifty feet ahead and waited until provincial constable W.E. Rogers of the Tillsonberg detachment arrived. The constable looked in both cars, then spoke over the radio. We stayed until the arrival of additional police and Coroner W.J. Nicholson, M.D., of Langton.

Dr. Nicholson had been on his way to meet Beattie for their golf game when Lierman and Goddyn drove away. Soon the village was abuzz with news of the robbery. Then came information about the two cars on the Kinglake Road, six miles from Langton. Nobody in the community knew yet about the murders. There was a rumour that Lierman and Goddyn were in the woods, pursuing the robber on foot. Dr. Nicholson was with a group of local residents who drove out to the Kinglake Road just to see what was going on. "Never did I dream I would be acting in an official capacity," he said later.

The Plymouth had twenty-seven bullet holes in it. Art Lierman, thirty-one, had been hit seven times, the fatal bullet going right through his heart. Bill Goddyn, twenty-three, had been shot five times, with four bullets hitting him in the head. Both men left behind wives and children.

The crime scene was soon swarming with police officers from Simcoe, Tillsonburg, Delhi, and Dundas. In the Meteor, which had been stolen in Windsor five days earlier, they found spent cartridge casings, the sun helmet and sunglasses, a green suit coat with white pinstripes, the .38 revolver, a notebook listing the back roads and communities between Windsor and Langton with a reference to a hideout, a torn shopping bag, and most of the remaining robbery loot. The fugitive's primary concern now wasn't money, but escape. If caught, he faced a trip to the gallows, and he was still heavily armed. Police still had no idea as to his identity.

Two OPP constables followed McAuliffe's footprints into the woods until they lost the trail in dense underbrush. At 6:30 p.m., Inspectors Len Neill and Alex McLeod of the OPP Criminal Investigation Branch arrived from Toronto to take charge of the manhunt. "It's a bad territory in which to find a man," an OPP spokesman told reporters. "The Kinglake district is rocky, scrub bush country with plenty of cover."

Hundreds of police officers and armed farmers spread out from the scene of the crime. A tracking dog was brought in from Leamington. Police set up roadblocks for miles around. They searched every vehicle and warned motorists not to pick up hitchhikers because they might be "shot to death by the desperado to get the car." Police told farmers in an area covering three townships to lock their doors and "shoot to kill the suspect on sight." Civilian pilots from the London Flying Club took to the air in small planes to search for the killer.

Fortunately, nobody acted on the "shoot to kill" order, or a few unwary tramps who got swept up in the dragnet might have become victims of mistaken identity. The tracking dog led one group to a schoolhouse. Taking no chances, the police shot the lock off and burst in with cocked revolvers and shotguns. The little building was empty, but the fact that the killer had been in the vicinity of a schoolhouse worried authorities enough that they ordered schools in the area closed and children kept home until the fugitive was caught.

After twenty-four hours of combing the countryside with no result, the manhunters were exhausted, sweat-soaked, and covered with mosquito bites. Officers manning the roadblocks and patrolling the country lanes had gone without food or sleep. Another OPP Inspector, Frank C. Kelly, arrived from Toronto. He had once been stationed in Simcoe and knew the country.

By now the robbery and the double-murder was news across Canada and in the United States, as well. Clifford Fanning, a sixteen-year-old Boy Scout from Mount Clemens, Michigan, arrived with his bloodhound, Doc Keen. The dog was something of a celebrity in the United States, with a record of sixty-three successful trackings. Now he and his young master were put on the trail of an armed fugitive. The story of the heroic boy and his dog made great copy for the newspapers. The Toronto *Star* reported: "Without a hint of fear, showing bravery rarely surpassed in the midst of battle, he [Fanning] led the exhaustive searches with levelled guns at his back and a killer at the other end of the trail. From the moment he entered the dense woods, he stood in constant danger of being suddenly caught in a murderous cross-fire."

If anybody had any qualms about putting a teenage boy between the posse and a man who had already murdered two people, it wasn't mentioned in the papers. Doc Keen led the police to two more schoolhouses, but the fugitive was gone. After a hard day on the trail, Clifford was worn out. He and Doc Keen went home. (The "Doc Keen" story appeared in newspapers of the time, but was disputed by Clifford Fanning when a National Film Board of Canada documentary about the case was being made in 1996.)

The police were perplexed over the fugitive's attraction to school-houses. Perhaps he hoped to find food in them. As the search widened, police did come across some signs of their quarry, and evidence that he was scrounging. He'd helped himself to a can of milk in a barn, eaten raw potatoes in a field, and left his footprints in the mud by a farmer's water pump. A telephone lineman reported seeing a man who seemed to be trying to hide in a ditch. A mile from Straffordville, a farmer named Bert Luce found a man sleeping in his haymow. Upon being disturbed, the stranger jumped up and fled into the woods. Luce was certain the man was carrying a Sten gun. The running man passed within a few feet of a neighbour, eight-year-old Donald Woods. The boy also reported seeing a gun in his hands. Police searched the barn and found a coat that witnesses identified as the one the bank robber had worn. There was nothing in the pockets but a couple of gnawed potatoes.

Still, after two days of rumours, alleged sightings, and clues, the killer remained at large. Local people were, as one resident put it, "scared skinny." Police were afraid the killer had slipped through their cordon and hopped a freight train. If so, no one might ever know who had killed Lierman and Goddyn.

By the afternoon of Saturday, June 24, Inspector Kelly was almost ready to admit that the fugitive had escaped the area, when the big break finally came. Graham Haggerty, a twenty-year-old resident of the little community of Vienna, and two OPP constables were searching along railway tracks north of Straffordville, when they saw a man run into the woods. One of the policemen fired three shots in the air to alert other parties. Then the three struck into the woods after the suspect. The officers plunged into the underbrush, while Haggerty followed a path that led to an old sawmill. Peering through the open door of a shack, Haggerty saw a figure huddled in a corner. He described what happened next for the Toronto *Star*:

> "Put 'em up or I'll kill you," I told him, and I meant it because I knew both Art Lierman and Bill Goddyn had been slaughtered when they got in the same position that I did late Saturday afternoon. The figure in the shabby clothes I was covering crouched down in the dim interior of the shack and his hand dropped down. I thought of that machine gun the men had been cut down with, and I drew back with my thumb the hammer of my deer gun — a .38-55 rifle.
>
> "I'm going to kill you right where you are," I shouted at him. I was talking his language now. He straightened up, raising his hands above his head and at the same time came through the doorway. "I didn't do anything," he mumbled.
>
> I got a good look at him. His clothes made him look like a bum, but he was too young. He had a good four-day stubble of red whiskers, and through the open front of his shabby coat I saw that he had nothing on underneath. His hairless chest was an angry patch of red scratches. He must have done a lot of running through blackberry bushes, I thought later. He didn't look scared, rather, sort of mean. He glared at me through his narrow eyes. Then the provincials rushed up and put the cuffs on him.

Soon more police officers arrived, along with their civilian helpers. The prisoner was hustled into a patrol car. To the disappointment of the civilians, the constables put an old rug over his head so his face couldn't be seen by anyone who might be called upon to identify the bank robber in a police line-up. McAuliffe was bruised and covered with insect bites.

His clothing was torn from his flight through brush and brambles. He was starving and he was sullen.

Locked up in the Norfolk County jail in Simcoe, McAuliffe refused to answer questions. The day after his arrest, he was placed in a lineup with fourteen other men of similar height and build, all wearing sun helmets and sunglasses. Nine of ten witnesses from the bank robbery identified him as the bandit.

Warned that he would be charged with armed robbery and with the murders of Art Lierman and Bill Goddyn, McAuliffe still refused to say who he was or where he came from. When an officer asked him how he got so badly scratched up, he snapped, "How do ya think? Eatin' berries!" Other than that, he'd only say, "I ain't done nothin'." However, after Inspector Neill kept pressing him for his name, he finally replied, "Frank West will do." He was officially charged under that name.

Police took "West's" finger and palm prints. They matched prints found on the Meteor. Moreover, they matched prints in the RCMP Identification Branch in Ottawa, taken from one Fred Walker of Windsor who'd been arrested for burglary in 1938.

The OPP investigators knew that "Frank West" and "Fred Walker" were aliases, but when they tried to get information about the prisoner's personal background, he'd only sneer that it was their business to find it. The police were able to do just that, thanks to a photograph of the suspect they circulated through the press.

Mrs. Emile Lezure, who kept a boarding house in Windsor, informed the RCMP that the man in the picture was a former roomer, Herbert McAuliffe. He'd stayed at her place for about two months. She also knew that he owned an old Ford that he kept in a rented garage.

Mrs. Lezure's information was the key that opened up the investigation. Police detectives learned that Joseph Herbert McAuliffe was a loner. He was a machinist who'd worked in various Windsor area factories and moved from one rooming house to another. But though he regularly changed his personal lodging, he'd kept the same rented garage for years. The garage held the secret of McAuliffe's hidden life as a fifty-cent-piece counterfeiter.

It was a double garage, because McAuliffe needed more than just a place to keep his car. He needed a private workshop. There, the police found a drill press, grinder, lathes, and cutting tools, as well as literature on coinage and a large number of unfinished counterfeit coins. In several hiding places they found guns and ammunition and parts of a Thompson submachine gun. Among the cache of ammunition were boxes of 9mm shells that could be used in a Sten gun. The police also found a pair of pants that matched the suit coat that had been in the Meteor.

At the same time that police in Windsor were searching McAuliffe's garage, ten-year-old Larry Holmes was looking for crows' nests in the bush just half a mile from the murder site. He stumbled upon a blue suit coat and a dirty shirt with narrow blue and white stripes hidden in a thicket of ferns. Realizing the clothing could be connected with the big crime story everybody was talking about, Larry went home to get his mother and older brother. Their search turned up a stash of $521 in one-dollar bills, and a Thompson submachine gun. Mrs. Holmes quickly informed the police.

This was a significant find. So far all of the evidence the police had collected was circumstantial. They had nothing that conclusively tied the suspect to the crimes. A competent defence lawyer would be able to challenge everything, even the finger and palm prints on the Meteor.

At the time of his arrest, McAuliffe was wearing a grey coat that had been stolen from a farm bunkhouse and he had no shirt. The coat and shirt Larry Holmes had found were positively identified as the ones the bank robber had worn. Most important was a thumbnail-size bit of tin-foil a constable found in the coat pocket. On it was a partial fingerprint that matched the print of the little finger of McAuliffe's left hand. The police now had proof, beyond the shadow of a doubt, that McAuliffe was the gunman.

McAuliffe's second pistol and the Sten gun that was the actual murder weapon were never found, but the Crown prosecutor had all the evidence he needed to make a strong case. McAuliffe went to trial in the Norfolk County Courthouse in Simcoe on September 5. He was defended by W.E. Ross, a young Simcoe lawyer involved in just his second important case. Ross made an argument for self-defence. McAuliffe fired back, he said, after Lierman had shot at him first.

There was conflicting testimony over whether or not Lierman had actually fired his gun. Witnesses had seen him holding the gun out the window of the Plymouth and said they had heard shots. But had those sounds of gunfire actually come from the .22 rifle? The constable who had first examined Lierman's rifle at the murder scene testified that the gun hadn't been recently fired and that it was in fact inoperable. The constable had found the rifle on the back seat of the Plymouth. Had the killer thrown it there after shooting the two men? Or had a wounded Lierman tossed it back there in a desperate attempt to show the bandit advancing on him and Goddyn with a Sten gun that they were unarmed?

McAuliffe was silent and presented a calm expression as more than sixty witnesses gave their testimony and Crown Attorney D.E.W. Tisdale introduced 102 exhibits. The jury retired on September 14 and took only three hours to reach a verdict of guilty on both charges of first-degree murder. When Mr. Justice R.W. Treleaven sentenced him to hang, McAuliffe's only betrayal of emotion was a slight twitching in his face.

The execution date was set for December 19. On October 3, with his case now in the hands of the highly respected Arthur Maloney, K.C., of Toronto, McAuliffe submitted a "Pauper's Appeal" on the argument that the trial judge erred on some points of law in his instructions to the jury. It was rejected first by the Supreme Court of Ontario and then by the Supreme Court of Canada. On December 4, when McAuliffe learned of the final failure of his appeal, he nonchalantly said, "Well, that's that."

Like so many other condemned prisoners, McAuliffe spent his last days seeking comfort in religion. He was visited by the aunt who had raised him, and by his father and sister, all of whom refused to believe he was guilty of murder. His only other visitor was a Roman Catholic priest. Because he was scheduled to hang six days before Christmas, McAuliffe's jailers said they would provide him with an early Christmas dinner if he wanted it. He didn't.

Nobody in Simcoe doubted that McAuliffe was guilty of murder, but the idea of a hanging taking place in their community didn't sit well with many of the residents. Some were opposed to capital punishment and called it "a barbaric hand-me-down from the stone age." Hundreds of them signed a petition — in vain — to have the death sentence commuted to life imprisonment. Others felt that "a central place of execution should be established where local people are not forced to participate in the affairs." Two hours before the execution, the municipal council made a request — which was granted — that the custom of having church bells toll to announce the carrying out of the death sentence not be observed.

Inside the jail, McAuliffe had to listen to the sounds of the gallows being constructed within a few feet of his cell. When the dreadful moment came for that last walk, he was offered a glass of whiskey, but refused it. McAuliffe went to his death without a word. The trap was dropped at 12:31 a.m. It wasn't a "clean" hanging. The executioner botched the job, and McAuliffe slowly strangled for seventeen minutes before he was pronounced dead.

The body was placed in a cheap casket that police officers accompanied under cover of darkness to St. Mary's Roman Catholic Cemetery. The constables needed flashlights to pick their way through the pathways of the snow-covered graveyard. Art Lierman and Bill Goddyn, who had bravely, if foolishly, met their deaths in pursuit of a criminal, had been laid to rest surrounded by mourning family and friends. For Joseph Herbert McAuliffe, the end result of that lethal pursuit was an unmarked grave.

CHAPTER 11
LUCIEN RIVARD:
The Great Escape

On March 2, 1965, Montreal's old Bordeaux Jail was the scene of an escape that would go on record as one of the most infamous in Canadian history. The ease with which two prisoners made their break was embarrassing enough for authorities at many levels of government. But what rocked the nation and brought about an international scandal was the fact that one of the escapees, Lucien Rivard, was already a key figure in allegations of political corruption that threatened to bring down the Liberal government of Prime Minister Lester Pearson.

Rivard, age forty-nine, had been in Bordeaux for almost ten months, fighting extradition to the United States where he was wanted on charges of drug trafficking. His fellow jail-breaker, Andre Durocher, age twenty-eight, had been sentenced to five years for robbery with violence. According to the story that appeared in the newspapers, at 6:20 p.m., Rivard and Durocher received permission from a guard, Sergeant Roger Beaupre, to get a hose so they could flood the jail's hockey rink. Ten minutes later, guard Noel Bonneville escorted Rivard and Durocher to the boiler room where the hose was stored. Durocher suddenly pulled a gun on him. "No tricks," Durocher warned. "This is serious." The weapon was made of wood and covered with black shoe polish, but it looked real enough to the guard. Rivard and Durocher tied him up with electric wire, along with two boiler attendants. Then they smashed through the door leading to the guards' target-practice room.

Guard Roland Gadoury was patrolling the lower inside jail wall at 7:15 when the two prisoners jumped him. They bound him with electric wire and black tape and took his twelve-gauge shotgun. Rivard and Durocher squirrelled their way across a ladder from the lower interior wall to the top of the twenty-foot-high main outside wall. Then they used the hose as a rope to slide down to the ground.

This story has become almost legendary. But how much of it is true is questionable. It was a spring night, with the temperature at 40 Fahrenheit (4.4 Celsius); not ideal for flooding an outdoor ice rink. (Inmates played broomball on it, not hockey, which the administration considered too rough.) Two days after the escape, a Bordeaux guard who preferred to remain anonymous told Toronto *Star* reporter David Proulx that it would have been impossible for Rivard and Durocher to have escaped without inside help. The going rate for buying one's way out of Bordeaux, he said, was $10,000. Rivard had access to that kind of money. He had plenty of it stashed away — proceeds from his various criminal activities. He also had strong contacts among the gang bosses of Montreal's notorious east end.

The escapees did in fact use a hose to get down from the top of the wall. A photograph of the wooden gun appeared in newspapers. Rivard worked in the jail's woodshop and could have made it there. But the hockey rink story seemed too contrived to many officials. There would be a lengthy investigation into just what happened before Rivard and Durocher went over the wall.

Once they were out of the jail, the two men ran across fields until they came to the intersection of Edmond Valade and Poincaré Streets, where there was a traffic signal. The first car to stop was a Dodge convertible driven by an accountant named Jacques Bourgeois, who was on his way to do some after-hours work at his office. Before he knew what was happening, both doors flew open and someone shouted, "Grab him!"

1952 police photo of Lucien Rivard, the career criminal whose escape from jail almost brought down a government.
THE ENCYCLOPEDIA OF CANADIAN ORGANIZED CRIME.

Bourgeois reached for the keys in the ignition, but was too late. Two men jumped in and forced him to the centre of the seat between them. A moment later, the car was racing down the street.

The stockily built, middle-aged man with the crew-cut hair who had seized the steering wheel seemed to be out of breath as he gasped, "Keep quiet! Don't get excited! We're armed, but we won't touch you." The next day, sitting in his home just two blocks from Bordeaux Jail, Bourgeois told reporters about his encounter with the jail breakers.

The car-jacker at the wheel asked him, "Do you know me?"

"I said I didn't know him and I didn't want to know him," said Bourgeois. "Then he said he was Lucien Rivard and he had just jumped the wall and escaped from Bordeaux. I looked at him again and then I remembered the pictures in the papers."

Bourgeois said that Rivard slowed down after putting some distance between himself and the jail. He actually seemed relaxed as he navigated the streets of Montreal, smoking a cigarette and offering one to Bourgeois. The frightened accountant, on the other hand, was anything but relaxed.

"I asked them several times to let me off," Bourgeois said, "but they replied each time not to worry. They would let me off in good time. I was more worried about the other fellow than about Rivard. He's the one who shouted, 'Grab him!' … He looked like a pretty rough customer."

Bourgeois reported that Rivard told him why he had escaped. "He said he was fifty years old and that he was expecting a pretty long sentence. He said he preferred to take a chance at breaking out rather than face the prospect of staying in jail until the age of sixty-five or seventy."

Bourgeois still feared for his life, even though Rivard had told him he wouldn't be harmed. He told the jail-breakers they could have the fifty dollars in his wallet. Rivard quietly replied, "We don't need your money."

Then, to Bourgeois's astonishment, Rivard gave him two dollars for taxi fare so he could get to his office. He even had a pencil and paper in his pocket so he could write down Bourgeois's office phone number. Rivard promised to call Bourgeois and let him know where he could find his car. Twenty minutes after jumping into his car, Rivard and Durocher dropped Bourgeois on Crémazie Boulevard at Montée St. Michel, and then drove away.

Bourgeois took a cab to his office. He arrived just in time to receive Rivard's phone call — fifteen minutes after the escapees had released him. Rivard told him his car was in the parking lot of a shopping centre at Montée St. Michel and Fleury Street. Bourgeois phoned the police and told them about his encounter with criminals. Officers found the car just where Rivard had said it would be. Inside were two pairs of jail-issue trousers. Rivard and Durocher had brought along a change of clothes. They had planned the escape down to the last detail. The fact that Bourgeois's car had been abandoned only a mile from the Pie IX Bridge suggested to police that the fugitives might already have escaped from Montreal Island. Considering Rivard's underworld connections, they could be almost anywhere and might even be out of the country within hours. Because of the "Great Escape," *Rivard* quickly became a household name, even to Canadians who might have paid only passing attention to the political controversy in which he was embroiled.

Lucien Rivard was born in Montreal on June 16, 1914. He was a high-school dropout, and spent some time working in Quebec's bush camps. Rivard's name first appeared in police records in 1933 when, at the age of nineteen, he received a suspended sentence for breaking into a storage shed. Two years later he was fined for loitering. In 1938, Rivard did his first stint in jail when he was sentenced to a year for attempting to break into a store and receiving stolen goods. He was back in prison again in 1943, starting a three-year stretch for burglary.

After that, Rivard managed to stay out of jail, but it wasn't because he had decided to go straight. He had been learning the ropes of living on the wrong side of the law and had made friends with influential people in the Montreal underworld. He'd found that there was more money to be made dealing drugs than in petty burglaries, and less chance of going to jail.

Rivard, known to his friends as "Moose," became associated with organized-crime figures like Giuseppi "Pep" Cotroni and "Monseigneur" Paul Mandolini. He started off in the illicit narcotics trade pushing "goof balls" (made from a variety of drugs including heroin, cocaine, amphetamines, and barbituates) in bars and pool halls. Over time he rose in the ranks to become a major figure in an international drug ring dealing mainly in heroin. Rivard was suspected of being an important player in dealings involving Montreal gangsters and the Corsican drug-smuggling organization known as the "French Connection."

In 1956, Rivard went to Cuba to manage a casino for Mondolini. He allegedly ran guns to the rebel forces of Fidel Castro, who was fighting to overthrow the dictator Fulgencio Batista. Rivard was arrested in 1958, imprisoned, and then expelled from Cuba.

Rivard returned to Montreal, none the worse for his Cuban adventure. He opened up a luxurious beach resort called Plage Ideal (Ideal Beach) on Île Jésus, north of Montreal. According to the Toronto *Globe and Mail*, it was a place much favoured by men "with strong appetites for wenching and drinking." Among the resort's patrons were Rivard's associates in the drug- and gun-trafficking business.

For a few years, Rivard lived the high life. He had a townhouse in a working-class neighbourhood in Montreal's north end, as well as a cottage on Île Jésus. He sported expensive suits and shoes and mixed with celebrities and high-profile gangsters, just like a figure from the Roaring Twenties. He always had a thick wad of cash from which he could peel off fifty- and hundred -dollar notes to impress his friends.

Rivard and his beautiful wife, Marie, thirty-two, were devoted to each other. They had no children, but Rivard was nonetheless a man to whom family ties were important. He supported a sister and gave her husband a part-time job as a gatekeeper at the resort.

Ties of a different nature were not only making Rivard wealthy, but also keeping him out of the clutches of the law. Not long after Rivard returned to Montreal from Cuba, he was arrested for possession of an unregistered handgun. A few words were spoken to the right people and the charge was quietly dropped. Sometime later, Rivard was charged with robbing a contractor of $5,000. When the case went to trial, Rivard's three accusers were suddenly stricken with loss of memory. Among law-enforcement agencies, Rivard became known as "The Brains."

However, Rivard's impunity was about to take a major blow. On October 10, 1963, a Montreal hoodlum named Michel Caron and his wife were crossing the border from Mexico into Laredo, Texas. An American customs agent thought Caron was acting in a suspicious manner and had the car searched. Hidden in the door panels were thirty-five kilograms of pure heroin. With the dope having an estimated value of more than $12 million once it had been cut and sold on the streets, the bust was one of the biggest in American history up to that time.

Mrs. Caron claimed to know nothing about the heroin. Her husband refused to talk to police. "I don't say nothing," he told them. "If I do, I'm dead." But the Texas police found a note in Caron's pocket in handwriting that was eventually identified as that of Lucien Rivard. They had also arrested another drug courier named Roger Beauchemin who admitted he'd been working for Rivard and who said Rivard ran a multi-million-dollar narcotics operation out of the resort.

Under police interrogation, Caron finally agreed to a deal. He would "sing" in return for a relatively light sentence of ten years and the promise of protection for his family in Montreal. Caron came to this decision even though a Montreal lawyer had flown to Texas to warn him of dire consequences if he "blabbed" to the police.

Caron said he earned his living as a "salesman and gambler." The address he gave as his place of residence was a house with which Montreal police were familiar. Officers had been called there for a variety of reasons and had sometimes been assaulted. Caron said that periodically he and other couriers working for Rivard went to Mexico on "holiday trips." They picked up shipments of heroin that had been transported from the Middle East via France and South America and smuggled it into the United States. Caron said that Rivard paid $3,000 for each trip a courier like him made.

Sometimes the couriers went to Paris, taking their cars with them. On the return voyage, the panels of the cars would be stuffed with heroin. On one occasion, according to Caron, a car that had just been unloaded from a transatlantic liner had caught fire on a downtown Montreal street. Rivard had coolly stood by and watched firemen put out the blaze, then called for a tow truck to haul the car away.

Caron's information led the RCMP to four of Rivard's criminal associates in Montreal. They were also looking for Mandolino, who was believed to have made a sudden trip to Italy. In the months to come, a joint investigation by the FBI and the RCMP would result in the cracking of a major international drug ring in which Rivard was connected to Carlo Gambino, head of one of the powerful Mafia crime families in the United States. A police raid on a Montreal bus terminal would turn up sixty-one kilograms of pure heroin hidden in a locker. Among those caught in the police net were a man who claimed to be an employee of the Uruguayan foreign ministry in Montreal, a French citizen who had previously been deported from the United States on drug charges and had then re-entered the country illegally, and the Mexican ambassador to Bolivia.

When Caron began to talk, information about the Canadian connection eventually reached the office of United States Attorney General Robert Kennedy. He personally called his counterpart in Ottawa to ensure that Caron's family would be protected. Kennedy also told Canadian officials that the Americans wanted Lucien Rivard.

RCMP officers arrested Rivard on June 19, 1964. As they led him to the car that would take him to Bordeaux Jail, Rivard called to Marie, "Don't worry. I won't be gone long."

Pierre Lamontagne, a Montreal lawyer and prosecutor who specialized in narcotics cases, was retained by the United States Department of Justice as its representative in the extradition process. Above all, the Americans wanted Lamontagne to make sure Rivard was not granted bail. They had no doubt that if Rivard got out of jail, he'd disappear. Rivard hired as *his* representative Raymond Daoust, who was considered to be one of the best criminal lawyers in Quebec.

While Daoust worked on getting him a bail hearing, Rivard had to put up with the inconvenience of being lodged in Bordeaux. He spent hours reading legal texts, concentrating on points of law concerning bail. Later investigations would reveal that Rivard bribed guards to allow him the use of a telephone. For twenty-five dollars he could make two calls a day. Rivard phoned Marie daily. He didn't say who else he called, but even though regulations allowed visits from family members only, Rivard had two visits from a known Montreal gangster. For one hundred dollars a week, Rivard's cell door would be left open until 11:00 p.m. The regulatory lockup time was 4:30 p.m.

In fact, Rivard was one of about forty inmates with the status of "VIP." He could roam the corridors freely and watch hockey games on the television in the psychiatric wing. He gambled for high stakes in dice games. Rivard had an electric hot plate in his cell so he could fry eggs and boil water for instant coffee if he got hungry between scheduled mealtimes. His hard cot was cushioned with two mattresses. Months later, when Bordeaux came under severe criticism for being a "Queen Elizabeth Hotel" for criminals, guards explained to the press, under the promise of anonymity, that the VIP system had been in place for a long time and wasn't their fault. They said that "big shots" like Rivard who had money and power could stir up a "bingo" (riot) if their privileges were hindered. They could even arrange for the transfer of any guard who threatened to upset the system. For those reasons, the guards said, they tolerated an arrangement that they didn't necessarily condone. Nonetheless, they admitted that some of the guards, who were notoriously underpaid, supplemented their meagre incomes by selling goof balls and liquor to inmates.

As a Bordeaux VIP, Rivard wasn't exactly suffering behind bars in a tiny cell. But he was certainly afraid of being extradited to the United States and he might have decided to explore alternative options in case Daoust wasn't successful. There would be evidence that Marie, who insisted that her husband was being framed by Roger Beauchemin because Rivard had fired him from a job at the resort, was also trying to help arrange bail. She allegedly approached influential people and borrowed large sums of money that could go toward a bail bond — or a bribe.

The Rivard case exploded into a national scandal on Monday, November 23, when Erik Nielsen, the Progessive Conservative MP for the Yukon, dropped a bombshell in Parliament. Nielsen, a former Crown prosecutor in Whitehorse, stood up in the House of Commons and charged that Raymond Denis, a former aide to René Tremblay, the immigration minister in Lester Pearson's Liberal government, had offered Pierre Lamontagne $20,000 to "go easy" in his opposition to bail for Rivard. Nielsen further charged that Guy Lord, recently a special assistant to Justice Minister Guy Favreau, had tried to "coerce" Lamontagne into throwing the fight against Rivard's bail by threatening to blacklist him from future government work. Nielsen told a stunned Parliament that the case involved people known to belong to "the international crime society known as the Mafia or Cosa Nostra."

"The fact remains," said Nielsen, "I can find no other way of putting it, that these tentacles of this international cartel dealing in narcotics extended into the very offices of two ministers of the federal government."

Nielsen's accusations resulted in a seven-month-long inquest headed by Quebec Supreme Court Chief Justice Frédéric Dorion. RCMP officers testified that Lamontagne had been in fear of his life when he reported the bribery attempt. He'd had threatening phone calls and said, "I may find myself at the bottom of the river."

Raymond Daoust told the inquest that his client was "outraged" when he learned that illegal means had been used to clear the way for his bail. There was speculation that the bribe had not originated with Rivard, but with American gangsters who were worried about what he might say if he were extradited to the United States. Whether or not Rivard was behind the bribe, a Jekyll and Hyde image of him took shape during the inquest. In his appearances before Dorion, Rivard was joking and affable. He was allowed to kiss Marie, and, according to a Toronto *Star* reporter, "her eyes shone."

But there was testimony from police officers that seemed to justify Lamontagne's fear that Rivard's "gang" would try to get rid of him. The police said at least two potential witnesses — men who were associates of Rivard — feared for their lives because of "Rivard and his boys."

The "Rivard Affair" shook the Pearson government, but in the end didn't topple it. Judge Dorion's report had scathing words for the conduct of several members of the Liberal party. Raymond Denis was convicted of attempting to obstruct justice and sentenced to two years in prison. Guy Favreau, who had failed to take appropriate action following the bribe attempt, was obliged to resign in disgrace. He died a broken man two years later. For all its in-depth probing, the Dorion inquest left many mysteries unsolved. The man who might have been able to answer some disturbing questions about government officials and the "tentacles" of organized crime wasn't talking. Lucien Rivard's number-one concern was getting out of jail before the Americans could get their hands on him. South of the border, he faced a possible forty-year sentence.

While the political storm raged, legal counsel for Rivard and three other men — Charles Emil Groleau, Julien Gagnon, and Joseph Jones — served a writ of habeas corpus. On December 4, 1964, the men were taken to court for the hearing. Reporters and photographers were waiting in the courthouse corridor. The prisoners didn't want their pictures taken. They snarled threats, lunged at reporters, punched and kicked photographers, and knocked cameras to the floor. Police got between the prisoners and the newsmen and ordered the latter out. Veterans of the press said they had not seen such a disturbance in the courthouse in many years.

The hearing was remanded to December 18. This time strict security measures were in place. Doors leading to the courtroom that were usually open were locked. Police officers shielded the prisoners from the press. The case was remanded again, but even though nothing dramatic happened, the name of the principal figure was still headline material. "Rivard Well Guarded at Montreal Hearing" reported the *Globe and Mail.*

Just how "well guarded" Rivard actually was would become the next big question in the Rivard Affair, and the focal point of yet another national scandal. The Dorion Inquest was still in progress when Rivard and Durocher made their sensational escape from Bordeaux Jail. Canadians woke up on the morning of March 3, 1965, to news that was more than stunning; it was an international embarrassment.

Rivard's escape infuriated a lot of people, including American authorities who were already growing impatient with the time the Canadians were taking to get through the extradition process. "We'll have to regroup now, and consider our position again," said one exasperated American official. "Ricard [*sic*] was the key to breaking this ring. I hate to think of him on the loose and in a position to operate again … This is a heck of a way to guard an important prisoner. The whole case is becoming ludicrous."

One of the Dorion inquiry lawyers, upon first hearing the news of the escape, said, "It's got to be a joke organized by the press." An editorial that appeared in the Toronto *Star* on March 3 lamented, "We hate to think what the escape of Lucien Rivard from Bordeaux Jail is going to do to Canada's image in the United States … the affair must leave Washington wondering what sort of banana republic is sprouting to the north."

People at all levels scurried to cover themselves and dodge any blame. Guards who were immediately suspended without pay pending an investigation complained they were being made scapegoats. "How am I going to feed my family?" asked guard Roland Larue, who spoke to the press in defiance of an order to keep quiet. "There was no payoff here, I'm sure of it. These two slugged a guard and made it over the fence. It doesn't look like a set-up to me."

In the House of Commons, Speaker Alan Macnaughton lost control of the proceedings as an outraged Opposition demanded Guy Favreau's immediate resignation. Favreau replied that Bordeaux was a provincial jail, not a federal prison, and therefore not his responsibility. He later suggested to the press that Rivard had inside help. But Claude Wagner, the attorney general of Quebec, told reporters, "It was not a case of complicity, but rather stupidity in some cases."

Suspicion fell on Marie Rivard as an accomplice. On the afternoon of Tuesday, March 2, she had gone to the jail and picked up a cheque for $2,000 — money Rivard had on deposit in his canteen account. The cheque was signed by Bordeaux's assistant governor, Antonio Pilon. Marie cashed it within minutes of leaving the jail. Then, even though she was being kept under surveillance by Montreal police detectives, Marie managed to disappear for a while.

After the escape, police suspected that Marie had joined Rivard in his flight from the law. But Toronto *Star* journalist Alan Edmonds found her at the Rivards' Montreal home. She'd been at the dentist, she said, and had a swollen face to prove it. When Edmonds asked what she'd done with the $2,000 she'd collected from the jail, Marie replied, "Ah, those reporters! They write all sorts of things, and they are not always true. Look, they say I am missing, that they are searching for me all last night. Why don't they look? I am here at my house from 4:30 p.m. on. I hear on the television that he [Rivard] escapes. I don't believe it. I can't believe it."

Marie's actions were nonetheless seen as suspicious. It just seemed too coincidental that she had picked up a cheque that emptied Rivard's canteen account the day before the escape and then cashed it. Could that have been travelling money he'd need once he got over the wall? Was that why Rivard told Jacques Bourgeois he didn't need his money when the car-jacking victim tried to give him the cash in his wallet?

The breakout quickly brought the Montreal Police Department, the Quebec Provincial Police, and the RCMP into the search for the fugitives. They watched roads, bus, and train stations, and the Montreal airport. Because of some oversight in communications, no one thought to inform police in Toronto. Not until four hours after the escape did the RCMP in Toronto learn about it from a television newscast. The implication in the press was that if Rivard slipped out of Montreal and got to Toronto's international airport, he could have boarded a plane and flown to anywhere in the world.

Rivard's whereabouts was anybody's guess. Some people believed he was still on Montreal Island, hiding out in some underworld lair. Others thought he was picked up by a small plane in a field outside the city. Reports of Rivard "sightings" started to pour into Montreal police head-quarters from all over.

The FBI began its own search in the United States. Agents watched the border crossings and airports. They thought Rivard would try to get to Mexico or Switzerland where he was believed to have a lot of money in secret bank accounts. The Americans were concerned that if Rivard got his hands on that money, he would then flee to a country like the Philippines, with which they had no extradition agreement.

American officials were close-mouthed about what they were doing to track Rivard down. However, the Canadian press reported that the FBI had several "unofficial channels" it could put to work. These included personal contacts with foreign law-enforcement officers, tipsters in foreign countries, and the extensive net of the U.S. diplomatic machine. There was one point on which the Americans were clear: if Rivard should be arrested in a country that had extradition agreements with both Canada and the United States, *they* wanted him *first*! But before anyone could lay claim to the man the Americans were now calling a "criminal mastermind," he had to be found.

Rivard knew very well that his escape would be a media headliner. He took advantage of this publicity by sending a letter, dated March 3, to Albert Tanguay, governor of Bordeaux Jail. The letter was in French, but an English translation was published in the Toronto *Star* and other newspapers.

Dear Sir:

A few words to let you know that it is not true that Andre Durocher and I stole $25 from one of your guards. I have never taken a cent from anyone poorer than myself. I had accumulated $460 during my 8 ½ months of detention and my companion Durocher had a similar amount. It would have given us pleasure to slip them (the guards) $25 because the poor devils receive a starvation salary.

It is also wrong to say that we used violence on them, because violence is strictly against my principles. Instead we were rather kind toward them, even lighting cigarets [*sic*] for them before we left, while making sure that their bonds were not too tight.

You always have been very good to everyone at Bordeaux. We sincerely regret all the trouble we are giving to everyone. You certainly did not deserve this, but I could see no other solution.

I see that I cannot obtain justice here. I am innocent. I have never seen or known the famous Michel Caron, being held in Texas.

Mr. Tanguay, never did any of your officers or guards help in our escape in any way whatsoever. It is regrettable, but I never had confidence in any of them, because it is known that they spend their time selling out one another to obtain a better position and salary. To summarize, don't punish your men because of us. They may have erred through negligence, but certainly did not help us to escape.

I hope they returned to you the 12-guage shotgun, because we dropped it on a lawn at the corner of Poincare and Ed. Valois to take over the car of Mr. Bourgeois, whom we did not molest in any way.

If I am lucky, I will be far away by the time you receive this letter. The escape was decided on suddenly at 4 p.m. yesterday March 2 without any help from the outside or inside. Hoping that you will believe me and that this short letter will help to enlighten you. Once again, excuse us.

Respectfully Yours

L. Rivard

Of course, Rivard's letter was meant as much for the public's eyes as for Tanguay's. His claim that he "never took a cent from anyone poorer than myself" gave him the image of a French Canadian Robin Hood, and editorial cartoonists gleefully portrayed him as such. Some people were taken in by the folk-hero pose, overlooking the fact that Rivard was suspected of being a major drug dealer, whose wares caused violence, misery, and death.

A Toronto *Star* editorial published on March 5 responded to Rivard's letter:

> "There is little enough for Canada to be proud of in the great bail-and-bribe scandal, but it has at least produced something this country had rarely had before — a rogue with style. Lucien Rivard's behaviour while breaking out of Bordeaux Jail was in the best tradition of gentleman highwaymen and pirates … It's plain that Mr. Rivard (we can't help calling him mister) differs from the ordinary run of shambling, mumbling thugs as Rex Harrison differs from John Wayne.

Newspaper readers of the time would have understood the sarcasm in the comparison with Harrison, a classically trained British actor; and Wayne, the rough-and-tough star of cowboy movies.

Guy Favreau announced on March 4 that the federal government was considering offering a reward for information leading to Rivard's recapture in hope that it would attract underworld "stool pigeons" who might otherwise be afraid to inform on a "big fish" like Rivard. Director Josephat Brunet of the Quebec Provincial Police said a reward would bring in a lot more tips. Then he added, "But the reward would have to be very large to encourage them, considering the people that are mixed up with Rivard." The government posted a $15,000 reward five days after the escape. Marie was indignant. "He is worth a lot more than that to me," she said. "He is priceless."

On the evening of March 4, Marie was interviewed by telephone on the CBC's *Observer*, a program that was aired across Canada. "I am sure he is innocent," she said. "I believe he escaped because justice was taking too long to reach him and because he hoped his escape would lead to a greater search for the truth of his guilt or innocence."

Marie described Rivard as a hard-working man with a heart of gold who often did the menial "joe-jobs" around the resort. She said Rivard's mother lived in the upstairs rooms of their Montreal townhouse and that the family had been trying to keep news of his troubles from her. Marie claimed she hadn't heard anything from Rivard since the escape. "He knows my telephone is tapped and that all letters I receive are previously checked."

Asked again about the $2,000 cheque, Marie said she'd put it in the bank because her house was surrounded by thieves. When she was told that a United States committee report on crime had identified Rivard as one of the "kings" of narcotics trafficking in North America, Marie impatiently responded, "They are completely nuts. My husband a king? He is a king, yes, but mine." She scoffed at the notion that Rivard was wealthy and said the only property he owned was the house and some shares in the resort.

That same night, Max Ferguson, a satirist who was best known for his radio work, performed a comedic sketch on TV in which he was a bungling Mountie who was thwarted in all of his attempts to arrest Lucien Rivard. The hilarious sketch concluded with "Rivard" escaping in a yacht and telling another notorious fugitive, crooked union leader Hal Banks, "We've got the booze, the women, the heroin and the marijuana. Let's get going."

The Rivard Affair had gone beyond the perimeter of a news item about crime and political corruption. It was seeping into the fabric of everyday life in Canada. While opposition MPs repeatedly stung Pearson's Liberals with barbed remarks about hockey rinks and pampered criminals, and more than three thousand police officers scoured Montreal, schoolchildren were discussing the Rivard case in Current Events period. Humorists like Toronto *Star* columnist Gary Lautens found the ongoing story to be a rich source of material. Another *Star* writer suggested that the weapons and gadget-packed Aston Martin driven by James Bond in the movie *Goldfinger* would be the perfect car for Lucien Rivard. Biff Rose, an American stand-up comic visiting Canada for the first time, told his audience in a Toronto nightclub that he'd like to meet Lucien Rivard because, "He can show me how to get out of Montreal." Rhinoceros Party founder Dr. Jacques Ferron said his party would run several candidates named Lucien Rivard in the next federal election. "The telephone book is full of them," he said.

Graffiti that said RIVARD WAS HERE was scrawled everywhere, especially in Montreal. Men checking into motels for extramarital trysts signed "Rivard" on the registers. Pranksters sent mocking postcards with Rivard's name on them to Guy Favreau and the RCMP.

Rivard had become a "celebrity criminal," and the newspapers cashed in. Everything about the outlaw was considered newsworthy. The Toronto *Star* ran an article on a study of Rivard's handwriting done by analyst Alf Hansen, who said the longhand, cursive script revealed him as impulsive, secretive, and fatalistic. "He's vain and enjoys playing to the gallery ... He's mentally sharp and logical. He's not easily fooled ... He's warm, friendly and outgoing, but he's not a gregarious type. He picks his friends carefully. Rivard is not a fearful man, and he'll take a chance. He's not a vicious man ... There are no conflicts here to indicate he would harm anyone. He likes people to think well of him."

Reporters spoke to Rivard's neighbours on Île Jésus, where he had a cottage on the resort property. The island had gained a reputation as a "haven for hoodlums" after Mayor Jean Drapeau launched a campaign to chase the gangsters out of Montreal. It had a history of violent crime, including the shooting death of a nightclub doorman. The accused killer, construction contractor Robert Gignac, who was now in Bordeaux Jail, had a villa just a few doors away from Rivard's cottage. He'd bought it from Rivard's brother, Paul. Gignac told the Dorion Inquest that he was a friend of Rivard's and the two of them had dabbled in real estate. Gignac also said he had contributed to Marie's bail fund for Rivard.

But not all of Rivard's Île Jésus neighbours were shady characters. Dr. Wilfred LaPointe, who had the cottage next door, was a retired dentist. "He [Rivard] was a private man," Dr. LaPointe told the press. "When he got drunk, he closed all his doors and windows and troubled no one. Me — I'm glad he escaped. Apart from the little mistake he made with narcotics he was a fine man and a good neighbour."

Retired letter carrier Remi DeCalles also sang Rivard's praises, calling him "a fine man, the best, the greatest." He added, "I was the most surprised man in the world when he was arrested."

But for all the good reports Rivard's Île Jésus neighbours gave inquisitive reporters, there was something odd about Dr. LaPointe's closing words. "I lived next to him for ten years, and I'm telling you he was a good fellow. Me — I'm just waiting to die. I've got arterial sclerosis and there's no stopping that. So why should I tell you a lie? I'd like to tell you more, but I can't. You mustn't talk."

Andre Durocher had his moment of national notoriety thanks to his part in the escape. As a criminal, Durocher wasn't in Rivard's league. Police believed Rivard had plotted the escape and recruited Durocher because he had been entrusted with the job of flooding Bordeaux's ice rink. Rivard would also have needed help in getting over the wall. On March 6, the Toronto *Star* provided its readers with a brief article on the jail-breaker who had practically become the forgotten man in the Rivard Affair.

Durocher had been in trouble with the police since 1953 when, at the age of nineteen, he'd been sentenced to a month in jail for petty theft. After that, his record was like that of most small-time crooks: in and out of jail for theft and burglary. At the time he met Rivard in Bordeaux, Durocher was appealing a five-year sentence for a robbery conviction. On December 11, 1963, he and a partner had hijacked a truckload of cigarettes and tobacco valued at $10,000. The driver wasn't harmed, but because Durocher's partner had a blackjack, the crime went into the books as "robbery with violence."

Durocher had never been known to carry a gun or any other weapon, but upon arrest he was labelled as "dangerous." One Montreal police detective described him as *"Un maudit bon voleur ... tout un moineau."* (A damn good thief ... quite a bird.) The police were certain that Rivard and Durocher had parted company soon after the escape. Rivard would have had no further use for someone he'd have considered a punk and might even have seen as a liability. The police had no more idea of where Durocher was than they did of Rivard.

Police received tips from far and wide. A gas-station attendant in Woodstock, Ontario, reported that he had filled up a car whose driver looked like Rivard and spoke with a French accent. The suspect turned out to be a Ukrainian-born scientist who lived in nearby London. A phone call from a concerned resident of Alexandria (in eastern Ontario) had the OPP on the lookout for a suspicious-looking car thought to be driven by Rivard. A Montreal businessman returning from a Florida vacation said he had seen Rivard in St. Petersburg. There were rumours that Rivard had been seen in the French islands of St. Pierre and Miquelon off the coast of Newfoundland. The government said it was investigating with the assistance of the French embassy in Ottawa. Rivard's status as a criminal of international importance struck home with Canadians when Interpol announced it was sending an agent to Acapulco, Mexico, to begin an investigation into his drug-smuggling activities.

Meanwhile, Quebec police were certain that Rivard was still in Montreal, even though they did investigate several tips claiming he was hiding in small Laurentian communities. Montreal police raided cafés, restaurants, and motels that were known criminal hangouts. Six people suspected of being connected to the escape were arrested. The idea was to shake up the underworld community and flush Rivard out. If nobody went for the reward, maybe someone would decide that Rivard was getting too hot to handle.

Île Jésus received special attention, since so many of Rivard's friends and associates lived there. One was Adrien Dusault, mayor of the community of Ville d'Auteuil. When the police knocked on his door, Dusault's son answered and said his father was away for the weekend.

The police also wanted to talk to Gilles Brochu, part owner of the Laval Service Club in Ville d'Auteuil. Detectives dropped in on him without warning and said, "You know what we're looking for." Brochu replied that he had a pretty good idea.

Brochu later boasted to reporters that he and Rivard were old friends. "We were arrested together once," he said. It surprised him that the police should visit him a full four days after the escape. "My impression is that they want to show you reporters that they're trying to find him," Brochu said.

Four detectives showed up suddenly at the home of Jacques Bourgeois. Two stationed themselves at the back door while the others went to the front. The police searched the house and grilled the accountant for more than two hours, trying to find out if he had any connection to Rivard prior to the night of the escape. Bourgeois told the press, "The house was checked. That is the only thing I am going to tell you about the visit."

Reporters later learned that the police had found a ring of fourteen keys belonging to Bordeaux on the floor of Bourgeois's car. *Montréal-Matin*, a popular tabloid, claimed an anonymous guard identified the keys as "masters" that could open any lock in the jail. However, a jail official said the keys could only open locks in the boiler room area. It had simply been the unfortunate Mr. Bourgeois's bad luck that the fugitives had dropped the keys in his car. The dramatic visit to his home was an indication of police desperation as days passed and they still didn't know where Rivard was. They were frustrated, too, by pranks such as the one pulled by a Montreal resident who'd lost a dispute with his neighbour over a parking space on the street. In revenge, he phoned in a false tip that Rivard had been spotted at the neighbour's house. "He figured we'd come charging up armed with machine guns and thought it a good way to get back at his neighbour," a police spokesman said.

Oddly enough, the police didn't search Rivard's Montreal townhouse until four days after the escape. Four Quebec Provincial Police detectives found Marie there, alone except for her Doberman pinscher, Gingo. They told her to tie the dog up or they'd shoot him. The officers left after finding nothing of use to them, but a group of RCMP plainclothes detectives kept watch outside. According to one observer, they "sauntered about, as inconspicuous in that unassuming neighbourhood as a duke at a peasant's ball."

A few days later, Marie agreed to an interview with Toronto *Star* reporter Robert Reguly. He was surprised by the rather plain furnishings in the Rivard home. Marie told him that the rumours of wealth were untrue. She said that when Rivard heard about a witness at the Dorion Inquest who testified that he had bank accounts in Mexico and Switzerland, he phoned her from Bordeaux and said, "We're supposed to be rich. Will you call that witness and get the number of my Swiss account so I could get at that money?"

Marie told Reguly she'd had no idea Rivard was going to escape, but she hoped he'd get away. She had her passport ready, she said, in case he phoned her to join him in some foreign country where Canadian and American authorities couldn't touch him. When Reguly asked which countries Rivard might go to, she replied, "I know my husband has friends in Cuba," and then would say no more on that matter.

Marie expressed fear that if Canadian police caught up with Rivard, they'd shoot him. "If he is cornered, he will surrender as, how do you say it in English, gallantly as he escaped. I know he is not armed. He never carries a gun."

Toward the end of the interview, Gingo barked and Marie rushed to the front door. It was her newspaper boy. She came back with a copy of *La Presse*. "She laughed," Reguly wrote, "on reading that the cops were stumped in the search for her husband."

On March 8, Rivard forfeited any legal right to fight extradition to the United States when he failed to appear in court. One day later, another political bombshell landed, this time in Quebec City. Opposition leader Daniel Johnson of the Union Nationale made charges in the Quebec National Assembly that Premier Jean Lesage's Liberal government may have been guilty of "complicity and connivance" in Rivard's escape. He said that Claude Wagner had hand-picked raids on suspected Rivard associates, and that some planned raids had been called off when police received orders from "higher-ups." One aborted raid, said Johnson, was to have been made on the home of a Liberal member of the Assembly.

Johnson said Rivard's escape had made Quebec "a laughingstock in all of Canada, in all America, and even in the whole universe." He called for an immediate debate. The motion was defeated by a vote of 51 to 17, but the Lesage government now had to quell new rumblings about the "tentacles" of organized crime reaching into high places.

On March 11, Jean-Noël Lavoie of the Quebec Liberals told the Assembly that it was his home that had allegedly been spared an RCMP raid. Lavoie was also mayor of the Île Jésus community of Chomedey. He was involved in a major libel suit concerning some suspect real-estate deals on Île Jésus, and Lucien Rivard's name had come up during inquiries into the case.

Lavoie claimed he hadn't been aware he'd been targeted for a police raid and had no knowledge of a "secret telephone call" that cancelled the raid. He accused Daniel Johnson of "trying to link me in one way or another with Mr. Rivard." He called on Johnson to "stop peddling malicious state-ments ... and stop spreading this venom."

Johnson responded that the federal Liberal party was being devoured by a "gangrene" that had spread to its "Siamese Twin," the Quebec Liberal party. Wagner answered, "I state on my honour and with all my sincerity that, according to the information in my possession at the moment, there was no plot on the part of politicians or anyone else to facilitate the escape of Lucien Rivard."

While politicians at every level were denying accusations of corrup-tion, Marie quietly sold the press a four-page letter she said her husband had mailed to her from Vancouver. It was dated March 6. Marie said she'd torn up the envelope and flushed it down the toilet in case the postmark could give the police a clue as to which part of Vancouver it had been mailed from.

Asked why she had sold the letter, Marie explained, "At the beginning, I gave interviews to anyone who wanted one. Now I mustn't forget I have to live. I have to eat and pay my taxes and I have no more income. I don't get the impression people will go down on their knees to offer me work once this is all over." (Before marrying Rivard four years earlier, Marie had been a telephone operator.)

The police immediately scoffed at the letter as a ruse to throw them off the trail. "Why should Rivard go to Vancouver?" asked Inspector Jean Gagnon of the Quebec Provincial Police. "Montreal is a big town. There are a million places he can hide out here where he has a lot of friends in the underworld."

In spite of their doubts about the letter's authenticity, the police grilled one of the detainees they'd picked up in a raid about the possibility that Rivard could actually be in Vancouver. Eddy Lechasseure was an ex-convict and Rivard's close friend and former business partner. He lived in Montreal's Rosemount suburb in an apartment he rented under the alias Eddy Hunter, the English translation of his name. When the police came calling on March 12, they allegedly found a blackjack on the premises and arrested Lechasseur for possession of an illegal weapon. Detectives interrogated him for several hours, but didn't disclose to the press whether or not he'd given them any useful information.

The heady allure of gold was added to the growing Rivard saga on March 18, with the report from an unnamed woman who'd been arrested by the Ontario Provincial Police in a case involving fraudulent bankruptcy charges. The woman, whose husband belonged to a Toronto gang, said that she and other gang members' wives would take trips to France and Italy and return to Toronto with "souvenir" packages. The packages, she said, were then forwarded by courier to Lucien Rivard in Montreal. She believed the packages contained gold bullion. Curiously enough, two days after Rivard's breakout, a United States senate sub-committee report had implicated him as a drug-smuggler and a dealer in illicit gold.

Throughout the political storms and police raids, creative minds with a flair for satire continued to find inspiration in the Rivard Affair. Impressionist Rich Little parodied Prime Minister Lester Pearson singing,

"Old Man Rivard, he just keeps running away." The comedy singing group The Brothers-in-Law included a song about Rivard titled "A Government Inquiry" on their album *Oh, Oh Canada*. A young housewife in St. Laurent, Quebec, named Anne-Marie Fauteux (later Namaro, died February 14, 2000) wrote "The Ballad of Bordeaux Jail," a humorous poem in the style of the nineteenth-century Canadian poet William Henry Drummond. The ballad describes how the clever "big wheel, Lou Rivard" confronts the cigar-smoking warden, and tells him:

> Pardonnez-moi, mon capitaine
> I did not stop to think
> But with your kind permission
> I would like to hose the rink

In the final stanza, the author refers to Rivard as "That Gallic pimpernel." The satirical poem was published in Canadian newspapers in the first week of April. The public laughed, but government officials and police were not at all amused. On April 9, in Montreal, a judge rejected habeas corpus petitions submitted on behalf of Rivard's associates: Groleau, Gagnon, and Jones. They could all now be sent to the United States.

Within a week, Marie claimed she'd had another letter from her husband. This one, she said, had been posted in Barcelona, Spain. She showed reporters the envelope, which did indeed have a Barcelona postmark, but the date and time were illegible. Marie wouldn't share the contents of the letter with the press because, "it could make trouble for him." She would only say, "He is waiting for something. He expects it in a few days ... When that happens, he will write me again and let me know where he is."

Once again, the police dismissed Marie's letter as a hoax. C.W. Harvison, retired head of the RCMP, said he believed Marie was using the newspapers to send messages to Rivard. He suggested it was a "decided possibility" that the Rivards had a pre-arranged code and communicated by means of press stories based on interviews with Marie.

Surprisingly, at that time Lucien Rivard wasn't at the top of the RCMP's "Most Wanted" list. That dubious honour went to Georges LeMay, who had vanished after pulling a $4 million bank robbery in Montreal in 1961. He was also a suspect in the mysterious disappearance of his wife, although police had no hard evidence that he was guilty of foul play. LeMay was arrested in Fort Lauderdale, Florida, on May 6. He was the first criminal to be caught through what was then called "satellite TV police power." The pioneering Early Bird satellite program sent images of suspects most wanted by the RCMP, the FBI, and Scotland Yard to TV viewers on both side of the Atlantic. A marina worker recognized LeMay's face and the bank robber was in the Dade County jail within hours.

As soon as the news of LeMay's arrest broke, the police in Fort Lauderdale were swamped with phone calls from Canadian newspapers. In addition to details about LeMay's arrest, they wanted to know if the Florida police had any leads on Rivard, who was known to be an underworld associate of LeMay's in Montreal. Robert Smith, captain of detectives in the Fort Lauderdale police department, said they didn't know anything about Lucien Rivard.

The local police had received circulars on LeMay, said Smith, but nothing on Rivard. They hadn't heard of this international criminal for whom even Interpol was searching. Smith said the detectives in his department were angry about having no information on Rivard, because they might have actually seen him without realizing who he was. LeMay was arrested aboard his yacht. As he was being taken in handcuffs to a police car, an unidentified man said to him, "Now George, you take care of yourself. You know what I mean?" The same man had been seen driving around Fort Lauderdale with LeMay. His description was similar to Rivard's.

Besides the possibility that a major drug smuggler might have slipped through their fingers, the thought that had the Fort Lauderdale detectives fuming concerned the potential loss of money. Unlike Canadian law-enforcement officers, American police officers were eligible to claim rewards. Rivard was worth $15,000! One of Captain Smith's detectives complained, "With that kind of a reward for Rivard, how come we haven't got circulars? He must be more important than LeMay, whose reward was only half as much."

Although Montreal police still said they were sure Rivard had never left the city, the press shifted its focus to Florida. A waitress in a Fort Lauderdale waterfront restaurant looked at prison mug shots of Rivard Canadian reporters showed her, and said, "Sure, I recognize him." She said he'd first shown up in the restaurant about a month earlier and had become a regular customer. Whenever he left, he always headed straight for the dock where LeMay's boat was tied up. He spoke with an accent she couldn't identify, and had "cold, dark eyes." The waitress said she hadn't seen the man since LeMay's arrest.

On May 10, the FBI announced it was searching for Rivard in Florida. If Canadian officials had been embarrassed over Rivard's escape, it was now the Americans' turn to blush after learning that Georges LeMay had been living in luxury on a yacht right under their noses and Rivard might have been his guest. "If Rivard is in the Fort Lauderdale area," quipped the Toronto *Star*, "he would be wise to hole up next to the police station."

Captain Smith argued, "We can't search for Rivard until we've been officially asked to do it." He went on to explain that it was only through a lucky tip brought about by the Early Bird program that they'd nailed LeMay. Prior to that, besides the circulars, the only information they'd had on him was a clipping from a Kenora, Ontario, newspaper. "If we had reason to believe a man we wanted was up in Canada," Smith said, "we would have plastered the place with information."

American authorities learned that LeMay had been in the United States for almost all of the four years since the bank robbery, but had gone to Montreal for Easter of 1965. He had re-entered the United States at Rouses Point, New York, on April 20, using false identification. The question was; could LeMay have helped smuggle Rivard across the border?

Reporters found LeMay's common-law wife, Lise Lemieux, a former Montreal nightclub singer, in a Miami hotel they said was "awash with French Canadian visitors." She agreed to talk to them in the hotel's bar, under the watchful eyes of two bodyguards. She told the reporters there was no need to worry about them, "as long as I'm smiling."

Lise said she had never heard LeMay mention Lucien Rivard. She denied that anyone named Rivard had ever been on their yacht. But she also insisted that LeMay was innocent of bank robbery. "I don't know where my husband got the money," Lise said. "But he did well in the real estate business in Montreal. My husband never told me anything he felt I shouldn't know."

The American government issued an "all states" warrant, signed by President Lyndon Johnson, for the arrest of Lucien Rivard. This document empowered any law-enforcement officer anywhere in the country to arrest the suspect in question on sight. It superseded all other warrants. The FBI refused to divulge whether it had any new information on Rivard.

In Canada, the press reported on May 10 that in December 1964 — while in jail — Rivard had arranged the sale of his share of Plage Ideal for $268,000. Marie claimed to know nothing about the sale. Where the proceeds were deposited was a mystery.

A tip on an illegal lottery-ticket racket led Montreal police to Andre Durocher on June 4. Four detectives went to an east-end address where they'd been told Durocher had a basement apartment. As they approached the building, Durocher's wife came out. She spotted the detectives and cried, "Andre! Get out! It's the swine from the police!"

Two policemen broke down the door and overpowered Durocher before he could get his hands on a weapon. A search of the apartment turned up four revolvers, several sticks of dynamite, and three Molotov cocktails. As Durocher was being taken away, he snarled, "You pigs! You took me by surprise, or they would have had to wipe you up with blotting paper." That, at least, was the account the police gave to the newspapers.

Durocher had died his hair red in a feeble attempt at disguise. The police were sure Rivard had dumped him right after the escape and that he probably had no idea where Canada's most wanted man was hiding. Marie, still willing to talk to any reporter, said, "I am sure he can't know anything. My husband must have got to know him in Bordeaux. I never heard anyone mention his name before that."

The police hoped Durocher would enlighten them on whether or not he and Rivard had inside help when they escaped. Instead, he told them a garbled tale of being in Spain with Rivard up until three weeks earlier. He even threw in a few Spanish words for effect. Durocher said Rivard had advised him not to return to Montreal, but then gave him $25,000.

Durocher had $1,100 on him, and had bought a brand-new car under a false name. Detective Sergeant Robert LeBlanc of the Montreal police department said it was "within the realm of possibility" that Durocher and Rivard had been in Spain, but not very likely. He didn't believe Rivard would have kept a small-time hoodlum like Durocher with him. There had been no passport among Durocher's belongings in the apartment. LeBlanc doubted he had even left Montreal. Durocher had most likely seen the newspaper articles about Marie's supposed letter from Spain, and had concocted a story. "I don't think we'll ever get much out of him," LeBlanc said. On June 4, 1966, Durocher would be found hanging in a prison lavatory, an apparent suicide.

An unnamed senior police official expressed the view that "Rivard is lucky if he is still alive today. He knows too much and is too well-known to be left lying around for too long." The notion that Rivard had enemies in the underworld soon became evident.

On June 18, Groleau, Gagnon, and Jones were secretly spirited out of Bordeaux Jail to be turned over to American authorities. It was a sudden move that caught the prisoners and their lawyers by surprise. Before they left the jail, Groleau was heard to remark, "Rivard is sending us down there, and he's going to pay for this one way or another."

The three men were put in handcuffs and leg irons. Eleven RCMP officers armed with rifles and shotguns took them by automobile convoy to the United States Air Force base at Plattsburg, New York. There, under heavy guard, they boarded a Coast Guard Globemaster aircraft for a flight to Texas. That night they slept in the small jail in Laredo.

Rivard's fellow escapee had been caught, and three of his partners in crime had been extradited. His name was in the papers and on the TV and radio news everyday as the Dorion hearings continued. But still the "Gallic pimpernel" remained elusive. Until July 16!

On June 11, a team of masked bandits struck the railway station in the tiny community of Larder Lake in northern Ontario, not far from the Quebec border. They seized five bars of gold bullion worth $164,000 that were being shipped from the Kerr Addison mine to the mint in Ottawa. The thieves then made a dramatic escape in a stolen light aircraft. The plane was eventually found 137 miles north of Montreal, but police believed it had made a stop near the city to unload the gold.

The OPP investigation soon focused on two men with long criminal records, Sebastian Boucher and Armand "Freddie" Cadieux. By the second week of July, Quebec Police and the RCMP had traced the pair to the community of Woodlands, a suburb of Chateauguay on the south shore of Lac St. Louis (the confluence of the Ottawa and St. Lawrence Rivers), about twenty miles from Montreal. An employee in a store there identified a photo of Boucher as that of a man who had recently been in the shop.

People had also seen a jeep which police believed belonged to Cadieux. The store clerk had seen another man with Boucher, and his description was similar to Rivard's. Of course, scores of Rivard "sightings" had been reported, but this man had been seen driving a 1956 Studebaker. Other tips had connected Rivard to such a car.

There were a lot of summer cottages around Woodlands, and investigators suspected the fugitives were using one of them, but they didn't know which. They couldn't just start banging on doors, as that might alert the quarry and give them a chance to flee — or make a stand in a blazing gun battle. So they quietly staked the area out.

Several officers disguised themselves as road crews for the municipal public works department. One policeman posed as a gardener, and another pretended to be a fishing guide, going from cottage to cottage in search of clients. All kept careful watch.

On Wednesday, July 14, the police spies noticed that one large cottage was in a relatively isolated location. Its owner, May Birch, lived in a nearby house. She told the police she had rented the cottage to a man the previous Monday. He had a young woman and an eight-year-old boy with him. She'd seen little of the man since then, and hadn't seen the woman and boy at all. Cars had come and gone, but she hadn't paid them much attention. However, the police learned that the people in the cottage shooed away anybody who wandered near. They decided the place was worth a closer look.

The officers who watched the cottage from concealment didn't have to wait very long before they spotted the man every cop in Canada and the United States was looking for: Lucien Rivard! They were the first law enforcement officers to knowingly lay eyes on the now-famous criminal since he had escaped from Bordeaux Jail. Rivard had dyed his grey hair black and was bearded, and he had put on about forty pounds, but there was no mistaking him.

Now that they had Rivard in their sights, the police couldn't afford any mistakes. Undercover officers kept watch on the cottage while senior police officials drew up a plan of action. The few people in the Woodlands area who were aware of the police presence, such as May Birch, hadn't the slightest idea that the police had located three major criminals in their midst.

The operation to capture Rivard, Boucher, and Cadieux was carefully planned and then carried out with military precision. It involved the RCMP, the Quebec Provincial Police, the Montreal Police Department, and one officer from the Ontario Provincial Police; a total of almost fifty men. At 1:00 p.m. on Friday, July 16, a call went out to the homes of RCMP, QPP, and Montreal police officers. They were told to report to Montreal police headquarters immediately, in civilian clothes. When they arrived, a constable took them to an upstairs room. Nobody was allowed near a telephone.

At 2:00 p.m. the officers were loaded into cars, four or five to a vehicle. Four cars carried German Shepherd police dogs. The officers weren't told anything about the operation until they reached Chateauguay. Only then did they learn that they were about to close in on Lucien Rivard. The police

Artist's sketch of the cottage where Lucien Rivard was captured, ending one of the biggest manhunts in Canadian history.
TORONTO *STAR.*

were armed with pistols, rifles, and machine guns, but senior officers gave strict orders that no one was to shoot except to protect their lives.

Roadblocks were set up to seal off the neighbourhood. A cordon of officers spaced twenty feet apart surrounded the cottage. The police dogs sat obediently silent, awaiting commands. Eight men made up the party that would actually carry out the raid. The occupants of the cottage were unaware of any unusual activity outside.

Shortly before 5:00 p.m., May Birch was entertaining a few visitors in her home when a party of police officers suddenly burst in. They told the startled people to sit quietly while they searched the house. When the officers were satisfied that none of the suspects were on the premises, they kept Mrs. Birch and her guests inside. Two hundred yards away, hidden from view of the house by a stand of trees, their colleagues were getting ready to move on the cottage.

At about the same time, a car towing a boat trailer pulled up at the Woodlands Yacht Club where an eighteen-year-old employee named Robin Burns was on duty. One of the men in the car asked if they could launch their motor boat there. They looked like a party of fishermen, and Burns thought they wanted to use the club's facilities for free. Then they showed him their RCMP badges. Burns later said he had never seen men get a boat into the water so fast. The police launch churned out onto the lake and took up a position, ready to cut off any attempt by the fugitives to escape by water. By this time, an RCMP light aircraft was circling overhead, in radio contact with the police on the ground.

When all was in readiness, the eight-man team rushed to the cottage. Four stayed outside to cover all exits. The other four burst through the front door with guns drawn. The first man they saw was Lucien Rivard. He immediately cried, "No, no! Don't shoot!"

Canada's most wanted man was taken completely by surprise. He was on his way to the kitchen, and wearing only a bathing suit when his long run from the law abruptly ended. "Flabbergasted" was the word a police official used to describe Rivard at the moment of his re-capture. "He looked dismayed ... after all, he hadn't sent us any invitations."

Boucher and Cadieux were also in the cottage, and they surrendered without any resistance. However, the radio message that went out to all of the police teams in the field was, "Rivard has been captured. Rivard has been captured. Return to rendezvous point."

The police in May Birch's house were grinning like schoolboys when they told the bewildered people they had just caught Lucien Rivard. Mrs. Birch was shocked to learn that she had rented her cottage to notorious criminals. "I guess it's just one of those things," she later told reporters who barraged her with questions. "I used to call the cottage Honeymoon Haven, but now I'm going to call it Rivard's Retreat."

The yacht club was over a mile from the cottage, so Robin Burns didn't know about the raid that had just taken place. He was surprised when the RCMP launch returned after less than half an hour. He asked the constables what they were doing. One of them said, "We'll tell you a little secret. We've got good news. We just captured Lucien Rivard."

"I rushed over to the cottage," Burns said later, "and looked over the fence. Then I saw Rivard. He was in the back seat of a car, wedged like a piece of baloney between two powerful Mounties."

Rivard was allowed to dress himself in a business suit before he was taken from the cottage in handcuffs. The police found no guns or ammunition on the premises. Rivard, Boucher, and Cadieux were taken to the Quebec Provincial Police headquarters on McGill Street in Montreal. Rivard was back in a cell, 136 days after his escape. When the sergeant who booked him in asked for his last residential address, Rivard smiled and said, "800 Gouin Boulevard." That was the address of the Bordeaux Jail.

Police spokesmen credited the success of the operation to the cooperation of the federal, provincial, and municipal police departments, and to the presence of a large number of officers. "We went in force and in that way prevented a siege. There was no siege, no violence, no injuries, nothing ... it was smooth sailing."

They wouldn't say if a tip from an informer had led them to the cottage. "If there were such a source, the police would take care that the finger is never pointed at him. His life would not be worth much otherwise."

The news of Rivard's capture flashed across the country, and early sensational reports were riddled with errors. One said the cottage had an arsenal of guns and ammunition. Wild rumours circulated as people in the streets and in bars and cafes spoke of nothing but Rivard's capture. One story had him fleeing across the St. Lawrence River in a fast boat, only to be overtaken by the RCMP. In another yarn, he slipped out of the cottage and was pursued through the woods by man hunters and dogs.

The three thousand residents of Woodlands were coming to grips with the dramatic event that had placed their community in the national spotlight. May Birch grew annoyed with the endless parade of curious "tourists" who wanted to see "Rivard's Retreat." To discourage them, she had a supply of large firecrackers that sounded like gunshots when they exploded.

Philip Goodyear, whose family was one of the oldest in the community and owned the land surrounding May Birch's property, wasn't at all pleased with all the publicity. "I'm not very happy about Rivard being captured in Woodlands," he complained. "How would you feel if they found him in your backyard?"

Prime Minister Lester Pearson, who was an experienced pilot, was flying an RCAF Vertol helicopter from Antigonish, Nova Scotia, to Halifax,

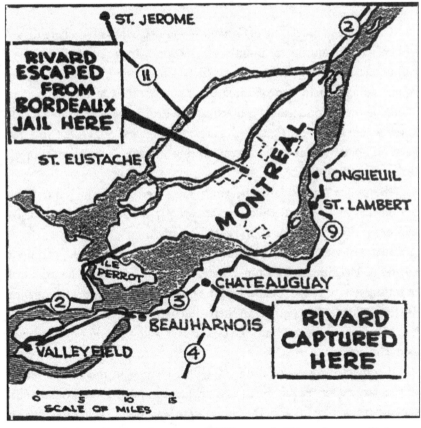

Overview of the area where Rivard was captured. While reports had him as far away as Spain, Rivard was about twenty miles from Montreal.
TORONTO *STAR.*

when his office received the news and informed him by radio. Pearson was jocular in a pair of messages he sent to Senator John Connoly. "Rivard caught at 4:45 confirmed," said the first communique. "Call an election at once." The second said, "There is no confirmation that he has already asked for bail."

After landing, Pearson issued a formal statement. "Very good news. I would like to congratulate the police authorities concerned. The law can now take its course and justice be served."

Understandably, Marie Rivard didn't share the prime minister's elation. She went to the grey stone building where her husband was being held, but was not allowed to visit him. A throng of newsmen rushed her, but all she said was, "I have nothing to say. Go away." Within a few days, Marie was permitted to see Rivard in what the press described as "a very touching reunion."

The police — indeed, all of Canada — were eager to know where Rivard had been hiding during his months of "freedom." They revealed that they'd had reports on him being in at least half a dozen countries, from Peru to Japan, sometimes in two or three different countries at the same time. When detectives questioned him, Rivard said, "I guess you really want to know where I've been. I guess it's been bugging you. So, I'll tell you. I've been on holidays. Naturally," he said with a chuckle, "I spent most of my time in la belle province."

The police said Rivard cheerfully answered all of their questions, but "always in an extremely clever, apparently well-thought-out, evasive manner ... Rivard told us a lot, yet told us nothing."

The Americans were delighted that Rivard had been captured. Lawrence Fleishman, the United States Customs agent who had the task of getting Rivard to Laredo, praised the Canadian police for catching him. Then he added, "You people up there don't realize what a big fish Rivard is ... The sooner we get him, the better. He's a key big shot of organized crime in North America."

If convicted on major drug smuggling charges in the United States, Rivard faced a term of as much as forty years in prison — a potential life sentence for a man his age. The expectation was that he would resume his fight against extradition. To the surprise of all, Rivard told his legal counsel he wanted to get out of Canada and take his chances in a Texas courtroom.

Rivard had pulled yet another trick out of his bag. At this stage, his extradition to the United States should have been a simple matter of stamping the papers. But now he faced criminal charges in Canada: escaping custody and, in the incident concerning Jacques Bourgeois, kidnapping and auto theft. Moreover, he could be an important witness in the still ongoing Dorion Inquest. In Texas, the case could boil down to a matter of Rivard's word against Michel Caron's.

In Ottawa, the Opposition demanded that Rivard be kept in Canada. They accused the Pearson government of trying to get rid of Rivard in what amounted to a political cover-up. The Conservatives said there was too much about the bribery attempt and Rivard's escape and long evasion of the law that was still a mystery. They also wanted to know where Rivard got the $16,500 that was in his possession when he was captured. (That money was later identified as part of the loot from a postal truck robbery in Montreal.) Conservative MPs like Erik Nielsen inferred there were shady deals going on between the Liberals and Rivard.

In spite of Opposition protests, the Canadian government agreed to deliver Rivard into the waiting arms of the Americans. The reasoning was pragmatic. If the Texas court found Rivard guilty, he'd be locked up in an American prison and would no longer be the Liberals' problem. Should he be acquitted, he'd still be deported as an undesirable, and could then be tried for crimes committed in Canada. That would take time, and meanwhile the uproar over the Rivard Affair would have died down.

While Rivard waited to be extradited, police searched the cottage and the grounds around it for the stolen gold. They found nothing. However, Boucher and Cadieux were held on charges of knowingly giving aid to a fugitive from the law. Cadieux was also wanted for forgery.

On July 22, a motorcade of police cars took Rivard to the Montreal airport where he was put aboard an RCMP aircraft. Accompanying him were two United States Customs agents and two Canadian police officers. At Plattsburg he was transferred to a Coast Guard plane. When the plane landed at Ellington Air Force Base in Houston, it was immediately surrounded by twenty United States Marshalls and customs agents with drawn guns. The heavy security was employed not out of concern that Rivard might try to escape, but to protect him from a possible Mafia "hit."

In a Houston courtroom, a judge read out the charges against Rivard, and set his bail at half a million dollars. When Rivard heard that, he chuckled and said, "I might as well forget it." Back in Canada, Marie was also in jail, waiting for her sister to pay $5,000 bail. Marie had been subpoenaed as a witness in the trial of Raymond Denis, and was being legally detained due to concern she would fail to appear in court. Marie was later allowed to leave Canada to attend Rivard's trial.

That trial date was set for September 7, and then was postponed. For much of the time, Rivard was kept in an undisclosed location out of concern that he could be the target of underworld assassins. When Rivard finally did have his day in court, his lawyer was unable to convince the jury of his innocence. On September 21, Rivard was found guilty of being the mastermind of an international heroin smuggling ring. When he heard the verdict, Rivard seemed unmoved, but he blew a kiss to Marie. Sentencing was set for a date in November.

By that time, Canada was in the midst of a federal election. From his jail cell in Texas, Rivard wrote to journalist Ron Haggart of the Toronto *Star*, and Haggart ran the letter in his column on November 11:

> As you know I've been out of circulation since June 19, 1964, except for a couple of months last spring when there 10 million eyes looking for a $15,000 reward. Then, I was really out of circulation … I do not know the program of any of the political parties … There's no doubt they all have a good program, but I can't sincerely give you my predictions. I do not know what goes on outside of here, as I am kept incommunicado; even my wife does not know where they are keeping me. Canada is a big, prosperous country … it's the best country in the world to live in, and let's hope they will keep it that way … I suffered a lot of wrongs in Canada and very bad publicity. I do not hold a grudge against anybody. I forgive them all … many times a little lie becomes a big story, and naturally there's always a victim.

Rivard was sentenced on November 12: twenty years in the federal penitentiary in Atlanta, Georgia, plus a fine of $20,000. His partners

Gagnon and Jones were sentenced to fifteen years each, and Groleau to twelve years. Caron, whose arrest in Laredo had sparked the whole affair, got ten years. Soon after Rivard began serving his sentence, the warden told him that he and Marie would not be allowed to correspond in French. All letters had to be in English. "Bilingualism is something they have yet to hear about in the United States," Marie said in an interview. "It's a good thing we both speak and understand English. Lucien writes very well in English, but I have a little trouble writing in that language."

Marie and Rivard wrote to each other almost daily until he was paroled and deported in January of 1975, having served nine years of his sentence. Rivard made Canadian newspaper headlines again when he arrived at the Montreal airport. Marie was there to meet him. New controversies swirled around Rivard when the Quebec government decided not to press charges for escaping custody, kidnapping, or car theft. Nor would there be any investigation into Rivard's possession of a large sum of stolen money at the time of his capture in 1966. Once again there were rumours about friends in high places.

After that, Rivard lived quietly in the Chomedey area, refusing requests for interviews. Once, a reporter spotted him in Montreal's old courthouse and asked what he was doing there. Rivard replied that he just wanted to see what it was like to walk through that building without wearing handcuffs. Rivard died at the age of 86 on February 3, 2002, taking to the grave many secrets concerning organized crime and political corruption — or so a lot of people believed.

Rivard's legacy was extraordinary for a Canadian criminal. In December 1965, he topped Prime Minister Lester Pearson as "Canadian Newsmaker of the Year." He became one of only a handful of underworld figures to have an entry in the *Canadian Encyclopedia* and mention in the *Dictionary of Canadian Biography*.

As a heroin smuggler, Rivard was involved in a despicable business. But his Great Escape and his cavalier bearing as a "Gallic Pimpernel" turned him into a folk hero, though he championed no cause but his own. He summed it up best himself in a letter he sent to Lester Pearson, dated March 30, 1965, when he was the most hunted man in Canada. "Life is short, you know. I don't intend to be in jail for the rest of my life."

CHAPTER 12
MICKY MCARTHUR:
"I'd Rather Die with a Gun in My Hand"

Mitchell Gordon "Micky" McArthur once stated that a criminal's most deadly weapons are intelligence and charm. Only five-foot-six in height, weighing just 130 pounds, and having what police called a "baby face", McArthur didn't look like a hardened criminal. But the smooth-talking hoodlum had an outgoing personality with charm to spare. If cunning can be said to be synonymous with intelligence, then McArthur was gifted.

In the autumn of 1977, McArthur was using both "weapons" in a scheme to defraud Toronto jewellery stores of expensive gems and watches by means of down payments of stolen cash coupled with counterfeit certified cheques. Dressed in a conservative three-piece suit and black leather overcoat, McArthur was confident he could hoodwink any store clerk or manager. He had false identification, and he timed his visits to jewellery stores on Yonge Street to hours when banks would be closed so no one could try to verify his cheques by phone. In case of trouble, McArthur also packed a Browning automatic pistol.

McArthur spent several days setting up the scam. He opened a bogus bank account and chatted with sales clerks as he presented himself as a respectable man of means. But his plan went disastrously wrong on the afternoon of November 11, starting with his visit to Gold's Jewelers. The saleswoman there said she'd have to get the manager's approval before she could accept McArthur's cheque. McArthur waited a couple of minutes. Then, sensing that something was wrong, he walked into the manager's office and demanded his cheque back. The manager said he'd already phoned the police.

McArthur fled from the jewellery store and went to the hotel he'd been using as a base of operations. He changed into a different suit, and then walked to Chapman Brothers Jewellers, another target on his list. Unfortunately for McArthur, the word on him was already out. He found himself face to face with Constable Brian McNeil of the Metropolitan Toronto Police Department's Fraud Squad.

McArthur pulled his gun, and McNeil lunged for it. McArthur fired, and the bullet shattered McNeil's kneecap. McArthur would later say that he had intended only to shoot at the floor as a warning to the officer. He said it was McNeil's own fault he got wounded. "He should have let me go."

When McArthur's gun discharged, the recoil spring popped out, rendering it useless. Another Fraud Squad officer who was posing as a salesman drew his revolver and placed McArthur under arrest. McArthur claimed later that in the Don Jail police officers beat him because he had shot a cop. Soon he was on his way to Millhaven, Canada's new maximum security "super prison" near Kingston. McArthur wasn't just a would-be crook who had bungled a job, and this wasn't his first trip to Millhaven. He was one of Canada's most wanted men, with a long criminal record and a history of prison escapes.

Micky McArthur was born in 1952. His father had deserted the family before his birth. McArthur's earliest years were spent with his mother and older sister living with an aunt in Galt, Ontario (now part of the city of Cambridge). Then his mother met a man named Harry McArthur who became Micky's stepfather. More children came along as the family moved around, first to Orrs Lake, and then Paisley. Harry proved to be a violent drunk who abused his wife and "disciplined" the children with an electrical cord.

Young Micky learned to hate authority. He was often in fights at school. If the other kid was too big, Micky would pick up a rock. He was in and out of foster homes. Hard experience taught him when to fight back, and when to run and hide. By the time the McArthur family moved to Walkerton in 1964, Micky had a reputation as a problem kid.

McArthur's first crime as a teenager was forging a cheque for ten dollars. That got him six months in the Bowmanville Training School east of Oshawa. There, he met Steve Faust, who would become his brother-in-law and partner in crime. Bowmanville did nothing to cure McArthur of his delinquency. His next stop was the Ontario Provincial Reformatory in Guelph, where he served eighteen months for three break-and-enter convictions. His pal Faust was there, too. McArthur would later blame the reformatory for turning him from "a mean little training school kid into an insensitive, totally amoral and vicious young punk."

Not long after his release from jail in Guelph, McArthur was sentenced to fourteen months in the Burwash Reformatory for auto theft. McArthur hated being incarcerated, but he would later regard his youthful misadventures as important learning experiences for a young man who had chosen to live a criminal lifestyle. It was in jail that he learned from "experts" such skills as picking locks, hot-wiring cars, obtaining foolproof false identification, and giving police the slip.

After his release from Burwash, McArthur went to Toronto. The idea of honest work was repugnant to him. He got money from break-ins. When he wanted a car or motorcycle, he'd steal one. To deceive the police, he altered the license plates. "My artistry was almost perfect," McArthur boasted later. Nonetheless, after a while he felt that the Toronto police were on his trail, so he moved to Galt. There, he stole so many vehicles, the local police thought a professional theft ring was in operation.

McArthur had numerous close calls with police, leading them on what he considered a merry chase. Faust was often his accomplice in break-ins and wild joyrides in stolen cars. Then one day while McArthur was visiting his mother's apartment in Galt, two policemen came to the door with warrants for his arrest for the robbery of a convenience store in Burgoyne, a community about twenty-four miles west of Owen Sound. McArthur put up a fight before he was finally handcuffed.

The next day, two OPP constables put McArthur in a car for the trip to the Bruce County jail in Walkerton. McArthur didn't think he would get a long sentence for the petty Burgoyne robbery, but he was determined not to go back to jail. When his escort made an unscheduled stop in the village of Harriston, McArthur took advantage of the lucky break and a lack of diligence on the officers' part to escape from the car and flee into the woods.

A police posse with a tracking dog was soon after him. McArthur used every trick he had seen in movies to throw them off his trail. He hopped fences, doubled back on his tracks, and waded through creeks. He found the only trick that actually worked was running up the middle of a highway. Once he'd thrown the hunters and their dog off his scent, McArthur stole a famer's car. As he put it, he was "freedom bound." But it was the false freedom of a man on the run. He could have gone straight after Burwash. Instead, he was a wanted man.

McArthur travelled back and forth across Canada by hitchhiking, hopping freight trains, and stealing cars. Whatever he needed, he stole. To use his own metaphor, the world was a big shopping mall and everything in it was free. For a while he worked under a false name in a trendy salon in Toronto, cutting hair in the daytime and pulling burglaries at night. That rare venture into employment ended when a customer he'd known in his school days recognized him.

Worried that his old acquaintance might inform on him, McArthur got out of Toronto in a hurry. He went to Walkerton, where he continued his career as a late night thief, once again in partnership with Faust. One of their targets was a garage whose owner had once been McArthur's landlord. McArthur felt justified in robbing the garage because the owner had never offered him a job. Again, he was the quarry of many police chases, and had incredible luck in evading capture again and again. But the inevitable happened when, in the wee hours of November 20, 1972, OPP officers burst into a cottage in Collingwood Township and surprised McArthur in bed. They took him to the Walkerton jail. Faust soon joined him.

By this time, local boy Micky McArthur had become something of an outlaw folk hero to some people in the Paisley and Walkerton areas, even though he was definitely no Robin Hood. He was implicated in more than a hundred criminal incidents in five counties that police knew of, and he had been the suspected fugitive in more than thirty police chases. McArthur seemed like a character from a Hollywood crime/action movie, and he revelled in his notoriety. He didn't even consider himself a criminal. In his own opinion he was "just young, fun-loving and incredibly wild." But he was still hell-bent on staying free.

On the night of April 24, 1973, McArthur and Faust became the first prisoners ever to break out of the Walkerton jail. They would never reveal who smuggled in the hacksaw blades they used to cut through bars. In spite of a search that included dogs and aircraft, the pair got away. They put plenty of distance between themselves and Walkerton, and then they cracked the safe in a grocery store in Sudbury. The swag was $11,500!

McArthur went through his share of the money quickly, travelling around the country and purchasing (for a change) a brand new sports car. He broke into a supermarket in Woodstock, Ontario, but was foiled by a safe he couldn't crack. A few weeks later he was in Vancouver, when a tip led the RCMP to his motel room. Faust had already been arrested in Sault Ste. Marie.

Returned to Walkerton, McArthur and Faust were convicted on several charges including escaping custody, and each was sentenced to three years and three months. Then they were sent to Sudbury where they were given another two years and three months for the grocery store burglary. But McArthur had no intention of spending the next five-and-a-half years in prison.

On July 10, 1973, McArthur and Faust were in the back of a sheriff's car, on their way to the Kingston Penitentiary. Two officers sat up front. Using a safety pin (or so he later claimed) McArthur quietly picked the locks on his and Faust's handcuffs and leg manacles. Near Whitby, the prisoners suddenly pounced on the officers and overpowered them. They left the dazed men at the side of the road and escaped in the sheriff's car.

Left: Micky McArthur was the first prisoner to escape from the Bruce County Jail in Walkerton, Ontario.
EDWARD AND JANE COBB.

Right: Cell window through which Micky McArthur made his escape from the Bruce County Jail in Walkerton, Ontario, on April 24, 1973.
EDWARD AND JANE COBB.

Micky McArthur had done it again! But this time his "freedom" was short-lived. Four days later the police tracked him and Faust to a friend's home in Kitchener. By the time the courts were finished with them, they were looking at nine years each in Kingston. Micky couldn't believe it. "This wasn't justice!" he wrote later. McArthur didn't think he belonged in prison with *real* criminals. Nonetheless, he entered Millhaven — the Mill, as inmates called it — as prisoner number 9864. By McArthur's reckoning, he had reached "the big time."

As a relatively good-looking young man, McArthur knew that he would be a target for sexual predators. He put on a "weird" act to keep potential attackers away. He worked out with weights, and befriended a hard case who put the word out that McArthur was not to be bothered. McArthur began to feel a strain on his friendship with Faust, who was associating with inmates Micky regarded as "low lifes." Eventually, McArthur was transferred to the Collins Bay Penitentiary, and Faust was sent to the Warkworth Institution at Campbellford.

McArthur never stopped thinking about escaping, but decided he would "obtain my freedom the right way and for the correct reason — on parole and gainfully employed." But when, after three-and-a-half years the parole board turned him down because of his record, McArthur became impatient. "I had had enough of their nonsense. I had been a model prisoner and was set to go straight. I deserved a parole and I was determined to see to it that I received one — no matter how."

On the night of December 21–22, 1976, using improvised tools such as a sledgehammer made from a broom handle and a fifty-pound weight from the gym, McArthur broke out of his cell. He managed to get over the prison wall undetected and fled on foot across the countryside. Once he was clear of the Kingston area, McArthur spent a few days hiding in the home of "a loyal family member." All he needed, he said later, was a gun so he could pull a robbery and then rent an apartment. He broke into a Canadian Tire store in Cambridge and stole a shotgun and a supply of shells. He was just leaving when Waterloo Regional Police arrived. It was Christmas night, and Micky was in custody again. A few days later he was transferred to the Kitchener jail. He was warned not to do anything foolish.

To McArthur, "foolish" meant staying behind bars. Once again, he somehow obtained hacksaw blades. On the evening of February 22, 1977,

McArthur and two other prisoners escaped. The other two were soon caught, but McArthur burglarized a car dealership and then fled all the way to Montreal.

McArthur now decided he would go straight and stay out of jail. He registered under an alias with an employment agency, and for a while supported himself as a labourer earning minimum wage. Then the work dried up and he found himself unemployed and broke. As McArthur put it, "I'd rather die with a gun in my hand than starve in the streets."

McArthur fled Montreal after a shoplifting incident almost landed him back in jail. He went to Saskatchewan, where he helped a friend escape from the Prince Albert Penitentiary. All the while, he kept himself in funds through robbery. McArthur then went to Toronto where he paid a cosmetic surgeon the hefty price of $1,000 to alter his facial features.

Satisfied with the results of the surgery, McArthur returned to Saskatchewan. On November 2, he drove a stolen car to the little community of Hague, north of Saskatoon. The prairie town had a bank that he'd been wanting to rob for a long time. McArthur casually walked in, showed a pistol to the manager, single teller, and lone customer, and walked out with $7,000. After his unpleasant experience with the employment agency in Montreal, the ease with which he pulled the Hague robbery convinced McArthur once and for all that working was for fools. Nine days later, he was apprehended in Chapman Brothers Jewellers in Toronto.

McArthur spent the next six years behind bars. He generally behaved himself, though he made a suicide attempt by slashing the arteries in the crooks of his arms. He tried to alter his fingerprints through a painful self-administered procedure involving a razor blade and drain cleaner. McArthur was shunted around from Millhaven, to Collins Bay, to the Frontenac Minimum Security Institution adjacent to Collins Bay, and to the Pittsburgh Farm Annex outside Joyceville. He participated in the Save the Youth Now Group (STYNG), a volunteer organization of inmates who spoke to young offenders about "the cruel realities of a criminal lifestyle or career."

In 1983, McArthur became eligible for parole. As a reward for his good behaviour, he was released. McArthur was elated to be out of jail at last, and this time without having to constantly look over his shoulder or worry about a knock at the door. But past lessons didn't seem to sink in with Micky McArthur.

By this time, McArthur's sister Janet had been married to Steve Faust for several years, but the marriage had gone bad. Faust was unemployed and broke, and told McArthur he planned to rob the Royal Bank in Hepworth, near Sauble Beach. McArthur later claimed that he tried to talk Faust out of it, but to no avail. McArthur himself had been, in his own words "robbing banks like they were going out of style." However, he didn't think Faust had the competence to pull a bank robbery on his own, so he decided to go with him to make sure he didn't get caught.

McArthur planned the holdup carefully, and told Faust to follow his instructions without question. No one was to get hurt, he said, as he gave Faust a 30-30 carbine. McArthur would be armed with a sawed-off shotgun. They stole a Datsun station wagon and a motorcycle. McArthur picked the morning of August 8, 1983, when the bank would have a shipment of cash ready for pick-up by a Brinks truck. Using theatrical make-up, McArthur disguised himself to look like a black man, and Faust to look like a "mutant." They had a scanner that allowed them to pick up police radio communications so they'd be warned of approaching cops.

They entered the bank at 10:15. McArthur shouted, "This is a stick-up! This is the real thing! We're here for the Brinks pick-up. Open the treasury. We're not leaving without the money. If the police come, we're taking hostages. We mean business."

The head teller opened the vault, and McArthur made bank employees fill a backpack with bundles of money. While they were doing that, he heard over his scanner that police were already on the way. Either a bank employee had pressed a button, or someone outside had realized something was wrong in the bank. Faust, who was a bundle of nerves, cried, "Let's go! We're running out of time."

With the backpack stuffed, the bandits fled from the bank and jumped into the Datsun. As they roared along Hepworth's main street, they saw a pick-up truck in the wrong lane, coming straight at them. The driver was clearly trying to block their escape. McArthur swerved up onto the curb to get around the truck. Then he saw in his rear view mirror that the truck had turned and was following them. He jammed on the brakes and yelled to Faust, "Hit him!"

He meant for Faust to get out of the car and put a bullet into the truck's engine block or a front tire. Instead, in his panic, Faust turned in his seat and fired a shot that blew out the Datsun's back window. Exasperated, McArthur stepped out from behind the wheel and pumped three shotgun blasts into the front of the pickup.

Rae Patterson, the truck driver, later reported, "I hit the floor of the truck, and by the time I crawled out the passenger door, they were gone." His windshield was smashed, and the front of the truck's body was peppered with buckshot marks. "I feel pretty stupid now, " Patterson said. "A guy could get killed doing that. The next time I'll think twice. I now know what a target feels like."

Four miles from Hepworth, McArthur and Faust ditched the car and retrieved the motorcycle from a hiding place in the bush. They wiped off the makeup, changed clothes, and made a successful getaway. Their take was $80,000.

McArthur buried most of the loot. He allowed himself and Faust $5,000 each to live on for a few months until things cooled down. His plan was to use the money to open a couple of salons in Western Canada so they both could go straight. He advised Faust to lay low and not make himself conspicuous by spending a lot of money.

But in an attempt to save his crumbling marriage, Faust blew his $5,000 buying Janet expensive gifts, like a fur coat. Of course, the police wondered where an unemployed parolee got the money. One night they picked a drunken Faust up in Toronto's Union Station. It didn't take them long to get a confession out of him. Faust told them where the money from the Hepworth robbery was hidden, and that he had pulled the job with his brother-in-law, Micky McArthur. Bitter over this betrayal, McArthur later wrote, "When he (Faust) was arrested, the police had to slap him twice: once to get him talking and once to shut him up." On October 13, 1983, McArthur was back in Millhaven. He had barely set foot inside his cell when he began to plan another escape.

McArthur spent a year studying every aspect of the prison's security systems. He learned the guards' routines. He exercised and ran to get into top physical shape. He quietly collected equipment he'd need, like a pair of cleated soccer shoes. On October 13, 1984, one year after his return to Millhaven, a heavy fog provided McArthur with the opportunity for which he'd been preparing.

Using a device he'd made from blocks of wood, mop handles, and nylon ropes, McArthur bent two of the bars on his cell window to create a space he could squeeze his wiry frame through. Then he armoured his torso, shins, and wrists with hard coverings made from layers of newspapers and glue. These would protect him from razor wire. Over them he wore olive coloured pajamas that would blend in with the grass in the prison yard.

McArthur dropped to the ground from his second storey window. Everything was enveloped in thick fog. He made his way to a place he'd already chosen at the inner fence. "I hit the chain links at full speed and scrambled for the top as if I were on fire," McArthur wrote later. "Counting on a little finesse and a lot of speed, I scaled the second fence for all I was worth."

There was a moment of panic when McArthur's pants snagged on the wire, but he tore loose and dropped to the other side. He ditched the homemade armour, and then he ran. The alert went out the next day for "an extremely violent cop hater who won't give up." Once again, slippery Micky eluded the posses, dogs, and helicopters.

For a while, McArthur made his base in Portland, Oregon, crossing the border occasionally to rob a bank in Canada when he needed money. But he didn't limit himself to Canadian banks. On April 29, 1985, he and a partner raided a bank in Mobridge, South Dakota, for $76,000 U.S. Soon after, the FBI arrested McArthur's partner for a bank robbery in Montana. They connected him to McArthur, and Micky had to high-tail it from Portland back to Canada. He allegedly attempted to break his pal out of the jail in Miles City, Montana, but the plot didn't work out.

Just after Christmas 1985, McArthur robbed a Toronto Dominion bank in Edmonton. Then on January 2, 1986, he drove to a farm outside Delisle, Saskatchewan, to dig up $81,000 in stolen negotiable bonds he'd buried there. The RCMP had been closing in on him, and had the place staked out. Two years and three months after his escape from Millhaven, McArthur was back in jail, this time the Edmonton Maximum Security Prison in Alberta.

Because of his reputation as an escape artist, McArthur spent a long time in solitary confinement in "Edmonton Max." He eventually found himself back in his old lodgings in Millhaven. There, to "save my sanity," as he put it, McArthur wrote his autobiography, *I'd Rather Be Wanted Than Had: The Memoirs of an Unrepentant Bank Robber*. McArthur's story, written with pencil stubs on the backs of official complaint forms he scrounged from guards, was published as a 243-page book in 1990. Often poignant, sometimes funny, it gives the reader an eye-opening look into a life spent on the wrong side of the law. However, even though McArthur sometimes admits to having been a fool, more than anything else he seems to brag about his crimes. He dismisses most bank robbers as amateurs, while he sees himself as a professional. When it comes to prison escapes, he deems himself without equal. He says he wasn't concerned about police chases, "because I was better equipped and trained than ninety-nine percent of all police officers."

Some noteworthy points in McArthur's criminal career didn't make it into the book. He was suspected in the disappearance in the early 1980s of a Kingston drywaller named Tom Gencarelli. No trace of Gencarelli was ever found, and police believed he was murdered. Sometime after McArthur's book was published, he was actually charged with the murder. However, a key witness for the Crown died before the case could go to court, and the charge was dropped. McArthur had also threatened to kill witnesses to the Hepworth bank robbery. When he escaped from Millhaven, those people were given special police protection out of concern that he might try to go after them. These and other instances belie McArthur's claim in his book that he tried to avoid violence. In fact, McArthur's single most violent moment of criminal behaviour was yet to come.

McArthur was let out of prison on a statutory release in June 1994, and took up residence in Kingston. At 7:30 pm on October 20, McArthur and an accomplice entered the Bank of Montreal on the Port Perry Plaza on Scugog Street in Port Perry, a small community on Lake Scugog, north of Whitby. One carried a pistol, and the other a high-powered hunting rifle. They ordered manager Alan Knight to open the safe. When Knight refused, one of them shot him in the knee. The injured man opened the vault.

A man outside heard the shot and summoned the police. When the bandits ran out with a pillow case stuffed with $50,000, they heard sirens. They ran through strip plaza's parking lot, which was almost surrounded by buildings and fences. They'd almost reached the Canadian Tire store at the south end of the parking lot, when two police cars roared onto the scene. In one were constables Mark McConkey and Warren Ellis of the Durham Region Police. In the other, an unmarked car, was Detective Paul Mooy. McConkey and Ellis hadn't even had a chance to get out of their cruiser when the bandits unleashed a fusillade. McConkey had his jaw smashed by a bullet. Fragments of bullet struck Ellis in the head. Both constables had their faces lacerated by glass from the shattered windshield. Mooy was just getting out of his car when a rifle bullet almost took his arm off. Two hundred metres away, on the other side of Scugog Street, real estate agent Debra-Ann Taylor was sitting at her typewriter when a stray rifle bullet pierced her office window and hit her in the back.

With three police officers down, the robbers dashed across the parking lot and between two buildings to a place where they'd left two stolen bicycles. They pedaled furiously to the home of an elderly couple, Harry and Marjorie Pearce. The bandits kicked the door in and ripped the telephone cord out of the wall. Then they forced seventy-five-year-old Harry to drive them away in his Volkswagen van. They released him, and then drove to a location where they had a getaway car parked. By the time police found Harry Pearce's van, the bandits were long gone. But witnesses had seen the car in which they fled.

It would later be said that the robbers had turned quiet Port Perry into a "war zone." Debra-Ann Taylor and Constable Ellis were airlifted to hospitals in Toronto; she to have a bullet removed from a lung, and he to undergo several hours of surgery for the removal of bullet fragments that were imbedded between his skull and his brain. Knight, Mooy, and McConkey were treated for serious but non-life threatening wounds in the Port Perry hospital.

Early the next morning, police acting on a tip arrested McArthur at his Kingston residence. Elsewhere in the city, officers arrested Micky's brother Angus, 28, whom they believed was the accomplice. Both were taken to jail in Oshawa. When they were brought before a magistrate for a bail hearing, a reporter asked Micky what his next book would be called. "*Frame!*" he shouted. "We didn't do these things. The police are lying. They are trying to frame us. They set us up — police set us up."

The brothers were tried for armed robbery and five counts of attempted murder. Angus was acquitted, but Micky was found guilty and sentenced to life in prison. Before being led away, he smirked and fired imaginary guns at police officers in the courtroom. At the time of this writing, Micky McArthur is still in jail. He has not identified his accomplice in the Port Perry holdup. The $50,000 has never been recovered. Remarkably, a court action to have McArthur declared a dangerous offender failed.